D0824963

DIGITAL CONTENT CREATION • COMPOSITING • IMAGING • VIDEO

IT WORKS FOR US

Whether you are a 3D artist using Autodesk Maya to produce cinematic quality animation or a graphics designer creating artwork for digital publishing, the ATI FireGL series of graphics accelerators delivers industry leading performance, ground-breaking features, and unprecedented visual fidelity for the most demanding workstation users.

ATI FireGL workstation graphics accelerators feature up to 1GB of memory — an industry first. In addition the highly parallel rendering architecture, innovative ring bus memory system, and vibrant 10-bit graphics pipeline capable of displaying over a billion colors will greatly improve your productivity.

With the graphics horsepower for today's professional applications and tomorrow's technology innovations, it's no wonder that animators, modelers, and designers rely on ATI FireGL graphics for superior performance, outstanding image quality, and exceptional value.

Visit ati.com/firegl to find out how ATI FireGL graphics can work for you.

ATI FireGL

1GB FRAMEBUFFER

ati.com

©Copyright 2006, ATI Technologies Inc. All rights reserved. ATI, FireGL and Avivo are trademarks and/or registered trademarks of ATI Technologies Inc.

© COPYRIGHT 2006 AUTODESK, INC.

ALL RIGHTS RESERVED.
THIS PUBLICATION, OR PARTS THEREOF, MAY NOT BE REPRODUCED IN ANY FORM, BY ANY METHOD, FOR ANY PURPOSE.

AUTODESK, INC., MAKES NO WARRANTY, EITHER EXPRESS OR IMPLIED, INCLUDING BUT NOT LIMITED TO ANY IMPLIED WARRANTIES OF MERCHANTABILITY OR FITNESS FOR A PARTICULAR PURPOSE REGARDING THESE MATERIALS, AND MAKES SUCH MATERIALS AVAILABLE SOLELY ON AN "AS-IS" BASIS.

IN NO EVENT SHALL AUTODESK, INC., BE LIABLE TO ANYONE FOR SPECIAL, COLLATERAL, INCIDENTAL, OR CONSEQUENTIAL DAMAGES IN CONNECTION WITH OR ARISING OUT OF PURCHASE OR USE OF THESE MATERIALS. THE SOLE AND EXCLUSIVE LIABILITY TO AUTODESK, INC., REGARDLESS OF THE FORM OF ACTION, SHALL NOT EXCEED THE PURCHASE PRICE OF THE MATERIALS DESCRIBED HEREIN.

AUTODESK, INC., RESERVES THE RIGHT TO REVISE AND IMPROVE ITS PRODUCTS AS IT SEES FIT. THIS PUBLICATION DESCRIBES THE STATE OF THIS PRODUCT AT THE TIME OF ITS PUBLICATION, AND MAY NOT REFLECT THE PRODUCT AT ALL TIMES IN THE FUTURE.

AUTODESK TRADEMARKS
THE FOLLOWING ARE REGISTERED TRADEMARKS OF AUTODESK, INC., IN THE USA AND OTHER COUNTRIES: 3DEC (DESIGN/LOGO), 3DECEMBER, 3DECEMBER.COM, 3D STUDIO, 3D STUDIO MAX, 3D STUDIO VIZ, 3DS MAX, ACTIVESHAPES, ACTRIX, ADI, AEC-X, ALIAS, ALIAS (SWIRL DESIGN/LOGO), ALIAS|WAVEFRONT (DESIGN/LOGO), ATC, AUGI, AUTOCAD, AUTOCAD LT, AUTODESK, AUTODESK ENVISION, AUTODESK INVENTOR, AUTODESK MAP, AUTODESK MAPGUIDE, AUTODESK STREAMLINE, AUTODESK WALKTHROUGH, AUTODESK WORLD, AUTOLISP, AUTOSKETCH, BACKDRAFT, BRINGING INFORMATION DOWN TO EARTH, BUZZSAW, CAD OVERLAY, CAN YOU IMAGINE, CHARACTER STUDIO, CINEPAK, CINEPAK (LOGO), CIVIL 3D, CLEANER, COMBUSTION, CONSTRUCTWARE, CREATE>WHAT'S>NEXT (DESIGN/LOGO), DESIGNSTUDIO, DESIGN|STUDIO (DESIGN/LOGO), DESIGN YOUR WORLD, DESIGN YOUR WORLD (DESIGN/LOGO), EDITDV, EDUCATION BY DESIGN, FBX, FILMBOX, GMAX, HEIDI, HOOPS, HUMANIK, I-DROP, INTRODV, KAYDARA, KAYDARA (DESIGN/LOGO), LUSTRE, MAYA, MECHANICAL DESKTOP, OBJECTARX, OPEN REALITY, PORTFOLIOWALL, POWERED WITH AUTODESK TECHNOLOGY (LOGO), PROJECTPOINT, RADIORAY, REACTOR, REVIT, SKETCHBOOK, VISUAL, VISUAL CONSTRUCTION, VISUAL DRAINAGE, VISUAL HYDRO, VISUAL LANDSCAPE, VISUAL ROADS, VISUAL SURVEY, VISUAL TOOLBOX, VISUAL TUGBOAT, VISUAL LISP, VOICE REALITY, VOLO, WHIP!, AND WHIP! (LOGO).

THE FOLLOWING ARE TRADEMARKS OF AUTODESK, INC., IN THE USA AND OTHER COUNTRIES: ALIASSTUDIO, AUTOCAD LEARNING ASSISTANCE, AUTOCAD SIMULATOR, AUTOCAD SQL EXTENSION, AUTOCAD SQL INTERFACE, AUTODESK INTENT, AUTOSNAP, AUTOTRACK, BUILT WITH OBJECTARX (LOGO), BURN, CAICE, CINESTREAM, CLEANER CENTRAL, CLEARSCALE, COLOUR WARPER, CONTENT EXPLORER, DANCING BABY (IMAGE), DESIGNCENTER, DESIGN DOCTOR, DESIGNER'S TOOLKIT, DESIGNKIDS, DESIGNPROF, DESIGNSERVER, DESIGN WEB FORMAT, DWF, DWG, DWG LINKING, DWG (LOGO), DWG TRUECONVERT, DWG TRUEVIEW, DXF, EXTENDING THE DESIGN TEAM, GDX DRIVER, GMAX (LOGO), GMAX READY (LOGO), HEADS-UP DESIGN, INCINERATOR, LOCATIONLOGIC, MOTIONBUILDER, OBJECTDBX, PLASMA, POLARSNAP, PRODUCTSTREAM, REALDWG, REAL-TIME ROTO, RENDER QUEUE, SHOWCASE, STUDIOTOOLS, SUBCONTRACTOR DESKTOP, TOPOBASE, TOXIK, VISUAL BRIDGE, VISUAL SYLLABUS, AND WIRETAP.

AUTODESK CANADA CO. TRADEMARKS
THE FOLLOWING ARE REGISTERED TRADEMARKS OF AUTODESK CANADA CO. IN THE USA AND/OR CANADA AND OTHER COUNTRIES: DISCREET, FIRE, FLAME, FLINT, FLINT RT, FROST, GLASS, INFERNO, MOUNTSTONE, RIOT, RIVER, SMOKE, SPARKS, STONE, STREAM, VAPOUR, WIRE.

THE FOLLOWING ARE TRADEMARKS OF AUTODESK CANADA CO., IN THE USA, CANADA, AND/OR OTHER COUNTRIES: BACKBURNER, MULTI-MASTER EDITING.

THIRD-PARTY TRADEMARKS
MENTAL RAY IS A REGISTERED TRADEMARK OF MENTAL IMAGES GMBH LICENSED FOR USE BY AUTODESK, INC.

WWW.3D.SK COPYRIGHT 2006.
ALL OTHER BRAND NAMES, PRODUCT NAMES, OR TRADEMARKS BELONG TO THEIR RESPECTIVE HOLDERS.

Autodesk

Acknowledgements

Primary Authors:
Rob Magiera, Loïc Zimmermann

Contributing Authors:
Mike Ahmadi, Petre Gheorghian, Rob Ormond,
Bob Gundu, Marc-André Guindon

Art Direction:
Michiel Schriever

Sr. Graphic Designer:
Ian McFadyen

Cover Image:
Rob Magiera

Development & Copy Editor:
Erica Fyvie

Technical Editor:
Diane Erlich

DVD Production:
Julio Lopez, Roark Andrade

Jr. Project Manager:
Skye Bjarnason

Project Manager:
Carla Sharkey

Product Manager, Learning Tools & Training:
Danielle Lamothe

Director, Packaged Services:
Michael Stamler

A special thanks goes out to:
Mariann Barsolo, Carmela Bourassa,
Sylvana Chan, James Christopher,
Robert Lin, Vivien May

We would also like to thank Dan Pressman,
creator of Captain Bob's Extreme Shark
Cage Adventure in Chapter 8 and the Alien
Creature in Chapter 9.

"I'd like to thank Jonas Thornqvist for
this workflow; I've seen him working this
way on many characters for a production,
and the results were definitely top notch."
-Loïc Zimmermann

Bonus textures for Loïc Zimmermann's
sections provided by www.3d.sk. All textures
in this section © Copyright 2006 3d.sk.
All rights reserved.

Autodesk Paint FX Plug-in Acknowledgements:

Plug-in Development:
Roy Lovejoy, Amalgamated Coders, Inc.

Contributing Plug-in Development:
David Israel

Testing & QA:
Julio Lopez, Christine Medina,
David Lau, Bruce Hickey

Special Thanks:
Jason Walter, Duncan Brinsmead

Primary Authors

Rob Magiera, Noumena Digital

Rob Magiera is recognized as one of the foremost computer artists in the world today. He is president and founder of Noumena Digital at www.studionoumena.com, a full-service digital art studio specializing in high-end CG for print. Noumena opened its doors in 1986 and shortly thereafter, Rob began his exploration of 3D with Alias® software.

Unlike many of his colleagues who work solely with Adobe® Photoshop® and Illustrator® software products as their primary tools, Rob has spent more than a decade exploring the unique capabilities that 3D modeling software can bring to the illustrator's craft. He uses Maya® software to create the core elements of his illustrations, but also for composition and experimentation. He feels that it is an exciting time to be a CG artist because most of the technical problems have been solved and if you can dream it, you can do it. As an artist he finds that incredibly liberating.

Some of his clients include American Express, Intel, Microsoft, Asymetrix, Nintendo, Koss Electronics, AT&T, Sprint, and the 2002 Winter Olympics. Rob's unique blend of 3D techniques and sophisticated compositing consistently push the boundaries of the modern still image.

Magiera has done lectures and presentations around the world on the use of Maya as an illustration tool, sharing what he has learned about ways to expand the digital artist's tool box.

In 2005, Rob was honored as a Maya Master, an industry and peer recognition award. These individuals have defined the shape of 3D as we know it today. Rob is the first illustrator to receive this award.

Loïc Zimmermann, e338

Loïc Zimmermann is a freelance CG master, character modeler, and illustrator based in France. In 1997, he received his Master of Fine Arts degree with first class honours from ESAA of Troyes. Since then, he has worked on a range of projects, both freelance and in-house, for various companies. For three years he worked at a small company called Okenite, initially as a CG artist and then as a lead modeler. Okenite, www.okan3d.com, specializes in film, multimedia and architectural design. He spent six months in Italy working on the CG feature *Dear Anne: The Gift of Hope*, to be released later this year. He also served as artistic director at Sparx animation (www.sparx.com) in Paris.

His freelance projects have included creating an entire CG fashion show, for which he modeled and rigged three characters, devised clothing simulations, created props, rendered lighting, and directed. He has also illustrated a cover for the comic book adaptation of the Sony Pictures® film *Silent Hill*. He is currently preparing another comic book for September 2006, as well as exhibitions for later this year.

His work has won several industry awards including: the Bolino (videoClip) award, selected by TrèsCourts at the Festival Très d'esprit in Paris (2004), and a special award for the film *Plaisir d'apprendre* at the Festival of Institutional Video of Creusot (2001). As well, his work was featured on the back cover of *Exposé2*, the preeminent book for the CG arts industry.

To learn more about Loïc and see his portfolio, visit his web site at www.e338.com.

Foreword

Danielle Lamothe Product Manager, Learning Tools & Training

For many people, the impression of Autodesk® Maya® software is one of dazzling special effects and animations that provide the backbone for huge productions and the world's best video games. Maya is used by the biggest and best studios and has become such an integral part of making today's movies, the Academy of Motion Pictures awarded the software an Oscar in 2001. But 3D film projects and video games are not the only domains where artists are pushing the boundaries of what Maya can accomplish. Increasingly, talented 2D artists are adding Maya to their toolkit, extending their options and creating unparalleled imagery.

3D Tools for Photographers, Illustrators, and Graphic Designers covers a wide range of techniques and workflows used by real-world artists creating compelling 2D images. Unlike other Maya books, the focus here isn't on learning the entire Maya toolset. Rather, the specialized focus in this book will allow you to develop your Maya skills and understand how you can use Maya in conjunction with Photoshop tools. Based on the techniques of artists such as Rob Magiera of Noumena Digital, Loïc Zimmermann of www.e338.com and others, this book explores the wide variety of options 3D can open for you.

Even if you aren't convinced that adding 3D to your process is the right step, you'll find exciting new creative possibilities within the pages of this book. Exclusively available in *3D Tools for Photographers, Illustrators, and Graphic Designers* is the Autodesk Paint FX for Photoshop plug-in, providing you with over 190 brushes that you can start using in Adobe® Photoshop® right away. The only limits are your imagination.

Table of Contents

Project 1
Photo-realism

Project 2
Workflows Introduction

Project 3
Special Effects

Project 4
Yatoer, the Bus Stop Boxer

About this book

Thank you for choosing *3D Tools for Photographers, Illustrators & Graphic Designers*. This book is intended to provide the 2D software user an introduction to 3D and Maya. This book is based on the real world techniques of working artists. Therefore, while we've made an effort to include workflows that are easy for a beginner to follow, some lessons may be challenging at first. Pay special attention to the comments at the beginning of each section in order to gauge the lesson's complexity. You may find it helpful to do the simpler lessons at first and, as you gain additional familiarity with Maya, to move on to the more advanced sections later on.

Updates to this book

In an effort to ensure your continued success through the lessons in this book, please visit our Web site for the latest updates available: www.autodesk.com/learningtools-updates.

For updates to the **Paint FX Plug-in**, please visit www.autodesk.com/3dtools.

Software Packaging

This book is based on working in Autodesk® Maya® and Adobe® Photoshop®. In order to use this book, you should have one of the following Maya software applications in addition to Adobe Photoshop:

- Maya Complete
- Maya Unlimited

- Maya Personal Learning Edition

Note: *Some functionality in this book is not compatible with Maya Personal Learning Edition software. Common issues occur in the use of specific resolution settings. A suggested work-around is to set your resolution to the next closest setting available to you. Plug-ins, such as in Lesson 8: Flash Format Output, also require a fully-functioning version of Maya software.*

DVD-ROM

The DVD-ROM at the back of this book contains several resources to accelerate your learning experience including:

- Autodesk Paint FX Plug-in
- Support files - including pre-built shaders and tools specific to workflows explored

- Interview with Author Rob Magiera
- Maya Personal Learning Edition 7
- Bonus Textures from 3d.sk

Installing support files – Before beginning the lessons in this book, you will need to install the lesson support files. Copy the project directories found in the support files folder from the accompanying DVD-ROM onto your computer.

Autodesk PaintFX Plug-in

This plug-in is compatible with Mac OSX and Windows systems. It is exclusively available through this book and includes numerous brushes that you can start using in Adobe Photoshop right away. Create trees, flowers, lightning, fire, clouds, smoke and other elements with a few simple brush strokes. Save time, energy and frustration by achieving the results you want effectively and efficiently. You'll benefit from over 190 brushes you can't find anywhere else including:

- Jet trails
- Daisies
- Ferns
- Raw meat
- And many more...

Installation Instructions

1. Copy the PaintFX Plug-in folder to your Photoshop Plug-in folder.

   On **Mac** it's located here: *Mac HD:Applications:Adobe Photoshop:Plug-Ins*.

   On **Windows** it's located here: *C:\Program Files\Adobe\Photoshop\Plug-Ins*.

2. Restart Photoshop.

System Requirements

Macintosh 	Windows 
Apple Mac OS X 10.3 or later	Microsoft Windows 2000 or XP
PowerPC G3 or later	Intel® Pentium III processor or later
128MB RAM or higher	128MB RAM or higher
Video card with at least 16MB of Video RAM	Video card with at least 16MB of Video RAM
Monitor displaying at least 1024 x 768 pixels	Monitor displaying at least 1024 x 768 pixels
Adobe Photoshop 7 or later	Adobe Photoshop 7 or later
3-button Mouse	3-button Mouse

Introduction
Understanding Maya

To understand Autodesk® Maya® software, it helps to understand how Maya works at a conceptual level. This introduction is designed to give you the story of Maya. In other words, the focus of this introduction will be on how different Maya concepts are woven together to create an integrated workspace.

While this book teaches you how to model and render in Maya, these concepts are explained with great detail. However some topics such as animation, which is covered in the introduction, are not elaborated upon in this book, but they give you an idea of the powerful tools available to you with Autodesk Maya software.

You will soon learn how the Maya software architecture can be explained by a single quote-"nodes with attributes that are connected." As you work through this book, the meaning of that statement becomes clearer and you will learn to appreciate how the Maya interface lets you focus on the act of creation, while giving you access to the power inherent in the underlying architecture.

Introduction

The user interface (UI)

The Maya software user interface (UI) includes a number of tools, editors and controls. You can access these using the main menus or special context-sensitive *Marking Menus*. You can also use *shelves* to store important icons or hotkeys to speed up workflow. Maya is designed to let you configure the UI as you see fit.

To work with objects, you can enter values using coordinate entry or you can use more interactive 3D manipulators. Manipulator handles let you edit your objects with a simple **click+drag**.

The Maya UI supports multiple levels of *undo* and *redo* and includes a drag+drop paradigm for accessing many parts of the workspace.

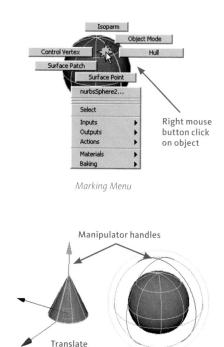

Right mouse button click on object

Marking Menu

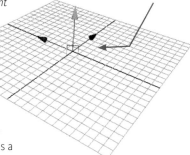

Maya manipulators

Working in 3D

In Maya, you will build and animate objects in three dimensions. These dimensions are defined by the cardinal axes that are labeled as X, Y and Z. These represent the *length* (X), *height* (Y) and *depth* (Z) of your scene. These axes are represented by colors – red for X, green for Y and blue for Z.

In Maya, the Y-axis is pointing up (also referred to as *Y-up*).

As you position, scale and rotate your objects, these three axes will serve as your main points of reference. The center of this coordinate system is called the *origin* and has a value of 0, 0, 0.

Origin: 0,0,0

The cardinal axes

UV coordinate space

As you build surfaces in Maya, they are created with their own coordinate space that is defined by U in one direction and V in another. You can use these coordinates when working with *curve-on-surface* objects or when positioning textures on a surface.

One corner of the surface acts as the origin of the system and all coordinates lie directly on the surface.

You can make surfaces *live* in order to work directly in the UV coordinate space. You will also encounter U and V attributes when you place textures onto surfaces.

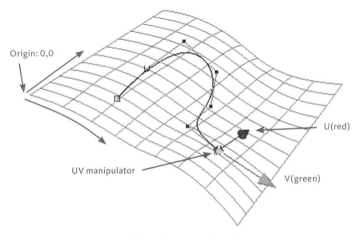

UV coordinates on a live surface

Views

In Maya software, you visualize your scenes using view panels that let you see into the 3D world.

Perspective views let you see your scene as if you are looking at it with your own eyes or through the lens of a camera.

Orthographic views are parallel to the scene and offer a more objective view. They focus on two axes at a time and are referred to as the *top*, *side* and *front* views.

In many cases, you will require several views to help you define the proper location of your objects. An object's position that looks good in the top view may not make sense in a side view. Maya lets you see multiple views at one time to help coordinate your project.

Introduction

Perspective view

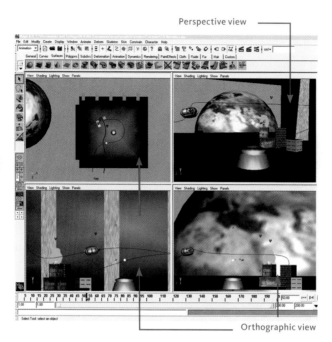

Orthographic view

Orthographic and Perspective views

Cameras

To achieve a particular view, you look through a virtual camera. An Orthographic camera defines the view using a parallel plane and a direction while a Perspective camera uses an *eye point*, a *look at point* and a *focal length*.

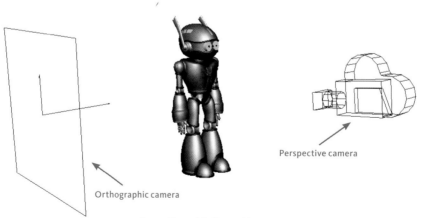

Orthographic camera

Perspective camera

Perspective and Orthographic cameras

Image planes

When you work with cameras, it is possible to place special backdrop objects called *image planes* onto the camera. An image plane can be placed onto the camera so that as the camera moves, the plane stays aligned.

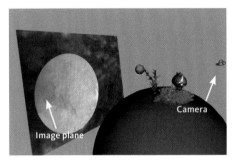

Image plane attached to a camera

Image plane seen looking through the camera

The image plane has several attributes that allow you to track and scale the image. These attributes can be animated to give the appearance that the plane is moving.

THE DEPENDENCY GRAPH

The system architecture in Maya software uses a procedural paradigm that lets you integrate traditional keyframe animation, inverse kinematics, dynamics and scripting on top of a node-based architecture that is called the **Dependency Graph**. This node-based architecture gives Maya its flexible procedural qualities.

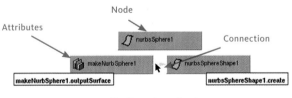

The Dependency Graph

Above is a diagram showing a primitive sphere's Dependency Graph. A procedural input node defines the shape of the sphere by connecting attributes on each node.

Nodes

Every element in Maya, whether it is a curve, surface, deformer, light, texture, expression, modeling operation or animation curve, is described by either a single node or a series of connected nodes.

A *node* is a generic object type in Maya. Different nodes are designed with specific attributes so that the node can accomplish a specific task. Nodes define all object types in Maya including geometry, shading and lighting.

Shown below are three typical node types as they appear on a primitive sphere:

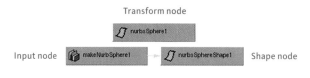

Node types on a sphere

Transform node

Transform nodes contain positioning information for your objects. When you move, rotate or scale, this is the node you are affecting.

Shape node

The shape node contains all the component information that represents the actual look of the sphere.

Input node

The input node represents options that drive the creation of your sphere's shape, such as Radius or End Sweep. This is sometimes referred to as its DNA.

The Maya UI presents these nodes to you in many ways. To the right is an image of the Channel Box, where you can edit and animate node attributes.

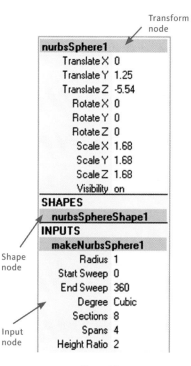

Channel Box

Node tabs

Attribute Editor

Attributes

Each node is defined by a series of attributes that relate to what the node is designed to accomplish. In the case of a transform node, *X Translate* is an attribute. In the case of a shader node, *Color Red* is an attribute. It is possible for you to assign values to the attributes. You can work with attributes in a number of UI windows including the *Attribute Editor*, the *Channel Box* and the *Spread Sheet Editor*.

One important feature in Maya is that you can animate virtually every attribute on any node. This helps give animation power to Maya software. You should note that attributes are also referred to as *channels*.

Connections

Nodes don't exist in isolation. A finished animation results when you begin making connections between attributes on different nodes. These connections are also known as *dependencies*. In modeling, these connections are sometimes referred to as *construction history*.

Most of these connections are created automatically by the Maya UI as a result of using commands or tools. If you desire, you can also build and edit these connections explicitly using the *Connection Editor*, by entering *MEL*™ (Maya Embedded Language) commands, or by writing MEL-based expressions.

Understanding Maya

Pivots

Transform nodes are all built with a special component known as the **pivot point**. Just like your arm pivots around your elbow, the pivot helps you rotate a transform node. By changing the location of the pivot point, you get different results.

Pivots are basically the stationary point from which you rotate or scale objects. When animating, you sometimes need to build hierarchies where one transform node rotates the object and a second transform node scales. Each node can have its own pivot location to help you get the effect you want.

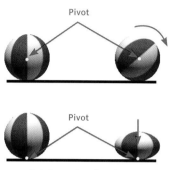

Rotation and scaling pivots

Hierarchies

When you are building scenes in Maya, you have learned that you can build dependency connections to link node attributes. When working with Transform nodes or joint nodes, you can also build hierarchies that create a different kind of relationship between your objects.

In a hierarchy, one transform node is *parented* to another. When Maya works with these nodes, Maya looks first at the top node, or *root* node, then down the hierarchy. Therefore, motion from the upper nodes is transferred down into the lower nodes. In the diagram below, if the *group1* node is rotated, then the two lower nodes will rotate with it. If the *nurbsCone1* node is rotated, the upper nodes are not affected.

Object and joint hierarchy nodes   *Object and joint hierarchies*

Joint hierarchies are used when you are building characters. When you create joints, the joint pivots act as limb joints while bones are drawn between them to help visualize the joint chain. By default, these hierarchies work just like object hierarchies. Rotating one node rotates all of the lower nodes at the same time.

You will learn more about joint hierarchies later in this introduction (see "Skeleton and Joints"), where you will also learn how *inverse kinematics* can reverse the flow of the hierarchy.

MEL scripting

MEL stands for *Maya Embedded Language*. In Autodesk® Maya®, every time you use a tool or open a window, you are using MEL. MEL can be used to execute simple commands, write expressions or build scripts that will extend the existing functionality in Maya. The Script Editor displays commands and feedback generated by scripts and tools. Simple MEL commands can be typed in the Command Line, while more complex MEL scripts can be typed in the Script Editor.

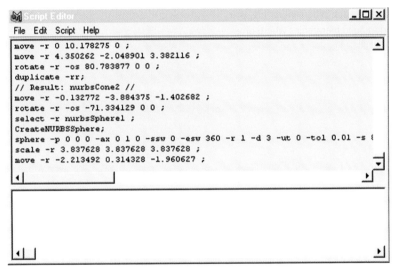

The Script Editor

MEL is the perfect tool for technical directors who are looking to customize Maya to suit the needs of a particular production environment. Animators can also use MEL to create simple macros that will help speed up more difficult or tedious workflows.

ANIMATING IN MAYA

When you animate, you bring objects to life. In Maya, there are several different ways in which you can animate your scenes and the characters who inhabit them.

Animation in Maya is generally measured using frames that mimic the frames you would find on a film reel. You can play these frames at different speeds to achieve an animated effect. By default, Maya plays at **24 frames per second**.

Keyframe animation

The most familiar method of animating is called *keyframe animation*. Using this technique, you determine how you want the parts of your objects to look at a particular frame, then save the important attributes as keys. After you set several keys, the animation can be played back with Maya filling motion in-between the keys.

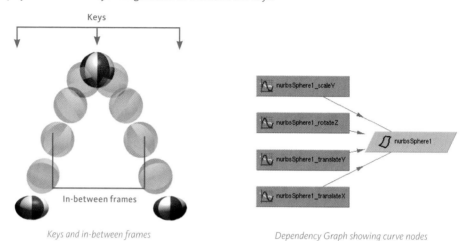

Keys and in-between frames

Dependency Graph showing curve nodes

When keys are set on a particular attribute, the keyed values are stored in special nodes called *animation curve* nodes.

These curves are defined by the keys that map the value of the attribute against time. The following is an example of several animation curve nodes connected to a transform node. One node is created for every attribute that is animated.

Once you have a curve, you can begin to control the tangency at each key to tweak the motion in-between the main keys. You can make your objects speed up or slow down by editing the shape of these animation curves.

Generally, the slope of the graph curve tells you the speed of the motion. A steep slope in the curve means fast motion while a flat curve equals no motion. Think of a skier going down a hill. Steep slopes increase speed while flatter sections slow things down.

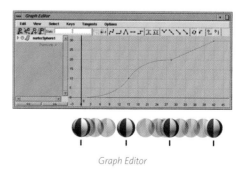

Graph Editor

Path animation

Path animation is already defined by its name. You can assign one or more objects so they move along a path that has been drawn as a curve in 3D space. You can then use the shape of the curve and special path markers to edit and tweak the resulting motion.

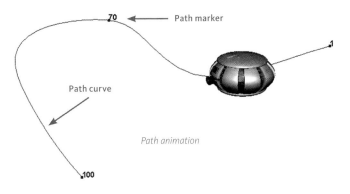

Path marker

Path curve

Path animation

Non-linear animation

Non-linear animation is a way to layer and mix character animation sequences non-linearly - independently of time. You can layer and blend any type of keyed animation, including motion capture and path animation. This is accomplished through the Autodesk® Maya® Software Trax Editor™.

Trax Editor

Reactive animation

Reactive animation is a term used to describe animation in which one object's animation is based on the animation of another object.

An example of this technique would be moving gears when the rotation of one gear is linked to the rotation of other gears. You can set keys on the first gear and all the others will animate automatically. Later, when you want to edit or tweak the keys, only one object needs to be worked on and the others will update reactively.

In Maya, you can set-up reactive animation using a number of tools, including those outlined below:

Set Driven Key

This tool lets you interactively set-up an attribute on one object to drive one or more attributes onto another.

Expressions

Expressions are scripts that let you connect different attributes on different nodes.

Constraints

Constraints let you set-up an object to point at, orient to or look at another object.

Connections

Attributes can be directly linked to another attribute using dependency node connections. You can create this kind of direct connection using the Connection Editor.

*Diagram of
animated gears*

Dynamics

Another animation technique involves *dynamics*. You can set up objects in your Maya scene that animate based on physical effects such as collisions, gravity and wind. Different variables are *bounciness, friction* or *initial velocity*. When you playback the scene, you run a simulation to see how all the parts react to the variables.

This technique gives you natural motion that would be difficult to keyframe. You can use dynamics with rigid body objects, particles or soft body objects.

Rigid body objects are objects that don't deform. You can further edit the rigid body by setting it as either *active* or *passive*. Active bodies react to the dynamics, whereas passive bodies don't.

To simulate effects such as wind or gravity, you add *fields* to your dynamic objects.

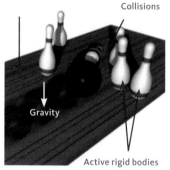

*Rigid body simulation of
bowling ball and pins*

Particles are tiny points that can be used to create effects such as smoke, fire or explosions. These points are emitted into the scene where they are also affected by the dynamic fields.

Soft bodies are surfaces that you deform during a simulation. To create a soft body, create an object and turn its points into particles. The particles react to the dynamic forces which in turn, deform the surface.

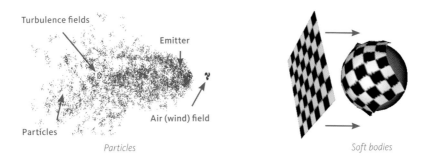

Particles   *Soft bodies*

MODELING IN MAYA

The objects you want to animate in Maya are usually built using either NURBS surfaces or polygonal meshes. Maya offers you both of these geometry types so that you can choose the method best suited to your work.

NURBS curves

NURBS stands for *non-uniform rational b-spline,* which is a technical term for a spline curve. By modeling with NURBS curves, you lay down control points and smooth geometry will be created using the points as guides.

Shown below is a typical NURBS curve with important parts labelled:

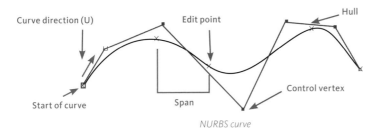

NURBS curve

These key components define important aspects of how a curve works.
The flexibility and power of NURBS geometry comes from your ability to edit the shape of the geometry using these controls.

Introduction

As your geometry becomes more complex, you may need more of these controls. For this reason, it is usually better to start out with simpler geometry so that you can more easily control the shape. If you need more complex geometry, controls can be inserted later.

NURBS surfaces

Surfaces are defined using the same mathematics as curves, except now they're in two dimensions – U and V. You learned about this earlier when you learned about UV coordinate space.

Below are some of the component elements of a typical NURBS surface:

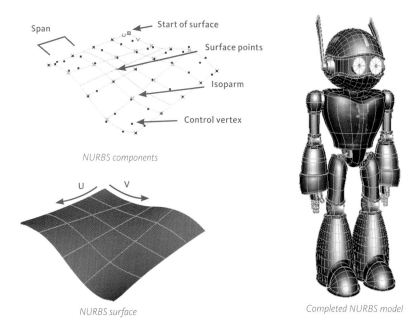

NURBS components

NURBS surface

Completed NURBS model

Complex shapes can be, in essence, sculpted using this surface type as you push and pull the controls to shape the surface.

Subdivision surfaces

Subdivision surfaces exhibit characteristics of both polygon and NURBS surfaces, allowing you to model smooth forms using comparatively few control vertices. They will enable you to create levels of detail exactly where you want.

Polygons

Polygons are another geometry type available in Maya. Whereas NURBS surfaces interpolate the shape of the geometry interactively, polygonal meshes draw the geometry directly to the control vertices.

Below are some of the components found on a polygonal mesh:

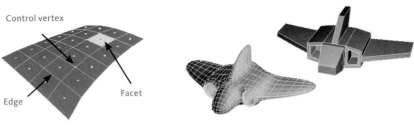

Polygon components   *Polygonal model before and after smoothing*

You can build up poly meshes by extruding, scaling and positioning polygonal facets to build shapes. You can then smooth the shape to get a more organic look for your model.

Construction history

When you create models in Maya, the various steps are recorded as dependency nodes that remain connected to your surface.

In the example to the right, a curve has been used to create a revolved surface. Maya keeps the history by creating dependencies between the curve, a revolve node and the shape node. Edits made to the curve or the revolve node will update the final shape.

Many of these nodes come with special manipulators that make it easier to update the node attributes. In the case of the revolve, manipulators are available for the axis line and for the revolve's sweep angle.

Revolve surface with dependencies

It is possible to later delete history so that you are only working with the shape node. Don't forget though, the dependency nodes have attributes that can be animated. Therefore, you lose some power if you delete history.

DEFORMATIONS

Deformers are special object types that can be used to reshape other objects. By using deformers, you can model different shapes, or give animations more of a squash and stretch quality.

Deformers are a powerful Maya feature; they can beare the deformers; they can be layered for more subtle effects. You can also bind deformers into skeletons or affect them with soft body dynamics.

The following lists some of the key deformer types available in Maya:

Lattices

Lattices are external frames that can be applied to your objects. If you then reshape the frame, the object is deformed in response.

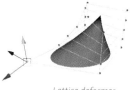

Lattice deformer

Sculpt object

Sculpt object lets you deform a surface by pushing it with the object. By animating the position of the sculpt object, you can achieve animated surface deformations.

Sculpt object deformer

Clusters

Clusters are groups of CVs or lattice points that are built into a single set. The cluster is given its own pivot point and can be used to manipulate the clustered points. You can weight the CVs in a cluster for more control over a deformation.

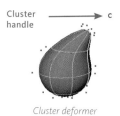

Cluster deformer

CHARACTER ANIMATION

In Maya, character animation typically involves the animation of surfaces using skeleton joint chains and inverse kinematic handles to help drive the motion.

Skeletons and joints

As you have already learned, skeleton joint chains are actually hierarchies. A skeleton is made of joint nodes that are connected visually by bone icons. Binding geometry to these hierarchies lets you create surface deformations when the joints are rotated.

Introduction

Inverse kinematics

By default, joint hierarchies work like any other hierarchy. The rotation of one joint is transferred to the lower joint nodes. This is known as *forward kinematics*. While this method is powerful, it makes it difficult to plant a character's feet or move a hand to control the arm.

Inverse kinematics lets you work with the hierarchy in the opposite direction. By placing an IK handle at the end of the joint chain, Maya will solve all rotations within that joint chain. This is a lot quicker than animating every single joint in the hierarchy. There are three kinds of inverse kinematic solvers in Maya: the IK spline, the IK single chain and the IK rotate plane.

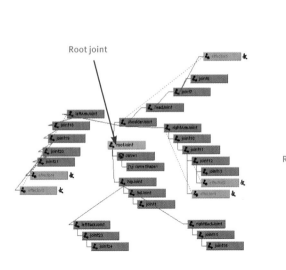

Character joint hierarchy

Joints and bones

Each of these solvers is designed to help you control the joint rotations with the use of an IK handle. As the IK handle is moved, the solver solves joint rotations that allow the end joint to properly move to the IK handle position.

Introduction

The individual solvers have their own unique controls. Some of these are outlined below:

Single chain solver

The *single chain solver* provides a straightforward mechanism for posing and animating a chain.

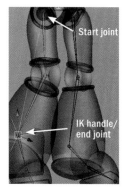

IK single chain solver

Rotate plane solver

The *rotate plane solver* gives you more control. With this solver, the plane that acts as the goal for all joints can be moved by rotating the plane using a *twist attribute* or by moving the *pole vector handle*.

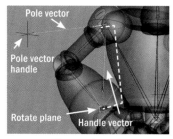

IK rotate plane solver

IK spline solver

The *IK spline solver* lets you control the chain using a spline curve. You can edit the CVs on the spline to influence the rotation of the joints in the chain.

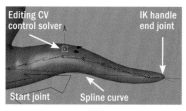

IK spline solver

Skinning your characters

Once you have a skeleton built, you can *bind skin* the surfaces of your character so that they deform with the rotation of the joints. In Maya you can use either *soft skinning* or *hard skinning*. Soft skinning uses weighted clusters while hard skinning does not.

Surface deformations

Flexors

In some cases, skinning a character does not yield realistic deformations in the character's joint areas. You can use *flexors* to add this secondary level of deformations to help control the tucking and bulging of your character.

Sculpt flexor

Lattice flexor

Flexors

RENDERING

Once your characters are set up, you can apply color and texture, then render with realistic lighting.

Shading networks

In Maya, you add texture maps and other rendering nodes to create shading networks. At the end of every shading network is a *shading group* node. This node has specific attributes on it, such as displacement maps and mental ray® for Maya ports, but more importantly, it contains a list of objects that are to be shaded by that network at render time. Without this node at the end of the network, the shader won't render.

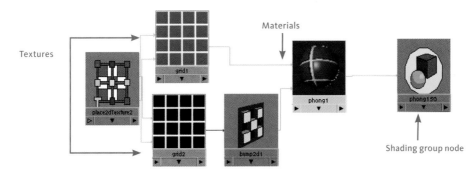

Materials

Textures

grid1

place2dTexture2

phong1

phong1SG

grid2

bump2d1

Shading group node

Shading group dependencies

Think of a shading network as a bucket into which you place all the color, texture and material qualities that you want for your surface. Add a light or two and your effect is achieved.

Texture maps

To add detail to your shading groups, you can *texture map* different attributes. Some of these include bump, transparency and color.

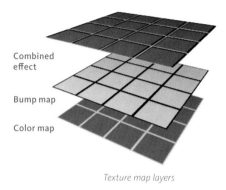

Combined effect

Bump map

Color map

Texture map layers

Lighting

You can light your scenes using any number of lights. These lights let you add mood and atmosphere to a scene in much the same way as lighting is used by a photographer. Maya lets you preview your lights interactively as you model, or you can render to see the final effect.

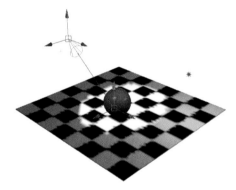

Light manipulator

Motion blur

When a real-life camera takes a shot of a moving object, the final image is often blurred. This *motion blur* adds to the animated look of a scene and can be used in Maya. Maya contains two types of motion blur – a 2 1/2 D solution and a 3D solution.

No motion blur

Motion blur

Motion blur

Hardware rendering

Maya includes *hardware rendering* that uses the power of your graphics card to render an image. This is a quick way to render, as the quality can be very good or it can be used to preview animations. You will need to use the hardware renderer to render most particle effects. These effects can be composited in later with software rendered images of your geometry.

Hardware rendering

A-buffer rendering

The Maya rendering architecture is a hybrid renderer. It uses an EAS (Exact Area Sampling) or A-buffer algorithm for primary visibility from the eye (camera), and then raytraces any secondary rays.

A-buffer rendering

Raytrace rendering

Raytracing lets you include reflections, refractions and raytrace shadows into your scenes. Only objects that have their raytrace options turned on will use this renderer. Raytracing is slower than the A-buffer algorithm and should only be used when necessary.

Raytrace rendering

How the renderer works

The Maya renderer works by looking through the camera at the scene. It then takes a section (or tile) and analyzes whether or not it can render that section. If it can, it will combine the information found in the shading group (geometry, lights and shading network) with the Render Settings information, and the whole tile is rendered.

As the renderer moves on to the next section, it again analyzes the situation. If it hits a tile where there is more information than it wants to handle at one time, it breaks down the tile into a smaller tile and renders.

When you use raytracing, each tile is first rendered with the A-buffer, then the renderer looks for items that require raytracing. If it finds any, it layers in the raytraced sections. When it finishes, you have your finished image, or if you are rendering an animation, a sequence of images.

Rendering of A-buffer tiles in progress

IPR

Maya includes an *Interactive Photorealistic Renderer* (IPR) that gives you fast feedback for texturing and lighting updates. *You will use IPR throughout this book.*

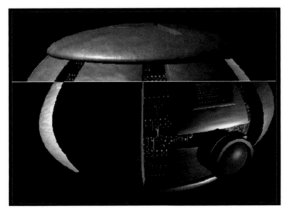

IPR rendering in progress

Conclusion

Now that you have a basic understanding of what Maya software is designed to do, it is time for you to start working with the application directly. The concepts outlined in this Introduction will be clearer when you experience them first-hand.

Project 1
Photo-realism

Probably the most often requested use of 3D is to create photo-realistic imagery, whether it's a rendering of a product, a realistic character, or creating some type of object that will be inserted into a photo of an existing scene. While high-end photo-realistic 3D work pushes the limits of modern computer graphics, very acceptable results can be obtained relatively easily and much quicker than you might expect.

You'll start by learning how to match the perspective of an existing photograph so that your models will look correct once composited. The next three lessons cover modeling and texture projection techniques that can be used in a multitude of ways to quickly and intuitively achieve high levels of realism.

Finally, learn how to 'degrade' the CG look of a 3D rendering by making adjustments to it in Photoshop, giving your rendered imagery the look of film. Using these tricks will enable you to create seamless composites of professional quality.

Lesson 1
Match Perspective

One of the most important benefits of using 3D is the ability to integrate digital models with existing photographs. Using this type of effect, you can seamlessly add props and creatures to a photographed environment. Maya gives you the ability to cast shadows and capture reflections from the 3D models on the objects in your picture, and, conversely, to capture reflections from your 2D photograph on your 3D models. One of the challenges in the integration process of 3D models with 2D photographs is matching the perspective angles from the picture with the camera used to render your objects in Maya.

In this lesson, you will learn the following:

- How to match your camera angles with an existing photograph;
- How to work with an image plane to match perspective;
- How to capture shadows on a photograph with the Use Background shader;
- How to use camera projections to capture reflections on 3D objects.

Setting up your Perspective camera

Prior to importing the existing photograph that will be integrated with 3D geometry, we will need to make some changes to the Perspective camera's attributes.

1 Start a new scene

- Select **File** → **New Scene.** Save your file as *Perspective_match.mb*.

2 Select your Perspective camera

- Maximize your Perspective view window.

- In the Perspective view menu bar, select **View** → **Select Camera.**

Selecting the Perspective View camera

3 Modify Perspective camera attributes to match the analog 35mm camera behavior

Since the original photo we are trying to match was shot with a 35mm camera, we have to change the settings of the Perspective camera to match the behavior of a 35mm analog camera.

- With the Perspective camera selected, go to **Window** → **Attribute Editor.**

- In the Attribute Editor window, open the Film Back section and choose **Film Gate** → **35mm Academy.**

- Scroll down to the Display Options section and turn on **Display Resolution**.

- At the bottom of the Display section set the **Overscan** to **1.6**. This will allow you to see boundaries of the area that will get rendered.

4 Change the image resolution and other rendering settings

In order to ensure a good match between the photograph that will be used and the 3D environment, we have to change the image resolution to match the size of the original image. The original image will then be imported onto an image plane and used as a visual reference while we are matching the camera position.

- In the Maya user interface, click on the Render Settings window.

Render Settings button, upper right side of screen

- In the Render Settings window on the Common tab, open the Image Size section.

- Enter the following values: **Width = 2000**; **Height =1210**.

- Set **Maintain Ratio** to **Pixel Aspect**.

- Make sure that the **Pixel Aspect Ratio** is set to **1.000**.

5 Import your photograph on an image plane

An image plane is a plane attached to the camera that enables the placement of an image file or a sequence of images into a camera view. Image planes are used extensively to create backgrounds and environments, but they can also be used as visual references for modeling or animation. We will import a photograph shot previously with a 35mm camera into an image plane attached to the Perspective camera. This image plane will be our visual reference while we match the Perspective camera position with our image.

- In the Perspective View menu bar, select **View** → **Image Plane** → **Import Image…**

- Retrieve the image called *Kitchen_2.jpg* and click **Open**. You should now see the image displayed inside resolution gate boundaries.

6 Change image plane settings

We will ensure that the image plane stretches correctly to the resolution boundaries, and that the image is only displayed in the Perspective view and none of the other camera views.

- In the Perspective view menu bar, select **View** → **Image Plane Attributes** → **ImagePlane1**.

- In the image plane attributes' section, set the Display to **looking through camera**.

- In the Placement section, set **Fit** → **Best** and click on **Fit to Resolution Gate**.

- The Perspective view should look like the following image:

Placing the photograph in the Perspective view

7 Creating a NURBS plane that will be used to capture shadows from the digital model

We will create a NURBS plane that will be used to capture shadows from the 3D teapot geometry that will be placed on the table. This plane will also help us to match the camera position with the perspective of the photograph.

- In the main Maya menu go to **Create** → **NURBS Primitives** → **Plane**.

- Scale the plane in the Channel Box: **Scale X = 20**; **Scale Y = 20**.

8 Change the shaded display in your Perspective view

Changing the display to X-Ray will allow you to see through the NURBS plane surface, making it easier to position the camera against the image.

- In the Perspective view menu bar, select **Shading → X-Ray.**

- In the Display menu, turn off the Grid (**Display → Grid**).

9 Matching the camera position

In order to be able to match the camera position we will have to use elements from the photograph as visual references. In this instance, we will use the base of the window frames as reference. We know that in reality the window frame base is horizontal and its sides form a 90 degree angle where the two windows meet. We will tumble and track with the camera (without translating or rotating the NURBS plane), until the sides of the plane geometry correspond with the bottom edge of the window frame in the picture.

- In the Perspective view, tumble and track (using the regular camera's navigation tools), until the NURBS plane created earlier lines up with the bottom edges of the window frames.

- Use the following image as a guide:

Perspective view matching the perspective from the photograph

10 Bookmark the camera position

Now that you have found the position of the camera that matches your image, you will want to bookmark it so you can return to this camera position when you want to render your image.

- In the Perspective view menu bar, select **View** → **Bookmarks** → **Edit Bookmarks...**

Creating a new bookmark for the camera

- Type **Match Perspective** in the name field and then press **Enter**. The position of the camera should now be bookmarked.

- To return to the bookmarked position simply select **View** → **Bookmarks** → **Match_Perspective.**

11 Creating the teapot Paint Effects stroke

We will use a Paint Effects brush to create the teapot geometry that will be placed on the table from the picture.

- Click on the Paint Effects shelf tab to make it active, and then click on the teapot brush.

Note: *If you don't have that brush available you can skip this step and import the Teapot.mb file into your current scene.*

Selecting the teapot brush

- **Click+drag** with the brush at the center of the table until you see the beginning of a teapot forming, and then release the brush by clicking on the Select Tool. A teapot should be now placed in your file.

12 Converting the teapot Paint Effects stroke to geometry

In order to have more control over how the teapot will render, you will convert the teapot Paint Effects stroke to geometry.

- With the Select Tool active, click on the teapot to select it.

- With the strokeTeapot1 node selected, go to **Modfy → Convert → Paint Effects to Polygons**. This will convert the teapot stroke into a group of three polygonal surfaces.

13 Position the teapot geometry

You will now adjust the position of the teapot geometry to better integrate it with the background image.

- With the Select Tool active, click on any part of the teapot. Now click on the up arrow key to pick the group node.

- Go to the side view and make sure that the teapot sits on the NURBS plane (on which it will cast a shadow), and that it looks like it is on the table.

Correctly placed teapot geometry

14 Create a Use Background shader for the NURBS plane

Since the teapot already looks like it is sitting on the table, we need to create a shader that will only capture its shadow at render time. This way, in the final rendering it will look as if the teapot is casting shadows on the table surface.

- Go to **Window** → **Rendering Editors** → **Hypershade** to open the Hypershade window.

- On the left side of the Hypershade window in the Create Maya Nodes section, click on the last node in the Surfaces, section called the **Use Background** shader.

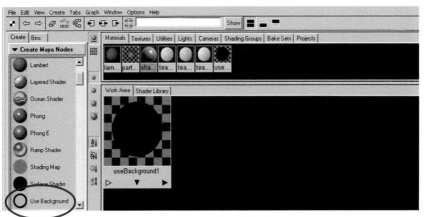

Creating a Use Background shader

- Select the NURBS plane.

- **RMB-click** on the Use Background shader icon in the Hypershade window and choose **Assign Material to Selection** from the pop-up menu.

15 Adjust the Use Background shader attributes

In order to capture shadows on the table surface and not reflections, we will have to make some changes to the attributes of the Use Background shader.

- Go to **Window** → **Rendering Editors** → **Hypershade** to open the Hypershade window.

- Select the Use Background shader. **Double-click** the Use Background shader icon to open the Attribute Editor window.

- In the Use Background attributes' section, set the **Reflectivity** = 0 and **Reflection Limit** = 0.

16 Create a second NURBS plane for generating reflections on the teapot

To get reflections from the table surface on the teapot, we need to make a copy of the initial NURBS plane (which was used to capture shadows on the table). This surface will only be visible in reflections.

- Select the NURBS plane.

- Duplicate it by going to **Edit** → **Duplicate**.

- Move the new surface very slightly above the original NURBS plane.

- Rename the new surface to *TableReflection*.

- Open the Attribute Editor for the new NURBS surface, and in the Render Stats section, turn off everything except **Visible In Reflections** and **Double Sided**.

17 Create a material for the second NURBS plane

We will create a lambert material and map its color with a camera projection. The camera projection node will place the area of the photograph containing the table on the surface used for reflections, and, as a result, will enhance the realism in our final rendering

- Go to **Window** → **Rendering Editors** → **Hypershade** to open the Hypershade window.

- Create a lambert material (from the left side of the Hypershade window), and rename it *TableCloth*.

- In the Attribute Editor window, click on the checker button on the right side of the color swatch to open the **Create Render Node** window.

- In the Create Render Node window under 2D Textures, click **As Projection** and then click on **File** to create an image file texture node.

- Click on the file node associated with the projection node and open *Kitchen_2.jpg*.

- Select the second NURBS plane and assign the new lambert material (TableCloth) to the selection.

> **Note:**   It might be easier to select the second NURBS plane in the Hypergraph window.

Lesson 1: Match Perspective

- In the Perspective view menu bar, select **View** → **Bookmarks** → **Match_Perspective**. It is important to set your camera in its bookmarked position before you link the projection node to the camera.

- In the Hypershade, select the TableCloth lambert material and click on the **Input and Output Connections** button (circled in the image below).

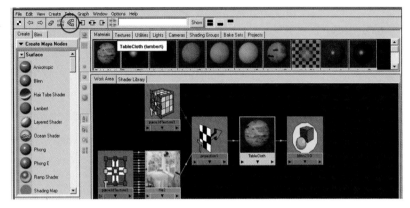

Displaying the input and output connections of a shader

- **Double-click** the projection node to open its Attribute Editor.

- In the Projection attributes section, scroll down to Perspective in the **Proj Type** menu.

- In the Camera Projection Attributes, scroll down to perspShape in the **Link To Camera** menu.

18 Create a material for the teapot that captures the reflections from the photograph

One very important factor when integrating a 3D character or object into an existing photograph or footage is capturing reflections from the elements that exist in the previously shot material onto the 3D assets. We will create a highly reflective material that replicates a chrome surface to capture reflections from the background image.

- Go to **Window** → **Rendering Editors** → **Hypershade** to open the Hypershade window.

- Go to the Create Maya Node side of the Hypershade window to create a blinn material, and rename it *TeapotBlinn*.

- Assign the *TeapotBlinn* material to the teapot geometry.

- Open the Attribute Editor window for the *TeapotBlinn* material. Set the color of the blinn material to black (**H** = 0; **S** = 0; **V** = 0).

- Use the values below for the following attributes:

  Diffuse = 0;

  Translucence = 0;

Translucence Depth = 0;

Translucence Focus = 0;

Eccentricity = 0.347;

Specular Roll Off = 0.700;

Specular Color to white (H = 0; S = 0; V = 1);

Reflectivity = 1.

- In the Raytrace Options of the Attribute Editor, set the **Reflection Limit = 4.**

19 Create additional surfaces replicating the walls in the room from the picture

To enhance the realism of the final rendering further, we will create two NURBS planes that simulate the walls in the photograph. This should be relatively easy to achieve since we have a bookmarked position for the camera and the picture contains enough visual reference, including the window frames and the edge where the windows meet.

- In the main Maya menu go to **Create** → NURBS Primitives → Cube.

- Scale the plane in the Channel Box to: **Scale X = 30; Scale Y = 30; Scale Z = 30.**

- In the Perspective view menu bar select **Shading** → X-Ray.

- Position the scaled cube until it matches the walls like in the image below.

Planes replicating the kitchen walls used to generate reflections

- Delete the bottom surface from the NURBS cube group.

Tip: *You could map the top surface with a light colored lambert shader and use it for reflections from the ceiling.*

Tip: *An option would be to use the front and left sides of the cube to cast reflections on the teapot geometry.*

- Open the Attribute Editor for the new NURBS surfaces, and in the Render Stats section turn off everything other than **Visible In Reflections** and **Double Sided.**

20 Create a material for the new NURBS surfaces

We will create a new lambert material for the cube faces along the walls with windows, and map its color with a camera projection. We will use the exact same technique as the one for creating the TableCloth material.

- Go to **Window → Rendering Editors → Hypershade** to open the Hypershade window.

- Create a lambert material (from the left side of the Hypershade window), and rename it *WallLambert.*

- In the Attribute Editor window, click on the checker button on the right side of the color swatch to open the Create Render Node window.

- In the Create Render Node window under 2D Textures, click **As Projection** and then click on **File** to create an image file texture node.

- Click on the file node associated with the projection node and open *Kitchen_2.jpg.*

- Select the two NURBS planes along the walls with windows (it might be easier to select in the Hypergraph window), and assign the new lambert material (*WallLambert*) to the selection.

- In the Perspective view menu bar, select **View → Bookmarks → Match_Perspective.**

- In the Hypershade, select the WallLambert material and click on the Input and Output Connections button.

- **Double-click** the projection node to open its Attribute Editor.

- In the Projection attributes section, scroll down to Perspective in the **Proj Type** menu.

- In the Camera Projection Attributes, scroll down to perspShape in the **Link To Camera** menu.

The wall geometry mapped with camera projections

21 Prepare the file for rendering in the Render Settings window

We will now choose the appropriate settings for the final rendering. The objects will need to be raytraced in order to capture real reflections. We will use mental ray as the rendering engine for the final rendering.

- Go to **Window** → **Rendering Editors** → **Render Settings** to open the Hypershade window.

- At the top of **Render Using,** scroll down the menu and choose **mental ray**.

- In the Common Tab, set your image format to **TIFF**.

- Set **Image Size** to **2000 X 1210.**

- In the mental ray tab, choose the following settings:

  Anti-aliasing = Quality:

  Min Sample Level = 0;

  Max Sample Level = 2.

- Raytracing :

    Reflections = 6;

    Refraction = 0;

    Max Trace Depth = 6;

    Shadow Trace Depth = 1;

    Scanline = On.

22 Rendering the image

To achieve a high degree of realism in your composite image, it is recommended to render the objects without the image plane and to layer them in Photoshop against the original photograph. It you render them again, the image plane will not have the ability to add film grain or to blur the edges of the objects against the background image (the objects look too sharp compared to the rest of the image). Before you render the image, you will also have to match the lighting from the original image. Rendering the file as it is with the default lighting will not give you the desired result. Proper lighting and shadows will add to the "realism" of the composite image.

Rendering using the raytracing algorithm and default lighting

The same file with the proper lighting will look very different.

The same scene file rendered with lights replicating the lighting from the photograph

Conclusion

In this lesson you learned how to use an image plane for matching 3D objects to an existing photograph. We also looked at the Use Background shader and the camera projection as useful tools for this type of effect.

Lesson 2
Texture Projection

Achieving high levels of photo-realism in computer generated models can be an extremely time-consuming and labor intensive task. If you have the luxury of unlimited time and a bottomless budget you are probably not concerned, but generally the demands of the real-world production environment require clever thinking and visual sleight of hand to produce efficient workflows.

Using scanned or photographed imagery as the source of texture maps can go a long way toward accomplishing this task, but simply applying the image to a surface will rarely yield satisfying results. By carefully manipulating the texture and creating the illusion of detail, you can quickly achieve a believable image. In this lesson you'll add height to a scan of a circuit board to bring it solidly into the 3rd dimension.

In this lesson you'll learn the following:

- How to use texture projection;
- How to use simple shapes to achieve complex illusions;
- How to model from a scan.

Lesson Overview

In this lesson you'll take a scan of a circuit board and make it 3D. The goal is to create a photo-realistic model that can be manipulated within 3D space, enabling you to use all of the Maya software tools to light and compose the scene. For this lesson you have been provided with a scan of the circuit board. If you are really ambitious and want to raise the difficulty level of this lesson, begin by finding a suitable circuit board of your own, scanning it and then following the steps of the lesson.

If you decide you're up to the challenge, begin by scanning the board you've located. One great advantage of having the actual piece to be reproduced in hand is that you have the best possible reference as you work toward your finished model.

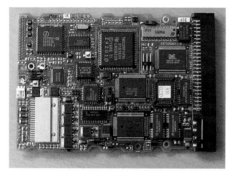

Scavenged circuit board from a dead hard drive

Circuit board on the scanner

These types of objects lend themselves perfectly to scanning. The advantages of using a scanner for image capture is that the lighting remains uniform across the surface and you don't have the issue of perspective distortion to deal with. Plus, it's fast and you can push the resolution as high as you like.

With the scan of your board open in Photoshop, make any rotation adjustment necessary in order to get the board horizontally and vertically aligned. Taking care at this stage will ensure precise alignment of the texture to your model when you are working in Maya.

Scanned circuit board

> *Tip*: *A fast way to square up an image is by using Photoshop's grid. From the menu, select* **View** → **Show** → **Grid**. *Then use the* **Transform Tool** *to rotate the image, aligning horizontal or vertical edges within the image to the grid lines.*

> *Tip*: *You can adjust the density of the Photoshop grid under Preferences.*

> *Note*: *Using the Transform Tool in conjunction with the grid is a good method for correcting perspective distortion in photographed textures. By changing the* **Transform Tool's** *settings to* **Distort** *or* **Shear**, *then stretching the corners of the image to align edges within the image with the grid, you can quickly square-up a distorted photo.*

1 Create a new scene file

- Open Maya. Set your project directory to *Project_01/Lesson_02_CircuitBoard*.

- If you just opened Maya you'll already have a new scene. If you are continuing from a previous lesson, make a new scene now by selecting **File** → **New Scene**, or from the keyboard press **Cmd+n** (**Ctrl+n**).

2 Make a polygon base for the circuit board

You need to create a base to project the texture onto, and this base needs to precisely match the dimensions of the scanned image.

- From the menu, select **Create** → **Polygon Primitives** → **Plane** → ☐.

- Set the settings to:

Width = 1.0	Subdivisions Along Height = 1
Height = 1.0	Axis = Y
Subdivisions Along Width = 1	Texture = Stretch To Fit

> *Note:* *The* ☐ *icon is the* **Option Box**. *Some menu items have this box icon which lets you access the options for that tool.*

- Click **Create**.

- Change the proportions of the polygon. In the **Channel Box**, change the **Scale X** value to **14.64** and the **Scale Z** value to **19.92**.

  These values are taken from the width and height pixel dimensions of the scanned image. If you are using your own scan, use those dimensions instead.

3 Set-up your workspace

- Change your workspace view by selecting **Panels** → **Saved layouts** → **Hypershade** → **Render** → **Persp Vertical**.

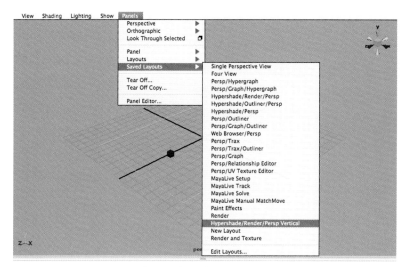

Changing the workspace layout

4 Create a projection shader

When you assign a texture to a surface, Maya will automatically fit it to that surface. In this case, you want to create a shader that will NOT automatically resize itself each time it is assigned to a new piece of geometry, so for that you'll utilize a planar projection shader that utilizes a 3D placement node.

5 Create a texture

- In the Hypershade, select **Create** → **Create Options** and make sure both **Include Shading Group With Materials** and **Include Placement With Textures** are selected.

- In the Create Bar under **Surface,** click once on the **Blinn** material icon to create a new material.

- In the **2D Textures** section, make sure the **As Projection** option is selected.

- Click on the **File** icon to create a file node.

- Select **Graph** → **Rearrange Graph** to display all of the newly created nodes.

All nodes are now visible in the work area.

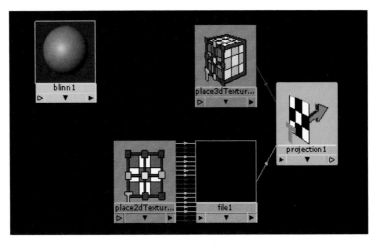

Newly created nodes in the work area

6 **Connect the nodes to create the shader**

- In the **Hypershade,** double-click on the **projection1 node** to open it in the Attribute Editor.

- In the Attribute Editor, open the **Projection Attributes** section. The default setting for **Proj Type** is **Planar**, which is what we want to use in this case.

7 **Load the texture image file**

- In the **Hypershade,** double-click on the **file1 node** to open it in the Attribute Editor.

- Click on the folder icon next to **Image Name** and open **sourceimages** → **CB_Scan-1.color.tif** to load it.

The shader nodes will update and show the texture file.

8 **Connect the projection node to the texture node**

- **MMB** the **Projection node** and drag it on top of the **blinn1 node**. Choose **Color** from the pop up menu to connect it.

- In the **Hypershade, double-click** on the **blinn1 node** to open it in the Attribute Editor.

- Scroll down to the **Hardware Texturing** section and expand it. Change **Texture Resolution** to **Highest (256x256)**.

9 Clean up the work area

- From the Hypershade menu, select **Graph** → **Rearrange Graph**.

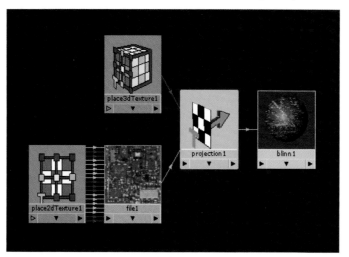

Hypershade menu

Assigning a shader

You have now created a shader that utilizes the projection node to lock down the position of the texture in 3D space.

The next step is to assign the shader to the polygon plane you made at the beginning of the lesson, and adjust it so it fits.

1 Assign the shader

In the center of the Perspective view you'll see a green texture placement icon. This is the 3D placement icon for the projection node. Note that it is currently pointing in the wrong direction – it should be pointing toward the polygon surface it has been assigned to.

- In the Perspective view, press the **6 key** to go into textured preview mode.

- **MMB** the **blinn1** texture node and drag it to the polygon plane.

  The texture is now assigned to the plane. It will show as stripes because the texture is being projected along the length of the poly plane rather than perpendicular to it.

2 Fit the texture to the plane

- Click on the **green placement icon** that is visible in the middle of the Perspective window to select it.

- Press the **E key** to select the Rotate Tool.

- Hold down the **J key** to constrain the rotation, click on the red arc (X rotation axis), and rotate the placement icon so that it is pointing straight down.

- Notice that the Attribute Editor updated to show the settings for the place3dTexture node. Under the **3D Texture Placement Attributes**, click on **Fit to group bbox**.

The texture placement icon resizes to fit the dimensions of the poly plane.

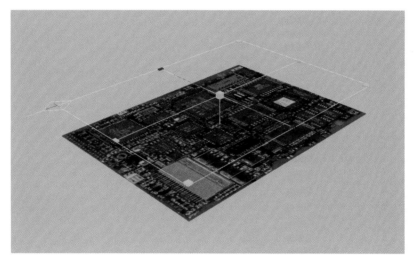

Circuit board shader assigned and fit to the polygon plane

3 Set-up your workspace

- Change your workspace view by selecting **Panels** → **Saved layouts** → **4 view**.

- In the top view, press the spacebar once (quickly) to zoom the window.

- Press the **6 key** for shaded texture preview.

4 Add a polygon cube to the model

- From the menu, select **Create** → **Polygon Primitives** → **Cube** to place a poly cube in the scene.

- With the poly cube still selected, press the **W** key to select the **Move Tool**.

- Move the poly cube to the center of one of the board chips.

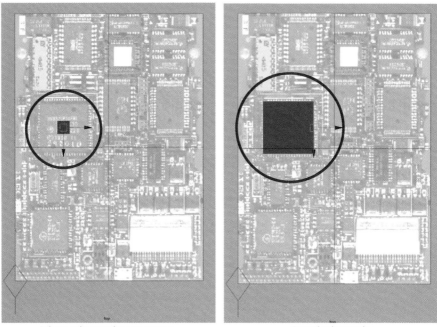

Polygon cube moved to new position   *Resized polygon cube*

5 Fit the cube to the chip

By using the projected texture as your guide, you can precisely fit the poly cube to the image. If Maya polygon modeling tools are unfamiliar to you, refer to the user's guide that came with the Maya software.

- **RMB** on top of the poly cube and select **Edge** from the pop-up menu.

- **LMB** to drag-select a side edge.

  By clicking and dragging a box to make your selection, you select both the top and bottom edges of the poly cube at the same time.

- Move the edge so it matches the corresponding edge of the chip.

- Repeat this action for the remaining edges.

Assigning textures using UV coordinates

This next step is done for technical reasons and is necessary to enable this particular projection technique to work. Textures are assigned to polygon surfaces by using *UV coordinates*. The UV coordinates essentially bind the texture to the surface so that when you move the surface, the texture moves along with the polygon. 99.9% of the time, that is exactly what you want to happen. In this instance, however, you want to be able to move and adjust the polygon "chips" without having the texture move with it, but rather for the polygon to simply pick up the texture as it is being projected.

Think of using a slide projector to shine an image on the wall, and then placing some type of object in front of it to pick up the projected image. The image rolls across the surface of the object as you move it. The same principle is at work here.

It is a simple matter of deleting the UV coordinates from the polygon shape and placing the shape in the path of the projected texture.

1 **Delete UV coordinates from the poly cube**

- With the poly cube selected, go to the menu and select **Polygon UVs** → **Delete UVs**.

- Assign the **blinn1** projected circuit board texture to the poly cube.

  The cube now has an odd-looking semi-transparent grey texturing to it. This is a warning texture indicating that the object no longer has any UVs assigned to it.

2 **Do a test rendering**

- Open the Render view window and do a test rendering.

  Notice that the poly cube has inherited the projected texture.

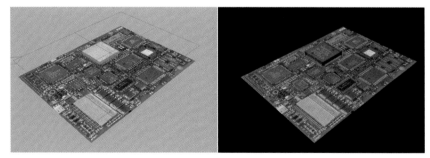

Textured preview and rendered view of the polygon cube

3   Duplicate the poly cube to make more chips

- Return to the zoomed top view.

- Click on the poly cube to select it.

- Press the **w key** to select the Move Tool, if it's not the current tool.

- From the menu, select **Edit** → **Duplicate** → ☐.

- In the options box, select **Edit** → **Reset Settings** and **Duplicate**.

4   Move the duplicated poly cube to another chip location

5   Resize the duplicated cube to fit

- Select and move the edges as you did earlier in this lesson.

6   Repeat

Repeat the above steps until you have created polygon shapes for all of the major chips on the board.

> **Tip:**   Change your selection to faces, and move the top face of every poly cube to vary its height.

> **Tip:**   Select the polygon shape and re-center the pivot point by going to the menu and selecting **Modify** → **Center Pivot**.

7   Save your work

- Name the model *CircuitBoard.mb* and save it in the **scenes** folder of the project directory.

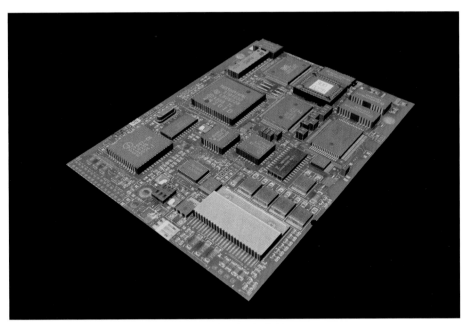

Circuit board with 3d chips

Conclusion

By now, you should have a good 3D replica of the circuit board. The more detail you add to the polygon meshes, the more realistic the result. Beveling the top and corner edges of the chips can add a nice edge detail that will pick up edge highlights when you render the image.

Now that the coarse modeling is done, a second level of surface detail and realism will be added by assigning additional features to the shader. That is the focus of the next lesson.

Lesson 3
Secondary Detail

In Lesson 2 you built a simple model of a circuit board that offered high levels of realism. Even though the results are fairly good, there remains a rather obvious CG quality to it. In this lesson you'll learn a few techniques that will let you take your images to the next stage of believability by adding secondary levels of detail.

In this lesson you'll learn the following:

- How to apply bump maps;
- How to use specular maps;
- How to "degrade" an image to make it more photographic.

Lesson Overview

In this lesson you'll continue with the model of the circuit board you built in Lesson 2.
If you are jumping directly to this lesson, you can start by opening *L3_CircuitBoard2_start.mb*
from the lesson's project directory.

1 **Set the project directory**

- Launch Maya and from the menu,
  select **File → Project → Set...** and
  navigate to the **Lesson_3_CircuitBoard2**
  folder. Click **Choose**.

2 **Open the file**

- Open the file you saved from Lesson 2
  (CircuitBoard.mb), or begin with the one
  provided: – *L3_CircuitBoard2_start.mb*.

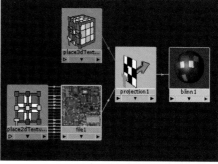

Selected nodes

3 **Set-up your workspace**

- Change your workspace view by
  selecting **Panels → Saved layouts →
  Hypershade → Render →
  Persp Vertical**.

4 **Graph the circuit board shader**

- **RMB** on the blinn1 shader and select
  Graph Network.

5 **Add a bump map and a specular map
  to the shader network**

By adding a bump map to the shader you
can add subtle detail to the surface that
would be impossible to model. It creates
the illusion of surface height variations
when the model is rendered.

In real life not all parts of a surface are
equally shiny or matte. You can mimic this
same quality in Maya through the use of a
specular map.

- In the work area, click once on the **file1**
  node to select it, hold down the **Shift**
  key and click once on the **projection1**
  node to add it to the selection.

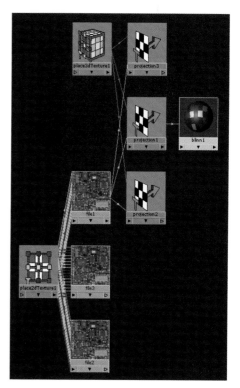

New nodes added to the shader network

- From the Hypershade menu, select **Edit** → **Duplicate** → **With Connections To Network**.

  This creates two new file nodes that have maintained their connections to single placement nodes.

- Press the **g key** to repeat your last action.

> **Tip**: The **g key**, by default, is assigned to "Repeat Last" and repeats the last action performed.

- Rearrange the graph.

6 Reconnect the new nodes

The new projection nodes are still connected to the original file1 texture node and need to be reconnected to file2 and file3 nodes. You'll use new image maps that were generated by making variations in Photoshop to the original scan of the circuit board. This is a very easy step to do but important to do correctly. Follow the next steps closely.

Establish new connections from the file nodes to the projection nodes. When done correctly, there will be a single green line going from each file node to each projection node. Make sure that file1 connects to projection1, file2 to projection2 and file3 to projection3.

- **MMB** on top of the **file3 node** and drag it on top of the **projection3 node**. Select **image** from the pop up menu.

- Repeat this step for **file2** by dragging it to **projection2** and connecting it to the **image** input.

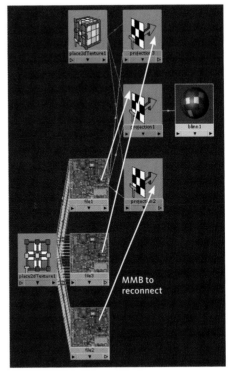

Reconnect the new nodes

Lesson 3: Secondary Detail

> **Note**: *Verify that your connections are correct by following the green lines between nodes: file1 to projection1, file2 to projection2 and file3 to projection3. If you need to make changes, **MMB+drag** the correct nodes to each other and Maya will automatically reconnect them.*

7 **Load the bump map**

- MMB on the **projection2 node** and drag it on top of the **blinn1 node**. Select **bump map** from the pop up menu.

- Click on the **file2 node** to load it into the Attribute Editor.

- Click on the folder icon next to **Image name** and select *CB_Scan-1.bump.tif* and **Open**.

  You've now loaded the image file that will be used for the bump map. If you want to see it in more detail, press the View button underneath the image name space and it will open in Photoshop.

Bump map image file derived from the original circuit board scan

8 **Adjust the bump map**

- Zoom in tight on a section of the board in the Perspective window so that you can see detail.

- In the Render view window, select **Options** and set the **Test Resolution** to **320 x 240**.

- Do an IPR render.

- Select the entire image.

- In the Attribute Editor, experiment with the Bump Depth slider and see how the setting effects the bump effect.

  *A setting of **0.75** seems to work well. You can set it where you like, but like anything good, don't overdo it.*

Specular map

9 **Add the specular map**

- **MMB+drag** the **projection2 node** to the **blinn1 node** and choose **specularColor** from the pop-up menu.

- Click on the **file2 node** to load it in the Attribute Editor, and load *CB_Scan-1.spec.tif* as the image file.

Notice how the IPR image updates to reflect the change to the shader network.

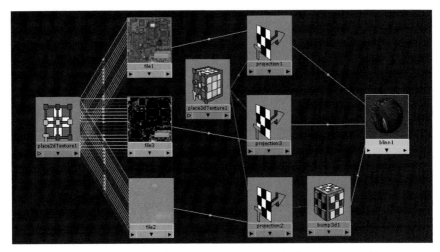

Updated shader network for the circuit board texture, with all its connections visible

Test rendering with bump map and specular map applied to the model

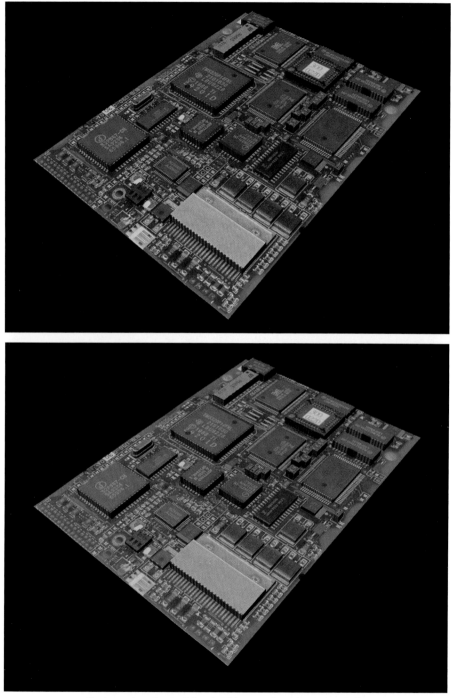

Top image shows the circuit board with bump and specular maps applied

These images have been rendered with a default light that Maya automatically creates when you do your first rendering. Custom lighting will take this image even further. Experiment by adding some lights to your scene and see how they affect the overall look. The IPR renderer is a fantastic tool for this type of exploration.

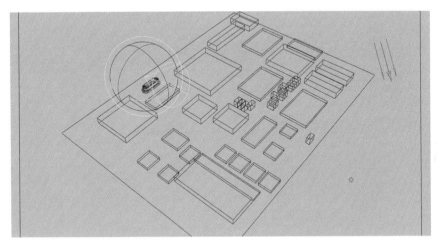

Three lights added to the scene

10 Set your Render Settings

- From the Render view menu, select **Options** → **Render Settings**.

- In the Image File Output section, make the **File Name Prefix** *CircuitBoard*.

  Maya will use the name of the scene file by default for the image name, or you can override it and give the rendered file a custom name, which is entered here.

- Change **File Format** to **PSD**.

- In the Image Size section, check **Maintain Width Height Ratio**.

- Change the **Width** to **1280**. The **Height** should automatically change to **960**.

- Click the **Maya Software tab**.

- Set **Quality** to **Production**.

- In the Multi-pixel filtering section, check **Use Multi Pixel Filter**.

  This filter is primarily used to prevent flickering of fine lines and details when rendering animation sequences, but softens the overall image unnecessarily for print applications.

- Close the Render Settings window.

- **Save** the scene.

11 Render the image and save it

- Change to the Rendering menu, then select **Render** → **Batch Render**.

Maya will now render the file and save it as **CircuitBoard.psd** *in the project directory* **images** *folder.*

Rendered image with lights and shadows

Now that you have the basic workflow and areas to address, how far you take it is dependent upon how much time you are willing to put into it. Adding details to the polygon chips will have the biggest impact on how "real" the model appears. Careful adjustment of the edge positions can also have a significant impact, as well as adjustments to the bump and shadow maps.

Note: *If you want to move the circuit board as a cohesive whole, you'll need to make it one single polygonal object that includes the texture placement node before doing so. Maya makes this easy to do. Select all of the poly chips and the board, then from the modeling menu select* **Polygons** → **Combine**. *This turns all of the separate parts into one polygonal object. Next, select the 3D texture placement icon in the scene,* **Shift-click** *to select the circuit board, and from the menu, select* **Edit** → **Parent**. *This groups the 3D placement node under the combined polygon node you just created, so when you move the model the projected texture moves with it and texture registration is maintained. Click on the circuit board and you'll see that all the parts become selected and are treated as one piece, which can now be moved, rotated and scaled.*

Making the rendering "photographic"

One of the big "problems" with CG imagery is that it's generally too perfect. Razor sharp edges, super-crisp details and smoothly graduating colors are just a few of the things that make CG elements pop out, rather than blend in, when integrated into photographic environments.

To combat this it is necessary to degrade the quality of the rendered imagery to match the photograph you intend to composite it with. This next section offers a few techniques that you can use in Photoshop to bring the rendered image more in sync with the environment you want to place it in.

1 **Open the rendered CircuitBoard.psd image**

- Launch Photoshop.

- Navigate to the **Lesson_3_CircuitBoard2** → **images** directory and open *CircuitBoard.psd*.

  If you are using the image provided with this lesson, navigate to the **Lesson_3_CircuitBoard2** → **Photoshop** *directory to find the image file.*

- In the **Layers** tab, **double-click** the **Background layer** to convert it to a layer with transparency.

- From the menu, select **Select** → **Load Selection**. Change **Channel** to **Alpha 1** and click **OK**.

- From the menu, select **Select** → **Inverse**.

- Press the **Delete (backspace) key** to delete the selected area.

- From the menu, select **Select** → **Deselect**.

- From the menu, select **Layer** → **Matting** → **Remove Black Matte**.

  The rendered image is on its own layer and ready to be composited.

Maya rendering converted to a Photoshop layer

2   Open the environment image

- Navigate to the **Lesson_3_CircuitBoard2** → **images** directory and open *DirtCrown.psd*.

- Drag it into the *CircuitBoard.psd* window and make it the **Background** layer.

3   Adjust the color tint of the CircuitBoard rendering

- Click on **Layer 0** to make it active.

- From the menu, select **Image** → **Adjustments** → **Match Color**.

- In the Options box that pops up, make sure **Preview** is checked **on**. Under **Image Statistics**, change the **Source** to *CircuitBoard.psd*. Change **Layer** to **Background**.

- Adjust **Luminance = 130, Color Intensity = 100** and **Fade = 50**. Click **OK**.

  This modifies the circuit board color palette to better match the environment.

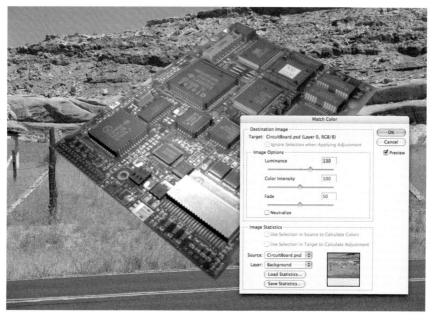

Using Match Color in Photoshop to rebalance the color of the circuit board

4   Soften edge sharpness

The edges of the circuit board are the sharpest item in the composition and look unnatural. Adding a slight blur will go a long way toward integrating the two layers.

- Select the **Blur Tool**. Choose a small brush size (13px, soft) and run it around the edge of the circuit board.

Tip: *You can do this quickly by loading the Alpha channel to select the circuit board shape. Then, click the Paths tab and from the options select Make Work Path. Click on Work Path and then from the options click on Stroke Path. A pop up box lets you choose which tool you want to use, but should show the Blur Tool if it is still your last selected tool. Click OK, and the Blur Tool runs around the edge of the circuit board.*

- Look over the image and manually soften any other edges you feel are too sharp.

5   Add grain to match the photo

This one is a really good trick and lets you precisely match the grain structure of the photo you want to composite your rendered elements into.

All photos have some type of a grain structure to them, whether from film or digital. Adding the same grain structure to the 3D rendered images is a subtle move, but goes a long way toward achieving a beautiful integration.

Note: *Look closely at the sky in the DirtCrown.psd image and you'll see the grain of that particular image.*

- Create a new layer and fill it with 50% grey by selecting **Edit** → **Fill**. In the pop up box, set contents to **50**% grey and Blending to **Normal**. Make sure this layer is at the top of the layer stack.
- From the menu, select **Filter** → **Noise** → **Add Noise**. Set the **Amount = 2%**, **Distribution = Gaussian** and check on **Monochromatic**.
- Set the **Blending Mode** to **Overlay**.

Tip: *50% grey in Overlay mode is neutral. The image underneath will get pushed lighter or darker as the pixels go lighter or darker from that midpoint.*

- Group the Noise layer and the Circuitboard layer by holding down the Option key and clicking on the line dividing the two layers in the Layer tab. The cursor will change when it's in the correct location. Click on the line to group them.
- Save your work.

    This will restrict the film grain to the circuit board only, and not add it to the background.

Note: *Grouping layers restricts the upper grouped layers to the opaque areas of the layer at the bottom of the group, effectively making the bottom layer a mask for the layers above it. This is a fast and intuitive method of restricting effects to only certain layers.*

On the left, with film grain added. On the right, without.

Final composited image

Conclusion

These are just some of the approaches that can be used when it comes to achieving photo-realism in your renderings, but the results are immediately apparent when you compare the image that you had at the end of Lesson 2 with the one you have now. The key points for achieving seamless composites are high attention to detail, particularly hard edges, and careful observation of how light works on objects in the real world.

Practice and experience will take you further. There were numerous techniques covered in these last two lessons that you should experiment on as you work through the rest of the book.

Lesson 4
Building Blocks

Photographing children is difficult enough, and when there are props or set dressing involved, composing the shot becomes even more difficult. In this lesson you will learn to simply focus on capturing the moment, and later use Maya to create a fun and unique set for the background. You will also learn how to use texture maps and displacement maps to add depth to the texture without having to model the detail.

The challenge of this lesson is to create realistic high-key lighting for the building blocks so it will match the style of lighting on the child. Notice the details like shadows and reflections.

In this lesson, you will learn how to:

- Create and texture the blocks;
- Change the environment color;
- Use the Final Gather feature from the mental ray Renderer;
- Composite images together in Adobe® Photoshop®.

Set your project

Before beginning any project, it is a good habit to set it up properly. This way, it will be easier to find your scene files and renderings.

- Transfer the support files directory for this lesson into the Maya projects directory.

- Select **File** → **Project** → **Set...**

- Navigate to the **BuildingBlocks** project directory.

- Press the **Choose** button.

- Save your scene as *BuildingBlockScene*.

Creating the floor surface

1. **Create a primitive plane**

This plane will be used as the floor underneath the blocks.

- From the **Create** menu, select **Polygon Primitive** → **Plane**.

- Scale the plane in the Channel Box in **XYZ** by **50**.

- Use the Channel Box to rename the plane to *Floor*.

- Turn the grid off by selecting **Show** → **Grid** from the panel.

- Turn on **Shaded Mode** by pressing **5**.

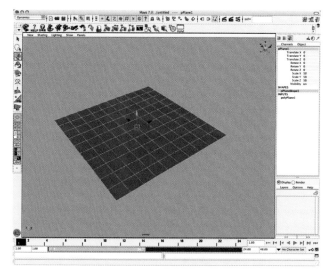

Polygon plane at the origin scaled by 50.

Creating the building blocks

1. **Create three polygon primitive cubes**

   The scene will have three polygon primitive cubes.

   - From the menu, select **Create** → **Polygon Primitives** → **Cubes**.

   - **Scale** the cube in the Channel Box by **5** in **XYZ**.

   - **Rename** the cube to *BlockOne*.

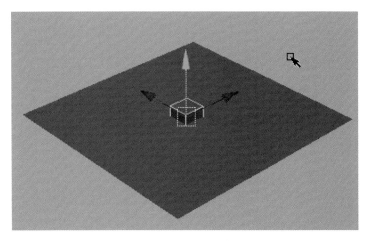

Cube at origin and scaled by 5

2. **Translate the cube to sit on the floor**

   You could use the Move Tool and the different camera views to align the cube to sit on the floor, but there is a more efficient method to align objects. Instead, you will use the Align Objects Tool.

   - Select the **Floor** and then **Shift-select** the **BlockOne**.

     It's important to select the floor first because you want the cube to move into position rather than having the floor move into position.

   - From the menu, select **Modify** → **Snap Align Objects** → **Align Objects** → ❏.

     The Align Objects Option window will pop-up.

Options set for the Align Tool

- Select the following options in this window :

    Align Mode to **Stack**;

    Align in to **World Y**.

- Click on the **Align** button.

    The cube should now be transformed in the Y-axis and be sitting on top of the floor.

3. **Duplicate the cube to create the second and third block**

    You will use the duplicate command to create the second cube.

    - Select only the cube.

    - From the menu, select **Edit** → **Duplicate**.

    Note: *At the moment it looks as if a duplicate cube has not been created. This is because it's sitting in the same location as the original.*

    - Use the **Move Tool** (**w** keyboard shortcut) and translate the new cube in the **Z-axis** next to the original.

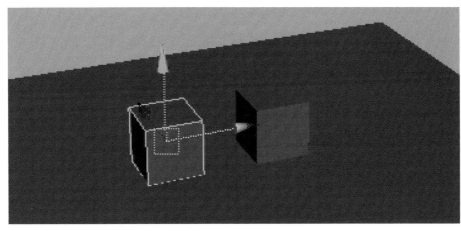

Duplicated cube

- Rename the new cube *BlockTwo*.

- With *BlockTwo* still selected, select **Edit** → **Duplicate** again.

- **Move** the latest duplicated cube along the Z-axis in-between *BlockOne* and *BlockTwo*.

- Rename this cube to *BlockThree*.

- **De-select** everything and select *BlockTwo*.

- **Shift-select** *BlockThree*.

- Select **Modify** → **Snap Align Object** → **Align Objects**.

   BlockThree should now be stacked on top of BlockOne and BlockTwo.

Note: *You may have noticed that you did not have to go into the options window for the Align Objects Tool this time. This is because the settings in the option window are maintained until you reset them. Since you used the same Tool setting as when you stacked the cube on the floor, you did not need to open the options window for the Align Objects Tool.*

4 Stagger and position the blocks

You will now slightly rotate and reposition the cubes using the Universal Manipulation Tool.

- Use the Universal Manipulator (Ctrl-t) to stagger the cubes slightly. Translate the cubes in X and Z, and then rotate them around the Y-axis.

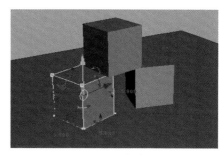

Staggered blocks

Texturing the blocks

The blocks are the only models you require for this scene. You will now apply material and texture attributes to them.

1 Create a lambert material for a cube face

Since the finish quality of the cubes will be more matte than glossy, you will use a lambert material node.

- Open the Hypershade window.

- From the Create Maya Nodes column, click on the **Lambert** surface.

- **Double-click** the blinn in the work area to bring up the Attribute Editor.

- Change the name to *LetterA***.**

2 Import a file texture

You will be importing a file texture to apply to one of the faces of the cubes.

- In the Hypershade, select the **LetterA** material node.

- In the Attribute Editor, click on the map button next to the **Color** attribute.

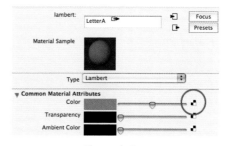

The map button

Project 1: Photo-realism

The Create Render Node window will pop-up.

- From the 2D Texture section, click on **File.**

  In the Attribute Editor, the attributes for the File node will appear.

- Click on the folder icon next to the **Image Name** field.

  This button will open a finder window where you will assign the texture.

- Select the file **A.tif** from the list and click **Open.**

  The Attribute Editor will update with the new texture.

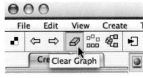

Folder icon for Image Name

3 **View the connections in the Hypershade**

You have now created a simple network connection using a shader. You can use the Hypershade to view this connection.

- In the Hypershade, click on the **Clear Graph** button.

- Select the **LetterA** material node in the Materials tab.

- Click on the **Input** and **Output Connections** button.

  This will graph all the connections to go into and out of the material node.

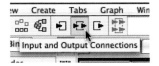

Clear Graph button

The Input and Output Connections button

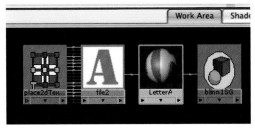

The node connections in the Hypershade window

4 Apply the texture to a face on a cube

If you were to assign this shader onto a cube, each of the six sides would be assigned the letter A. Instead, you will assign the texture to one face at a time.

- With your mouse over **BlockTwo**, **RMB-click**, and select **Face** from the pop-up menu.

- Click on the center of the front surface of **BlockTwo.**

- In the Hypershade, **RMB-click** over **LetterA**, and select **Assign Material to Selection** from the pop-up menu.

- Press **6** to view the scene in Shaded Texture mode.

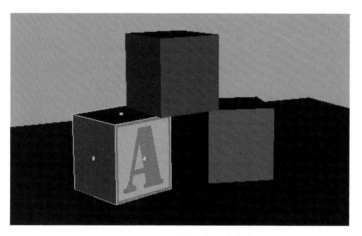

LetterA texture assigned to a face of BlockTwo

5 Create a material and texture node for the remaining surfaces

Repeat the previous steps for all the other surfaces. Keep in mind that you do not need to put the textures on the faces of the cube that you will not be seeing in the final render, like the bottom and back surfaces.

- Repeat steps 1 - 4 for the following letters: B, C, E, O, R, S, T, V.

Tip: *If you want to rotate the textures on any of the surfaces, graph the material node in the Hypershade, click on the* **place2DTexture** *node and change the* **Rotate UV** *attribute to either, 90, 180, or 270.*

Textures applied to main surfaces

Assign a material for the floor

The floor still has the default floor shader. You'll use a phong material because you want the floor to have reflections.

1   **Create a phong material node for the floor**

- **Double-click** the *floorMaterial* to open the Attribute Editor.

- Rename this to *floorMaterial.*

- In the Attribute Editor, click on the Color swatch to open the Color Chooser.

- In the Color Chooser, change the **H, S, V** values to **0,0,1**, to make the floor white.

- **MMB-drag** the **floorMaterial** onto the **floor** surface in the Perspective window to assign it.

2. **Perform a test render**

For fun, go ahead and do a test render just to see how the scene is coming along. You'll probably notice how unrealistic and bland the image looks. You'll also notice that the background is black instead of white.

Change the environment color

The background color is determined by an attribute within the camera node that is being rendered. In this case, the Perspective camera's **Environment** attribute needs to be changed to white.

1. **Open the Perspective camera's attribute window**

- From the Perspective panel menu, select **View** → **Select Camera**.

- Open the Attribute Editor, scroll down to **Environment**, and **open** the tab.

- Move the slider to white.

2. **Perform a test render**

- Click the **Render Current Frame** button again to see the effect of the white background.

Switch to mental ray Renderer

So far you have been using the Maya Software Renderer. mental ray® offers some unique features that are not found in the others like Global Illumination and Final Gather. In this lesson you will learn how to use the Final Gather feature to add more realism to the render. Final Gather also allows you to render a scene without lights! It can render the scene by turning every object into a light source so each object in a scene influences the color of its surroundings as in the real world. Even though you have not added lights to this scene, it has been illuminated. This is because the default setting in Maya is to add a default light if there is not one detected at render time. However, with Final Gather, lights are not needed so you will turn this default setting to off.

1. **Switch to the mental ray Renderer**

   You will switch from the Maya Software Renderer to the mental ray Renderer using the Render Settings window.

   Render Settings window button

   • Press the **Render Settings** button in the Status Line or Render view window.

   • In the Render Settings window, change **Render Using** to **mental ray**.

2. **Turn off the default light setting**

   Since you are going to be using Final Gather, you don't need to have Maya add a default light when you render.

   • In the **Common** tab, scroll down to the **Render Options** section.

   • Turn off the **Enable Default Light** option.

3. **Turn on Final Gather**

   You can quickly turn on the Final Gather options by using the Quality Presets.

   • In the Render Settings window, click on the **mental ray** tab.

   • From the **Quality Preset** pulldown menu, select **PreviewFinalGather**.

4. **Perform a test render**

   You will see a large improvement already using this renderer.

Final Gather rendering

Tweak the shader attributes

At this stage the render is looking quite good. You can start to adjust some of the default settings for the material nodes.

1. **Brighten the faces of the cubes**

   Without having to add a light to the scene, you can adjust the brightness of the blocks by adjusting the ambient color of their material node.

   - Open the Hypershade and select **LetterA.**
   - Open the Attribute Editor.
   - Click on the **Ambient Color** swatch.
   - Enter a value of **.3** for **V.**
   - Repeat this for the other letters.

   | *Tip:* | To adjust attributes of nodes that share the same attributes simultaneously, you can use the Channel Box. In this case, to adjust the ambient color of all the letter textures at once, Shift-select the materials in the Hypershade, and in the Channel Box, adjust the **Ambient Color RGB** to a value of **.3.** |

Transparency B	0
Ambient Color R	0.3
Ambient Color G	0.3
Ambient Color B	0.3
Incandescence R	0

2. **Adjust the diffuse value of the floor**

   The floor can have more realistic highlights by increasing the **Diffuse** value.

   - In the Hypershade, select the **FloorMaterial.**
   - In the Attribute Editor, increase the **Diffuse** value to **.95.**

3. **Perform a test render**

   This rendering has come a long way! But, there's still more you can do.

Adding more depth to the cubes

The rendering is looking more realistic due to Final Gather, however, you can definitely add more depth to the cubes using displacement maps. Displacement maps are grayscale textures you map to objects to create true surface relief (elevations and depressions) on an otherwise flat object. With displacement maps, depressions and elevations become part of the geometry of the object, changing the topology. This is unlike bump maps that only create the illusion of surface relief.

1. **Add a displacement map to the Block shader**

   In the source images folder for this project, there are accompanying grayscale images of the letters. These will be used as the displacement maps.

   - In the Hypershade, select **LetterA**.

   - Click the **Input Output Connections** button.

   - In the work area, select the **lambertSG** node.

   - In the Attribute Editor, click on the **lambertSG** tab.

   - Click on the texture map icon next to the **Displacement Map** field.

The Shading Group node in the Attribute Editor

- Click on **File** in the Create Render Node window.

  This step is similar to when you added the texture to the material node.

- Click on the folder icon next to the **Image Name** field.

Pre Filter Radius	2.000			
Image Name				
	Reload	Edit	View	

Use BOT

Folder icon for Image Name

- Select the file **A_bw.tif** from the list, and click **Open.**

  The Attribute Editor will update with the new texture.

2. **Perform a test render**

   Zoom in closely to LetterA to see what the displacement map is doing. You'll notice the default settings are somewhat problematic. The surface has detached itself from the cubes, and the overall quality could be better.

Default displacement settings need adjustments

3. Improve the quality of the displacement

The displacement map depth and position can be controlled by adjusting the Alpha Gain and the Alpha Offset.

- In the Hypershade, click on the **Textures** tab.
- Click on the black and white letter A.

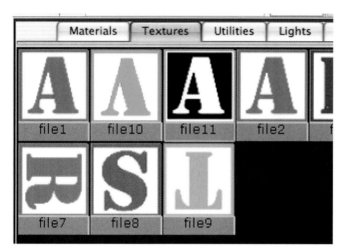

Select the black and white letter A in the Hypershade

- In the Attribute Editor, open the **Color Balance** section.
- Set the **Alpha Gain** to 0.3.

  This will reduce the depth of the displacement.

- Set the **Alpha Offset** to -0.3.

  This will set the overall displaced surface back the same amount of units as the set displacement above.

- In the Perspective window, select **BlockTwo.**
- In the Attribute Editor, open the **Displacement Map** sections, and set the following:

  Initial Sample Rate to 75;

  Extra Sample Rate to 35.

4. Perform a test render

The test will now show a much improved displacement and proper placement of the texture over the surface of the A. Notice the difference between the letter A and the other surfaces?

Much improved displacement mapping

5. Repeat the previous steps to create a displacement map for all the other surfaces

You can now go ahead and follow the steps you did for displacement mapping Letter A to all the other shading groups. Don't forget to match the rotation of the displacement maps with the texture maps. You can quickly verify that the rotations match by viewing all of them in the Textures Tab. Also, remember to increase the **Initial Sample Rate** and **Extra Sample Rate** for **BlockOne** and **BlockThree** as indicated in step 3.

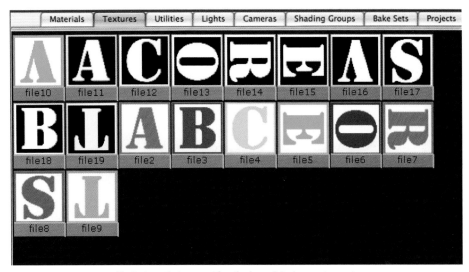

| Materials | Textures | Utilities | Lights | Cameras | Shading Groups | Bake Sets | Projects |

The textures that are used for all color and displacement mapping

Final render output

The last step before compositing this image in Adobe Photoshop is to set-up the final render settings. You will be using a higher quality preset and increasing the resolution.

1. **Open the Render Settings window**

   - From the Status Line or Render view window, click the **Render Settings** button.

   - Set the following attributes in the **Common** Section:

     Image Size to **Width 1500** and **Height 1200**.

   - Click on the mental ray tab and set the **Quality Presets** to **Production.**

   - Scroll down to the **Final Gather** section and toggle **Final Gather** to **On**.

     This option was deactivated when the Production preset was selected.

2. **Turn on the resolution gate**

   - From the Perspective panel menu, select **View** → **Camera Settings** → **Resolution Gate.**

   - Frame the scene to see the top surface of **BlockOne** and **BlockTwo**.

3. Render the scene

Go ahead and press the Render Current Frame button and relax. This render will take a little longer than the previous renders because of the higher resolution and increased quality settings.

4 Save your rendered file

From the Render view's menu, select **File** → **Save As...,** and save it to your hard drive.

Framing for the final render

Composite the image

The final stage is to composite the two images. Use the methods you are comfortable with for masking and layer the two images together.

The layered images in Adobe Photoshop

Conclusion

In this lesson, you learned how to add detail with texture and displacement maps without going through the time-consuming process of modeling detail. You also used the mental ray Renderer's Final Gather feature to add realism to your render. Finally, you composited your image in Adobe Photoshop and then layered the two images together.

Lesson 5
Using Photographic Textures

Using photographic images as the source of your texture maps is one of the most effective ways to achieve high levels of realism. While the obvious first choice may be to grab the digital camera and begin shooting pictures of the object you want to model and texture, there's a downside to that approach that can cause numerous problems later in the pipeline. The flatbed scanner sitting in your studio can be your tool of choice when it comes to yielding both fast and high quality results. In this lesson you will create the model, and in the following lesson learn how to apply textures that will achieve a high level of realism.

In this lesson, you will learn the following:

- How to build a model from a scan;
- How to use the image plane as a construction guide;
- Using history to automatically update your model.

Using Photographic Textures

Using photographic images for your textures can provide high levels of realism, but brings a unique set of challenges as well. Ideally, textures that will be applied to your model should be as flat and distortion-free as possible, with even light across the surface. Since you are adding your own light to the scene when it comes time to render, light information that is captured in a casual photograph can be the source of odd visual effects down the line.

Flatbed scanners vs. cameras

What makes a scanner such an ideal tool for this application is: even light distribution, no lens or perspective distortion, high detail and resolution, and it's fast.

Drawbacks are types of objects you can scan, both size and shape, and some materials which respond oddly to the scanner light.

Cameras are obviously excellent for the task, but take more set-up to achieve usable images for texturing. Listed below are some general guidelines:

- Make sure your light is as even and neutral as possible. Strong directional light and bright speculars will limit what you can do later on. Soft, ambient fill light will generally give the most versatile texture files.

- Shoot as square to the object as possible and with as long of a lens as feasible. Don't fill the entire frame, but plan to crop in on the central region. This will minimize perspective distortion toward the edges of your image, which will cause mapping problems later.

- Pay special attention to keystoning and minimize it as much as you can.

CREATING A MODEL FROM A SCANNED IMAGE

Set-up your scene

It's always in your best interest to take a few minutes to plan out a general overview of what you want to accomplish and the steps that you will need to follow to get there. As in previous lessons, begin by making a project directory to keep your work organized as you work. Add a folder for your scanned files so that everything is in one place.

In this lesson you will be making a photorealistic replica of a sealed ball bearing. The first step is to acquire a nice scan of the object, so begin by carefully laying your object on top of the scanner glass. Use the *bearing_top_raw.tif* file included on the accompanying DVD at the back of this book, or you can substitute another object in lieu of a bearing. For the purposes of this lesson, make sure that it is something round and flat, such as a coin or bottle cap.

1 **Open the image in Photoshop**

Check that it is perfectly square – occasionally some scanners will stretch the image – and adjust if necessary.

- Zoom in and drag guidelines to the border of the bearing on each side. Use the Selection Tool and drag a box to the guidelines.

- From the menu select **Select Image → Crop**.

- Save the file as *Bearing_top.tif.* in your **Lesson_05 → sourceimages** directory.

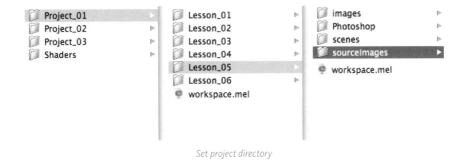

Set project directory

2 **Creating an image plane in Maya**

You will now use an image plane as the template image for model construction. Autodesk Maya allows you to assign an image plane to each camera view, but in this instance a simple overhead view is all you will need. You will now use the same image that was scanned for the texture.

- Begin by making sure you have a new scene open.

- Save the scene to the **Scenes** folder as *Bearing.mb*.

- Change your workspace to **4-view** by clicking on the workspace navigator on the left side of your screen.

- In the top view, select **View → Image Plane → Import Image Plane**.

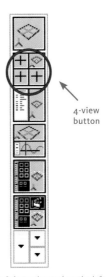

4-view button

The View Selector located on the left margin of the workspace

Adding an image plane

This will take you to the sourceimages folder in your project directory where you saved the cropped scanned image earlier. Open the **Bearing_top.tif** file.

3   Adjust the image plane settings

- In the Attribute Editor under Image Plane Attributes, make sure that **Display** is set to **Looking Through Camera**.

- Adjust **Color Gain** by clicking on the color swatch and setting **V** to **0.3**.

- Adjust **Color Offset** by clicking on the color swatch and setting **V** to **0.65**.

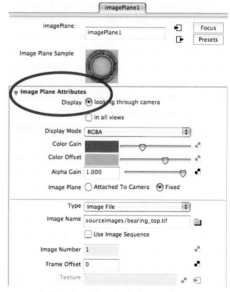

Setting the options for the image plane

4 Create curves for lofting

You will create the surfaces for the bearing by lofting a series of curves. By maintaining history throughout the construction process, it is very easy to make changes and fine-tune your model at a later stage. The changes will automatically ripple though your model with a minimum of effort.

- Mouse over the **top view** window to make it active, then quickly press the **spacebar** to zoom the window.

- From the menu, select **Create** → **NURBS Primitives** → **Circle** → ⬜, and set as shown in the following image:

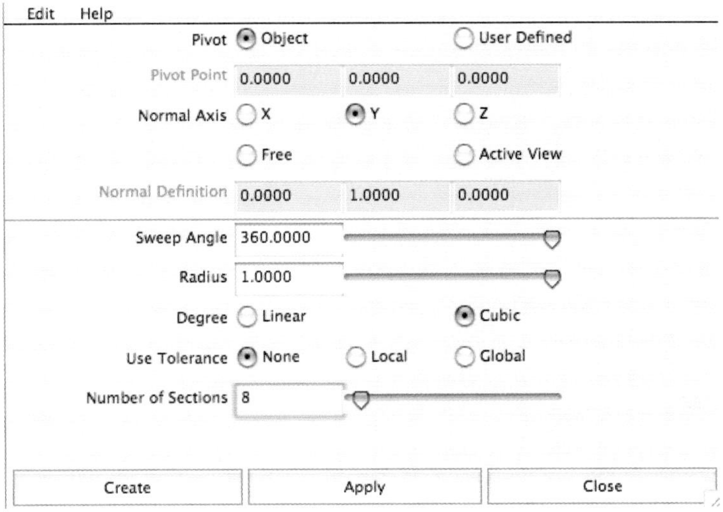

Edit Help			
Pivot ⦿ Object		◯ User Defined	
Pivot Point 0.0000	0.0000	0.0000	
Normal Axis ◯ X	⦿ Y	◯ Z	
◯ Free		◯ Active View	
Normal Definition 0.0000	1.0000	0.0000	
Sweep Angle 360.0000			🔘
Radius 1.0000			🔘
Degree ◯ Linear		⦿ Cubic	
Use Tolerance ⦿ None	◯ Local	◯ Global	
Number of Sections 8	🔘		
Create	Apply	Close	

Circle settings

- Click **Create**.
- Select Scale Tool **(r)**.
- From the center, scale the circle up to fit the innermost boundary of the bearing.
- From the menu, select **Edit** → **Duplicate** → ⬜.
- In the options, select **Edit** → **Reset**.

Note: *Selecting **Edit** → **Reset** will clear any previous settings and is a good habit to get into.*

- Click **Duplicate**.

- Scale the new circle to the next visible edge.

- Repeat this process by pressing the **g key**, which repeats the last action performed. Scale the new circle.

- Repeat until you have a circle for each major edge of the bearing image. You will be using these curves to define the depth changes for the surface you will be creating next.

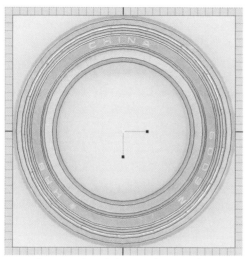

Creating circles and aligning to the image plane

5 **Make an instance of the curve set**

- Select the curves by dragging a box with the Selection Tool (**q**).

- Group the curves by selecting **Menu** → **Edit** → **Group** .

- In the menu, go to **Edit** → **Duplicate** ☐. Change **Scale y** to **-1**, and change **Geometry Type** to **Instance**.

  By scaling to a negative value (-1), you create a mirror image of the original that will behave exactly as a reflection would.

Note: *The Duplicate command lets you create a "real" duplicate or a lightweight "instance" of the original.*

This lets you create armies and forests full of duplicate objects without needing the memory or computing power to handle that much actual geometry.

An instance is like an alias or symbolic link in a file system. It doesn't have its own shape: it's just a visual pointer back to the original. However, each instance has its own transform node so it can have its own position, rotation, and scaling.

An instance stays linked to the original so when the original changes, the instance changes too. If you move a control point on the original, all instances automatically update. The instances do not have their own control points.

(In the Outliner an instance appears to have its own shape node, but it is actually shared with the original.)

> **Tip:** This can be used to your advantage when modeling objects that are symmetrical. By modeling only half of the object and creating an instance set to a negative value (**X-, Y-,** or **Z-** axis) for the mirror-image half, any changes you make to the one side are automatically reflected on the other.

Duplicate as instanced geometry

- Move the newly created group down **-5 units** in the **Y-axis**.

6 Loft a surface

Lofting is a method of creating a NURBS surface by using a series of curves to define its shape. A surface degree of 1 draws a straight line between two points. When the degree is set higher, such as 3, Maya will draw a smooth arc between the selected points. Surfaces can have different degrees assigned to each direction (U or V), which can help achieve the proper results. In this case, you will use a 3 degree setting for the direction that follows the curves (U), and a degree of 1 to go across from the inner to the outer edge (V). This will give you a smooth arc in one direction and sharp, defined edges in the other.

7 Set-up your workspace

- Change the top view window to a second Persp window. Select **Panels** → **Perspective** → **persp**. From the **Show** menu, check off **NURBS curves**. While still in that window, press the **5 key** to go into shaded view.

- Click in the original Persp window to make it active, and select **Show** → **NURBS surfaces**.

- Use the cursor to drag a selection box to select a few of the curves. Press the up arrow key to select the Group node.

  You could also open the Outliner window and select the group node there.

- From the menu, select **Surfaces** → **Loft** ❑. Go to **Edit** → **Reset**, then change the **Surface degree** to **Linear**, then **Loft**.

  You'll see the lofted surface appear in the shaded window.

- Select the curves that should be moved down to create the correct depressions in the surface. Notice that since the bottom curves are an instance, rather than a duplicate of the top set, any changes you make are reflected in both sets of curves.

- Repeat the selection process for the bottom set of curves. Press the up arrow key to traverse to the group node and loft.

  You are repeating the same sequence of steps that you did previously to create the top lofted surface, this time creating the bottom lofted surface.

- Now select the top outer curve. Hold the Shift key and select the corresponding duplicated curve. Press **g** to loft.

> **Note:** *In this example, when you select a curve, the corresponding duplicate instanced curve will also highlight. This can be confusing as it appears that both curves are selected when in fact only the first curve you clicked on is. You must select the second (target) curve by holding the Shift key and manually selecting it in order to loft a surface between them.*

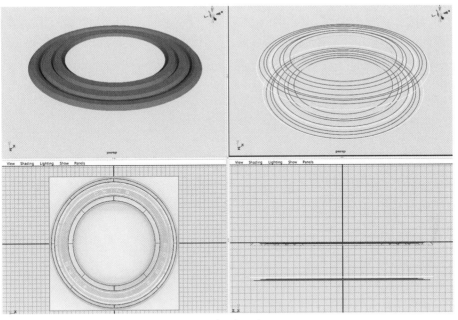

Lofting a surface from the curves

- Repeat the process for the inner curves.

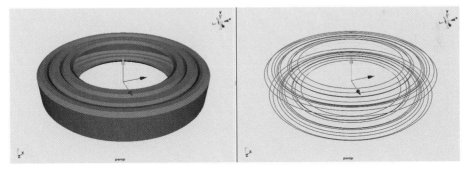

Lofting the remaining surfaces

Conclusion

You now have a NURBS model ready for texturing. By maintaining history throughout the process, you can modify the curves and see an immediate update in the lofted NURBS surfaces. Select a curve and move it to see how it affects the model, then undo **z**. This is an effective way to utilize the Maya built-in power when it comes time to fine-tune your model.

In the next lesson you will look at applying textures to achieve a believable level of realism.

Lesson 6
Texturing and Fine-tuning

Now that you've built a NURBS model that matches the object you scanned earlier, the next step is to make it look real, which you accomplish through texturing and lighting the model. The main reasons for scanning the bearing in the first place were to capture the surface texture image and apply the color to the model as a texture map. Photo-derived texture maps are a great resource if used intelligently since they bring all the nuances of the real world to your model, but you still need to add some extra touches to bring them alive. By playing close attention to the surface quality, light direction, and other small details that we take for granted in the world around us, you can pull off the illusion of reality in your CG models in fairly short order.

In this lesson you'll learn the following:

- How to precisely fit a texture to the model surface;
- How to fine-tune the texture;
- How to adjust model parameters for high definition rendering.

Applying the texture

1 Open the file

- Open the file that you saved from the last lesson, or use the one that was supplied on the DVD.

2 Set-up your workspace

One of the great strengths of Maya software is being able to fully customize the workspace to best suit your needs for specialized workflows. Experiment with different setups to find what is most comfortable for you.

- From the view selector on the left side of your screen, click on Hypershade/Render/Persp vertical. You can also access this by selecting **Panels** → **Saved Layouts** → **Hypershade / Render / Persp Vertical**.

This is an ideal layout for the texturing and rendering phase of a project.

- In the **Perspective view**, check **Show** → **NURBS surfaces** and make sure it is selected.

- Select **Show** → **NURBS curves** to hide them.

Hypershade / Render / Persp Vertical

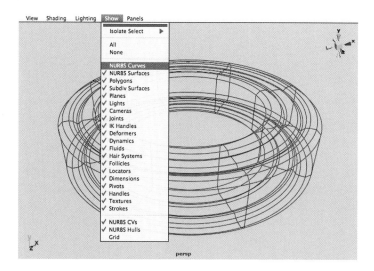

Selecting which components to make visible in the workspace

- Press **6** for textured preview mode.

Create a new material

What exactly is a shader? How is it different from a material? Where do textures and texture maps fit into all of this? Good questions! A shader is the full description of a surface appearance. In Maya these are aptly named *shader networks* or *shader groups*. The shader network includes all of the parts and pieces, description, settings and even lighting information that gives a surface its final appearance when rendered. A *material* is a collection of attributes that you apply to a surface to control how the surface appears when it is rendered. **Blinn**, **lambert** and **phong** are all examples of materials.

> **Note:** *Often you'll find the terms shader, material and texture all used interchangeably to mean what something is made of.*

A *texture* is an image that modifies surface detail. It can be derived from scanned or painted images or ones that are generated internally within Maya. A *procedural texture* is a texture that is calculated based on an algorithm or mathematical formula. They can be 2D or 3D. Noise, checker, ramp and wood are all examples of these. A *texture map* is an image that modifies the appearance of a surface, created from painted or scanned-in 2D images. These images are wrapped around the surface of a 3D object so that the patterns in the images curve and distort in a realistic manner. *Texture mapping* refers to the process of applying a 2D image to the surfaces of a 3D object.

The texture is mapped to the surface. *Utility nodes* are add-ons that are used to modify behavior or settings within the shader network. 2D placement, projection and multiply divide are examples of utility nodes. A node is a basic unit used to build data structures, like a building block. Maya creates, connects, evaluates and destroys nodes. At any moment, what you see in the Maya workspace is the result of the dynamic Maya node-based architecture, which continuously evaluates the web of nodes that underlie and comprise your work. Each node can receive, hold and provide information with attributes. A node's attributes connect to the attributes of other nodes, thus forming a web of nodes (node network).

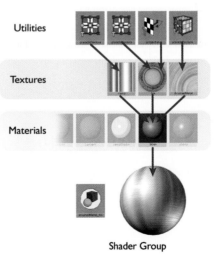

The various parts of a Maya shader

1 Create a new material

- In the Hypershade window, **create** a new **blinn material** by clicking on it once.

  A new material is placed in the Materials window and is also shown in the Work Area window below it.

- In the Materials window, **RMB** on the new blinn node and select **rename**.

- Change the name to *bearingTop_Tex*, then press **Enter**.

- Click on the *bearingTop_Tex* material to select it, and in the Attribute Editor click on the color node connector box.

Node connection icon in the Attribute Editor

- A **Create Render Node** window pops up. Make sure that **With New Texture Placement** is checked and change 2D Textures to **As Projection**.

- Select **File** to create a file node and connect it to your material.

Create a Render Node window

> **Note:** NURBS and polygons use different methods for assigning textures to a surface. When you create a texture that is applied to a NURBS surface, make sure that **With New Texture Placement** is checked. This creates a place2D texture node that lets you control how the material is mapped to the surface. With polygons the opposite is true – make sure that **With New Texture Placement** is off. Positioning the material on a polygonal surface is controlled through the UV Texture Editor. Maya will allow you to forego either of these conventions, but the results can be unpredictable.

Tip: *An easy way to make identical materials for use on either surface type (NURBS or polygon) is to start by creating your texture files **With New Texture Placement** enabled. This node is necessary for the NURBS shader. In the Hypershade, select the material and* **Edit** → **Duplicate** → **Shading Network**. *Graph the network and delete the* **place2DTexture** *nodes. You now have your polygon-friendly version. For more information on this, please refer to the Maya documentation.*

2 **Assign the scanned image as the color map**

- Click once on the bearingTop_Tex material to select it, then **RMB** and select **Graph Network**.

   The nodes and connections you just created appear in the work area window directly below the Materials window. Working with the graphed view of a shader is a very fast and direct way to access and edit the components of a shader's construction. By clicking a node, the Attribute Editor will update to show the contents and editable parameters for that node.

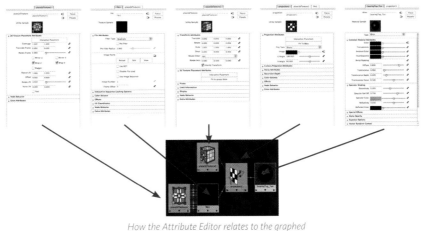

How the Attribute Editor relates to the graphed view of a shader network

- Click once on the **file1 node**, and in the Attribute Editor click on the folder icon next to the Image Name box.

   This takes you to the sourceimages directory.

- Select the *bearing_Top.tif* file and **Open**.

   The file1 node and the material update show the new texture assignment.

3 Assign the material to your model

- Using the **MMB**, **click+drag** the **bearingTop_Tex** material to the top of your bearing model.

The cursor will change to a hand when properly selected. Once the texture is assigned, notice that a green box icon has appeared in your scene. This is the icon for the 3D texture placement node and will let you intuitively place it. Notice the post that extends from the center of the icon. This is the direction of projection. You will need to reorient it so that it is projecting straight down onto the surface rather than cutting across it.

3D texture placement icon

- Click on the **3D Placement icon** to select it.

- Press **e** to select the **Rotate Tool**.

- Hold down the **J** key to constrain the rotation to even increments, then click on the red axis (X-axis) and rotate so that the icon post is pointing straight down. If you look in the Attribute Editor, you'll see that the transform attributes have updated so that **Rotate = -90 - 0 - 0**.

You can also manually enter changes to transform the node in this step.

4 Increase the quality of the texture preview

- Select the bearingTop_Tex and in the Attribute Editor go down to **Hardware Texturing** and expand.

- Change **Texture Resolution** to **Highest (256 x 256)**.

Project 1: Photo-realism

View Navigator

The preview texture is much better now and it becomes immediately apparent that the projected texture is much too small and needs to be scaled to fit the bearing correctly.

- Change to the top view by clicking the **y** (green) cone on the View Navigator.

- In the work area, click on the **place3DTexture node** to select it.

- In the Perspective window, press **R** to select the Scale Tool and, using the center square (yellow), scale the placement icon up so that it is the same size as the outer edge of the bearing.

The texture now fits the model correctly.

Texture scaled to fit the model

- Click the center square of the View Navigator to return to your Perspective view and zoom in.

5 Import a premade shader to apply to the bearing sidewalls

For this you'll import a shader that was made previously and reapply it to your model. Exporting shaders you like to a central library can be an invaluable resource when crunch time hits and you need to get something done in a hurry. The library that you develop over time will become one of your greatest assets and can be a huge influence on having a consistent look and style of your work.

- Go to **RenderDate** → **Shaders** and select **BrushedMetal.mb**.

- Click **Import**.

  A new material called BrushedMetal:BrushedMetal_plasticTex has been added to the materials window.

- Change the name to *brushedMetal_Tex*.

- **MMB+drag** the material to the bearing's outer sidewall to assign it. Do the same for the inner sidewall.

6   Do a preview render

In the window above the Perspective window (Render view window), check **Options** → **Test Resolution** and set it to **50%** (320x240). You'll use the Maya software renderer for the IPR preview.

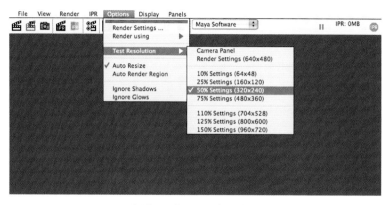

Setting up the test render options

- Click the IPR button.

  You'll see that the top doesn't look too bad, but the sides definitely need work.

7   Modify the *brushedMetal_Tex* shader

- With the IPR still active, go to the Hypershade window and **RMB** → **Graph Network** for the *brushedMetal_Tex* shader.

If you hold the cursor over the connection line to the material node, you'll see that a 3D procedural texture has been connected to the specular color of the material. This will work nicely to give the impression of a machine's metallic surface. Right now it's not showing up properly so you'll need to adjust it. Since there are no environmental reflections in this rendering, faking them will impart a much more metallic look to the surface.

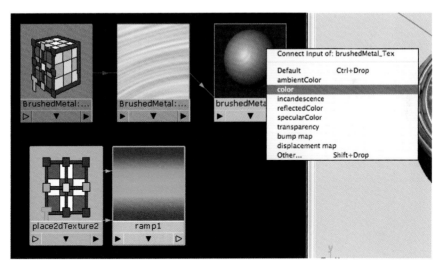

Graphed shader view in the Hypershade Work Area

- In the Create Bar (left side of Hypershade), expand **2D Textures** if it is not already open. Make sure that **Normal** is selected and click on the **ramp** texture.

A new texture node is created and appears in the workspace.

- **MMB** the **ramp** node and drag it to the material node. Select **Color** from the pop-up box.

Adding the Ramp texture to the shader

The shaded and IPR view updates show the ramp shader is now connected to the color channel. You'll now modify the ramp to look more like a metallic reflection.

- Double-click the **ramp** node to load it into the Attribute Editor.

- **Delete** the green color by clicking the box on the right side of the ramp.

- Change the red and blue colors to black and white.

The ramp is now a black and white gradation that runs from top to bottom on the model surface. You'll need to change the orientation so that it wraps around the circumference of the surface.

- Change the **Type** to **U Ramp**.

  Voila! Orientation is now correct. Now onto the "metal"...

- Blend the seam by having the gradation begin and end with the same color. Add some slight blue tints here and there. Look at the sample image to see the rough idea.

- Click on the **place2DTexture** node to select it, and in the Attribute Editor change the **Repeat UV** value to **4** and **1**.

Metallic ramp texture

This now has a much better metallic feel to it. Adjusting the specular color will bring out even more of the surface finish.

- Select the Placed3DTexture node. The placement icon is highlighted in the scene.

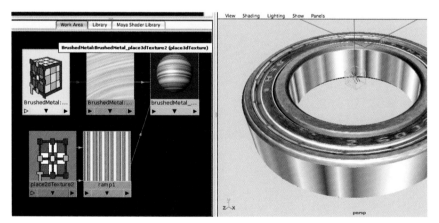

Click on the 3D texture placement icon to select it

- Press **r** to select the Scale Tool and scale up the texture placement icon.

  It's hard to see what effect this is having, so add a directional light and change the viewing angle to get a better look.

- Add a directional light by selecting **Create** → **Lights** → **Directional Light**. Position it however you feel looks best.

- Zoom the view to get a closer look at the sidewall.

- Click the IPR render to update the view.

Now you can see the surface striations. In the Perspective view, zoom back out and select the 3DTex placement icon again. The IPR renderer will hold the zoomed view while you make your updates.

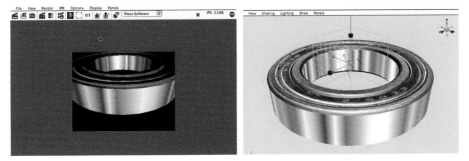

Resize the 3dTexturePlacement icon to change the appearance of the metal surface

8 **Add a directional light to the scene**

- Select **Create** → **Lights** → **Directional Light**.

- Position the light so that it fills in some of the shadow area.

- Decrease the **intensity** to 0.5.

9 **Adjust the shader**

Scaling the texture helped, but more contrast will make the striations pop better.

- In the graphed view of the *brushedMetal_Tex* shader network, locate the **BrushedMetal: Brownian node** and click on it to select it.

- In the Attribute Editor, expand **Color Balance**.

- Adjust the **Color Gain** to 0.85 and the **Color Offset** to 0.6.

10 Generate a higher quality rendering to inspect

- In the Perspective window, select **View** → **Camera Settings** → **Resolution Gate**.

- Zoom and pan the view so that it's nicely framed.

- In the Render view, select **Options** → **Test Resolution** → **Render Settings (640x480)**.

- Select the **Options** → **Render Settings** → **Maya Software** tab. Change **Quality** to **Production Quality**.

- Render the image.

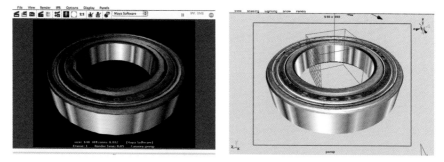

Test rendering in the Render view window

11 Refine geometry smoothness

In order for Maya to render an image, it must first subdivide the NURBS geometry into a fine polygon mesh. This is a behind-the-scenes process called *tessellation,* and it determines the overall smoothness of the final rendering. The beauty of NURBS is that it is a scalable model format in the same way that vector graphics are scalable. This gives you tremendous flexibility to push the model resolution up or down as needed and eliminate any faceting or "nickeling" (flat spots) that occur along the edges. Maya gives you direct control of tessellation settings so that you can optimize the output.

- Press **q** to change to the Selection Tool.

- Click the top surface to select it.

- In the **Attribute Editor**, expand **tessellation**. Select **Display Render Tessellation** and **Enable Advanced Tessellation**.

- Expand **Advanced Tessellation** and **Primary Tessellation** attributes.

- Change **Number U** to **12** and **Number V** to **1**.

- Select the outer sidewall and apply the same settings.

Tip: *A shortcut is to drag-select over all the geometry pieces, then select* **Menu** → **Window** → **General Editors** → **Attribute Spread Sheet**. *In the Attribute Spread Sheet select the Tessellation tab and all of your selected geometry will show there. Find the Number U and Number V values, then click the top of the column head to select all, and enter your new values, in this case 12 and 1. Make sure that* **Explicit Tessellation** *is set to On, otherwise those settings will not go into effect.*

- Select the column head and type 1 for **On** or o for **Off**.

Names   Layouts   Key   Layer   Help

| | | Transform | Translate | Rotate | Scale | Render | Tessellation | Geometry | All | ▼ |

	mooth Edg	Display Rende	Mode U	Number U	Mode V	Number V	Use Chord
loftedSurface	.99	on	Per Span # of	12	Per Span # of	1	off
loftedSurface	.99	off	Per Span # of	12	Per Span # of	3	off
loftedSurface	.99	on	Per Span # of	12	Per Span # of	1	off
loftedSurface	.99	off	Per Span # of	12	Per Span # of	3	off

Attribute Spread Sheet

- In the Render view, select **File** → **Keep Image** so that you can compare the results.

- Re-render the image.

- Using the slider bar under the Render view window, slide it back and forth to see the changes.

Move the slider bar left and right to cycle through saved renderings in the Render view window

12 Final adjustments

The image is looking much better, but could still use some fine-tuning. The scanned texture seems a bit dull and could use more contrast. The lighting could also be dialed in a bit better. Make these changes by tweaking the *bearingtop_Tex* shader.

- In the Hypershade, select *bearingTop_Tex* and **RMB** → **Graph Network**.

- Click **projection1**. This is your color input.

- **MMB+drag** to the material node. Select **specularColor** from the pop-up menu.

  You can have multiple connections from the same node to different inputs.

  Since the texture map is projected, make any additional connections to the material node from there. Although Maya will allow you to go directly from the file1 node and bypass the projection node, the results would not be aligned properly with the model.

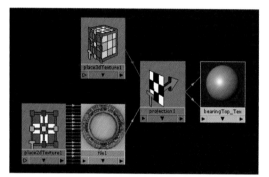

bearingTop_Tex graphed network

- Re-render the image.

This is much better, but the scanned image still seems a bit soft.

- Click on the **file1 node** to select it, then in the Attribute Editor expand **Effects** and change the **Filter** setting to **0**.

- In the Render view, select **Options** → **Render Settings** → **Maya Software** and uncheck **Use Multi Pixel Filter**.

- Re-render.

> **Note:** *Textures that are optimized for motion are often softened slightly to avoid flickering as the object moves. As Maya is principally an animation program, many of the defaults have been optimized for that purpose. With stills you often want your output to be as sharp as possible, but pay attention to not go too far or you'll wind up with aliased (pixelated) edges and transition areas.*

| Poor Tessellation | Smoothed Geometry | Modified specular and sharpened |

Note: *"In my own workflow I would now generate an even higher res image and inspect it closely. When I did that with this model I noticed some of the curves that I had placed originally weren't hitting in the correct places, but since I had maintained history it was very easy to fix by simply selecting, rescaling, and moving the curves in question. Attention to detail and taking the time to get things just right can make all the difference in the final outcome."*

-Rob Magiera

Tip: *Once a texture has been assigned to a NURBS surface, any changes you make to that surface will warp and stretch the texture. The effect is as if the texture had been painted on and now stretches with the surface. Sometimes that's desirable, but not in this case. To avoid it, select the surface with the texture, go to the Attribute Editor, and expand* **Texture Map** *and check* **Fix Texture Warp**. *This will keep the texture from warping and distorting as you make the adjustments. If you are curious as to how and why this works, read up on parameterization and fix* **texture warp** *in the Maya documentation.*

Conclusion

Maya is a deep program with lots of variables and tools, but you shouldn't let that scare you off. The tools and techniques covered in this lesson touch on the core functionality of Maya that I use in the majority of my work. Isolate the key tools and workflows and set your own preferences and you can quickly become comfortable using one of the most powerful computer graphics applications available today.

Lesson 6: Texturing and Fine-tuning

Project 2
Workflows Introduction

Much of the broad appeal of Maya software stems from its innate ability to be customized to fit anyone's workflow preferences. From how the interface is arranged, to maximizing use of the Alpha channel, you can (and should) tune Maya to work in the manner that is most comfortable for you.

In this section you'll learn how to use render layers to speed up your workflow. Then, you'll utilize the flexible output capabilities of Maya software to render Flash (.swf) files that are ready for Web deployment.

Finally, you'll finish the project by examining toon-shading techniques that will imbue your images with your personal look and style, without sacrificing any of the power that 3D has to offer.

Lesson 7
Compositing

One of the major benefits of working with Maya to create component pieces for compositing in an image editing program such as Photoshop is the pixel-for-pixel perfect Alpha channel that can be generated during rendering. More information on the Alpha channel in this lesson will clarify how to squeeze the maximum benefit out of it.

Much of this lesson will focus on Photoshop and putting its tools to use to perfect the rendered imagery that you derive from Maya. When it comes to an efficient workflow, it is often faster and more intuitive to let Maya do the heavy lifting, i.e. breaking your image into separate pieces that can then be recomposed later in the image editing / compositing program of your choice. For the sake of brevity I'll use Photoshop in my examples, but these principles apply to virtually any program that allows you to layer imagery to achieve a final result, including most video editing programs, such as Adobe® After Effects® and Adobe® Final Cut Pro® software products.

In this lesson you'll learn the following:

- What an Alpha channel is;
- How to use the Alpha channel to record transparency information;
- How to fix "halos" and "fringing" at compositing time;
- How to maintain perfect registration.

First, some background... *What's the deal with RGB and CMYK color spaces?*

If you have a basic understanding of the underpinnings of the imagery that you're working with, many of the esoteric or otherwise mysterious steps you must go though at times begin to make more sense. At least that's the general hope.

The vast majority of imagery that you deal with day in and day out on your computer is what is categorized as a *24 bit RGB color*. This is the basic building block of all color images that are displayed on modern computer systems today. Even CMYK images are in fact 24 bit RGB when viewed on the computer screen.

Computer monitors show color by starting at black (no color, no light) and gradually adding light energy in the form of primary colors consisting of red, green and blue. When a maximum of all three primaries are mixed, white is the result. This is known as *additive color, and it* happens to be exactly the opposite of printed color, which depends upon the reflected energy of an external light source to accomplish its task. *Subtractive color* (also known as reflective color) is essentially a light absorption process where various pigments or filters absorb certain colors and reflect back others. A blue paint would absorb all colors except blue, which is reflected back to the eye with the result of the object appearing to be blue. Black would be a total absorption of all light energy, which, incidentally, is why a black car gets so hot on a sunny day. White is a reflection of the full color spectrum.

Red, green and blue channels combine together to give the full spectrum of color

Here's how the math on this works out:

- Each color channel is allocated 8 bits of information: 8 bits for red, 8 bits for green and 8 bits for blue.

- 8 x 3 = 24, thus the name *24 bit color.*

- The 8 bits allow for 256 gradated steps going from black to white.

- When totaled, 256 x 256 x 256 = 16,777,216 possible color variations.

- As all modern mainstream computer systems are based on at least 32 bits, there are an extra 8 bits unspoken for; this means that 24 bit images are in actuality 32 bit images with an extra channel that can be used or not. This extra channel is called the *Alpha channel*.

- The most typical use of the Alpha channel is to record transparency information, which can be a huge asset when it comes time to assemble multiple pieces into one composited whole. Alpha channels have also been used to record other valuable data, such as depth information, but for the purposes of this lesson we'll stick with using the Alpha for transparency data.

Alpha channels and 3D

One of the great advantages of working with 3D images is that you can record the Alpha channel information as part of the rendering process, which provides you with a perfectly registered, built-in masking channel. Maya offers a great deal of control over how you choose to use the Alpha channel and this can greatly ease compositing efforts later.

The Alpha channel is in pixel-for-pixel perfect registration, but there are a few basic rules you need to follow for seamless composites.

If you have some experience with cutting and pasting images together, you've certainly encountered just how tricky making selections can be. Alpha channels make quick work of precisely isolating the image area you want to select.

RGB channel and Alpha channel edge anti-aliasing

Smooth edges are achieved by blending the colors along the edge to eliminate the stair-stepping ("jaggies") you would see otherwise. This works well when you are keeping everything flattened on one layer.

Object rendered on white background

White edge contamination "halo"

White contamination in the transparency

White contamination in the blur

Black contamination in the blur

No color contamination - correct color composite

No color contamination - correct transparency composite

In doing so, however, the foreground color gets mixed with the background color. This is where the headaches can start once you separate the rendered object from the background for compositing. I call this *color contamination*.

White edge contamination is often referred to as a "halo" and is a sure sign of a bad composite. The opposite effect is when you get a dark outline from having rendered on a dark background, often called "fringing".

So far, the effects of this are minimized as the color contamination is confined to a single row of pixels along the border of the object. But, add transparency or motion blur and all of a sudden your compositing efforts are ruined.

Fixing the problem

Fortunately, color contamination is an issue that can be easily corrected. By rendering your object over either a black or white background color, the black (or white) additive can be removed, and what you are left with is the pure color of the original. This method uses tools that are built into Photoshop specifically for this purpose.

1 **Open Photoshop**

   - Launch Photoshop and open the file **Donut_transparent.psd**.

      The file can be found in *Project_02/Lesson_7_Compositing/Photoshop*.

2 **Make the background a layer**

   - In the **Layers tab**, double-click on the **Background**. In the **New Layer** dialog box click **OK**.

   This converts the background from its default state to a layer that includes transparency.

> **Tip:**   *Holding down the Option key and double-clicking the lock icon for the background layer will convert it into a layer with transparency.*

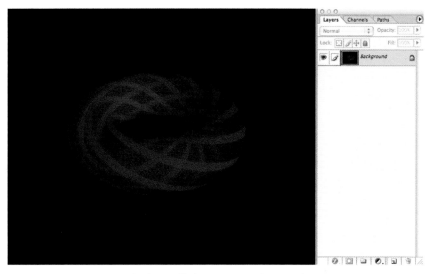

Rendered image file from Maya opened in Photoshop

3 Use the Alpha channel to make your selection

• Click on the **Channels tab**, then click on the **Alpha 1** channel to select it.

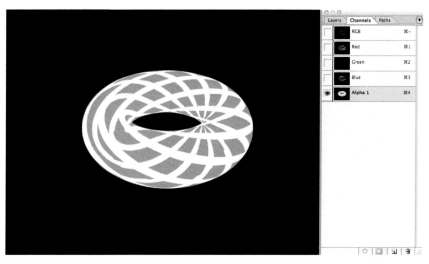

Alpha channel (masking channel)

Project 2: Workflows Introduction

- From the menu choose **Select** → **Load Selection**, then from the dialog box click **OK**.

  This loads the Alpha channel as the selection. The white areas are fully selected, the grey partially, and the black not at all.

- Switch back to the layer view by clicking on the **Layers tab**. Click on **Layer 0** to select it.

  You'll see that the rendered area is selected by the "marching ants" marquee.

- Invert the selection. From the menu choose **Select** → **Inverse**.

  You want to delete the black background, so the selection must be changed from the rendered area to the unrendered portion of the image.

- Delete the inverted selection by selecting **Edit** → **Clear** or simply pressing the **Delete (Backspace) key** on your keyboard.

4 **Remove the black color contamination**

- Turn off the selection. From the menu choose **Select** → **Deselect**.

- From the menu, select **Layer** → **Matting** → **Remove Black Matte**.

  *Notice how the color in the transparent area cleaned up when you did this. The black color contamination has been removed from the edge pixels as well. If you rendered on a white background you would use **Remove White Matte**.*

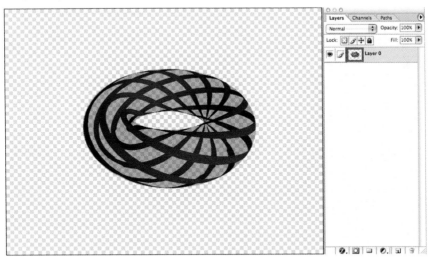

Alpha channel applied to the object with the black contamination removed

5 **Composite the image**

- Open *SeaShore.tif* from the Photoshop folder.

- Click in the *Donut_transparent.psd* window to select it.

- From the menu select **Layer** → **Duplicate Layer**. In the dialog box change **Destination Document** to **Seashore.tif**, then click **OK**.

6 **View your work!**

- Click on *Seashore.tif* to see how the composite came together.

> **Tip:** *Repeat this workflow a few times to get comfortable with it. Once you have it mastered, do it once more but this time record it as an Action and assign the Action an F key. This way, you'll have automated the entire process and made it a one-button solution for future needs.*

> **Note:** *A special note about layered Photoshop PSD files from Maya. When Maya generates a layered PSD file it does not automatically remove the black matte from each of the layers. You'll need to apply the* **Layer** → **Matting** → **Remove Black Matte** *operation as a separate step for each layer (when applicable), once you have the file open in Photoshop.*

Final composited image

Conclusion

Without correcting edge and transparency color contamination, your composites would be plagued with less than satisfactory results. The basic steps covered in this lesson will go a long way toward helping you achieve professional level work. Always pay special attention to how the edges come together and you'll quickly take your images to a new level.

Alpha channels are a powerful tool and can be used in almost limitless ways. Difficult masking tasks can be tackled by assigning the objects you need to isolate to a render layer, then assigning the TotalBlack and TotalWhite shaders (included on the DVD) to those objects in strategic ways. You can quickly render precision fitting black and white images that can then be put to work in Photoshop as masking (Alpha) channels.

Lesson 8
Flash Format Output

In this lesson you will learn how to use vector rendering in Maya and how to export the file in the .swf Flash format, which is a graphic format. The Swift3DImporter plug-in (available in the Vector Render window in Maya), gives you the ability to export images into FlashMX. The plug-in allows you to export with different render passes such as color, outlines, reflection, highlights and shadows, all of which FlashMX understands. Each pass is in a separate layer and can be accessed within FlashMX. These steps will happen automatically when you use the plug-in for export in the .swft format.

In this lesson you will learn the following:

- How to use the Swift3DImporter plug-in and export files to Flash format;
- How to use vector render overwrite options to change the Flash image output.

Opening the scene file

To start, you can use the scene file that was already created as a test file for this lesson. Open *DP2.Flash.mb* from the scene files in the Lesson 8 folder.

Maya scene dp2.Flash.mb

> **Note:** *You can use your own character for this lesson as well. If you do so, be sure that shaders are assigned to your geometry and that there is some animation on your character. Otherwise, the exported Flash file will not demonstrate your character properly.*

1 **Using Swift3DImporter plug-in**

Once your scene file is open, follow these steps to use the Swift3Dimporter plug in:

- In Maya, go to **Window** → **Rendering Editor** → **Render Setting**.

- Choose the Maya Vector option from the pulldown menu, right beside **Render Using**.

- From **Frame** → **Animation Ext** select *name.ext* (Multi Frame). Now select the Swift3DImporter option from the Image format menu.

- At this point, you can do a test render to check the results. Make sure your settings match the screen capture on the top right of the following page.

Render Settings window

After checking the test render and making any necessary adjustments, you can render the sequence using batch render. Go to the Rendering menu and select **Render → Batch Render**. The files will be saved under the image directory of your current project.

Once the rendering process has finished, you can import the images into FlashMX. Here you will see that every channel (color, shadow, highlights, reflection, etc.) has both a separate layer and a combined layer that shows the final image.

You can see the result by running the Flash demo file. First, you have to click on the Persp/Outliner layout to get your view like the image below.

Test render

Tip: *You can also monitor the progress of the batch render in the Script Editor window.*

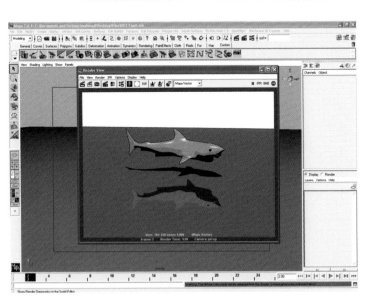

Perspective/Outliner windows

2   **Preview the Flash SWF in the Maya Browser window**

In the Outliner window, click on the Panels menu at the top of the window and go
to **Panel → Web Browser**.

- First let's switch our view to include the Outliner. From your persp view go to
  Panels → Saved Layout → Perspective → Outliner.

- Then from the Outliner window select **Panels → Perspective → Webbrowser**.

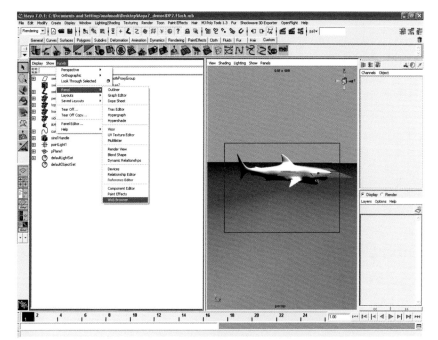

Change Outliner panel to Web Browser

- When the Web Browser window has loaded you can navigate through the Maya 7
  demo folder by clicking on **File → Open**, or just click on the open file icon in the top
  right corner.

- In the folder, open the file called *sharkFlash2.html*.

  *When the Flash file opens you can see that the shark animation is in Flash format. You
  can also see the options at the bottom of the Flash window. Click on each of the layers
  separately to see how the channel plays individually, or simply click on the **Full button** to
  see all the layers combined into a single layer.*

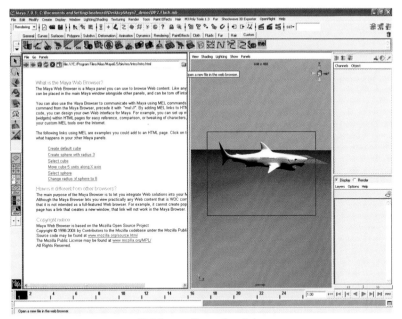

Web Browser/Perspective window

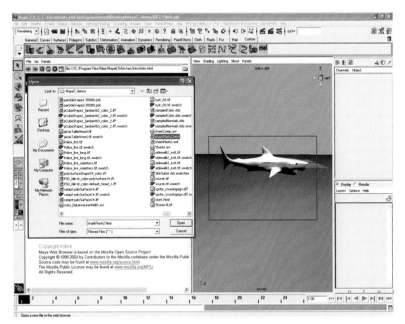

Opening sharkFlash2.html

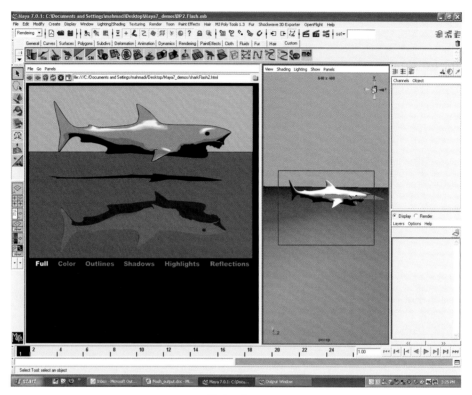

Flash swf. preview

Vector render overwrite

In addition to vector rendering, you have the ability to overwrite vector render attributes on individual objects.

- Select the object.

- Go to the Attribute Editor under the shader that has been assigned to the geometry.

- Open the Vector Renderer Control and enable the **Vector Render Overwrite**.

- In Vector Render Overwrite you can change attributes such as Edge Color and Edge Style.

Conclusion

Using the Swift3DImport plug-in allows you to convert your Maya file into FlashMX format files. The process is very simple and easy to set-up. Making use of the Swift3Dimport plug-in is very useful for low bandwidth and interactive controls with layers.

In the next lesson, you will learn about the toon shader.

Lesson 9
Create a Toon-shaded Character

This lesson teaches you how to assign and manipulate different toon shaders and toon outlines on a space alien character.

In this lesson, you will learn the following:

- How to use the high quality render mode in a viewport;

- How to assign and adjust toon fill shaders;

- How to assign and adjust toon outlines.

Set your project

Maya uses a project directory to store and organize all files (scenes, images, materials, textures, etc.) related to a particular scene. When working with a scene, you create and work with a variety of file types and formats. The project directory allows you to keep these different file types in their unique sub-directory locations within the project directory.

1 Launch Maya

2 Set the project

To manage your files, you can set a project directory that contains sub-directories for different types of files that relate to your project.

- Go to the **File** menu and select **Project → Set...**

- A window opens that directs you to the Maya projects directory.

- Open the folder *support_files*.

- Click on the folder named *toon shader* to select it.

- Click on the **OK** button.

- This sets this directory as your current project.

3 Load the scene

- Select **File → Open Scene →** *book_toon_file.mb*.

  This will open the scene containing the space alien that we will use to apply the toon shading.

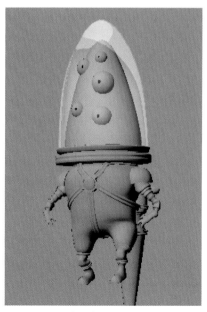

4 Turn on high quality display

In order to properly see the glass of the space alien helmet, you will turn on the high quality display option within the viewport.

- From the **Shading** pulldown menu within the Perspective viewport, select **high quality rendering**.

  The helmet should now appear in the viewport with proper transparent display and reflections. As well, any toon shaders that will be applied will appear correctly.

High quality Render view

TOON SHADING

Toon shading creates the look of 2D cel or cartoon animation using 3D modeling and animation software. Elements of the "toon" look include profile lines (outlines), border lines, crease lines, intersection lines and solid color shading. Combined, these elements recreate the look of traditional animation's "ink and paint" technique, where *ink* refers to lines and *paint* refers to shading.

Assigning the toon fill shaders

To start, you will assign different toon fill shaders to the various parts of the alien. The toon fill shaders represent the painted effect you would see with traditional cartoon rendering.

1 **Assign the Head fill shader**

   • **Select** the *head* geometry and then from the **Rendering** menu select Toon → **Assign fill shader** → **Shaded brightness two tone**.

2 **Adjust the Head fill shader**

   Now that you have assigned the shader you will adjust the colors and placement of the tones.

   • With the *head* still selected, press **Ctrl-a** to open the **Attribute Editor**. Choose the tab in the Attribute Editor called *shadedBrightnessShader1*.

   • Adjust the color and placement of the two tones by selecting the small round handles in the color adjustment ramp widget. Set the dark grey color to a dark green and the white color to a light green. Move the light green handle slightly more to the right.

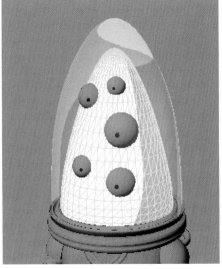

The first fill shader assigned

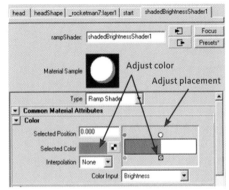

Adjust the ramp handles

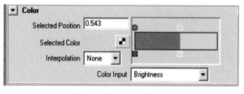

Setting the ramp colors

> **Note:** The handles in the color ramp can be removed by picking the small square at the bottom of each handle. Handles can be added by clicking anywhere within the color ramp.

3 Assign and adjust the Eye fill shader

- **Select** the five eyeballs and assign a new **Shaded brightness two tone** shader. Adjust the fill color white placement by moving it to the left.

The eyeball ramp

4 Assign and adjust the remaining alien body shaders

You will now repeat the same process you used for the head and eyeballs on the other body parts (with the exception of the jet pack, which will be explained in the next step).

- Repeat the assignment and adjust the procedure outlined in steps 2 and 3 for the other body parts, separating the shaders as follows:

  Adjust main **body, helmet rings, upper arms, lower arms, foot rings** to two tone brown/light brown;

  Adjust **shoulders, elbows, legs** to two tone brown/dark brown;

  Adjust **feet** and **hands** to two tone grey/dark grey;

  Adjust **body straps** to two tone light yellow/dark yellow;

  Adjust **body strap middle** (button) to two tone red/dark red.

Project 2: Workflows Introduction

The fill shaders assigned

5 **Assign and adjust the jet pack fill shader**

You will use a different type of fill shader called a rim light shader for the jet pack geometry. This shader will give the impression of a rim highlight.

- **Select** all the jet pack geometry and **assign Toon → Assign fill shader → Rim Light.**

- Adjust the ramp colors to a dark blue and a light blue and move the light blue handle slightly to the left.

The rim light shader ramp

Note: With this fill shader, you will notice a nice white rim lighting effect around all the jet pack pieces.

6   **Assign and adjust the thrust fill shader**

Lastly, you will use a solid color fill shader for the thrust geometry and then map a ramp to it.

- **Select** the *thrust* geometry and assign **Toon** → **Assign fill shader** → **Solid color.**

- In the Channel Box, map a ramp texture to the out color of the solid color fill shader and set the color to go from yellow to red.

- Save your scene.

   You have now finished applying the fill shaders and will move on to creating the toon outlines.

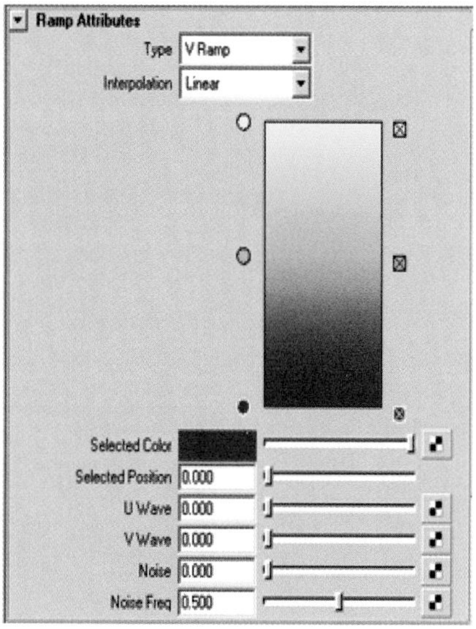

The thrust shader ramp

Assigning the toon outlines

The second part of creating a toon effect is assigning the toon outlines. The outlines represent the rendered edges of all the geometry.

1   **Assign the outlines**

- Select all of the alien geometry and then **Toon** → **Assign outline** → **Add new toon outline.**

Tip: *If the outlines do not appear in the viewport, check under the **Show** menu within the viewport to see if the display of strokes is turned on.*

2 **Adjust the outline attributes**

- Open the **Outliner** window and select the *pfxToon1* node.

- Open the **Attribute Editor** and set the following for the *pfxToon1* node:

    Turn **On** Intersection lines

    Line width to **.100**

    The toon outline attributes are very extensive and can result in a wide variety of effects. Feel free to experiment with the attributes or look at the toon examples provided by Maya under **toon → get toon example**.

3 **Save your work**

The toon outlines assigned

Conclusion

You have toon-shaded a character using Maya. You should now be able to render this character as you wish using the Maya Software Renderer. You should also be confident in applying these workflows to other geometry and experimenting with different looks and results.

Level 3 ▲ Advanced

Lesson 10
Render Layers and Strategy

In Project 3 Lesson 13, you will investigate Paint Effects as a modeling method in some depth. If you are continuing from that lesson, open the model that you saved at the end of it (Oaktree.mb). If you are starting with this lesson to learn about render layers, open the scene file that has been provided for you on the accompanying DVD, *L10_Oaktree_Start.mb*. This lesson will cover Maya render layers and the Maya-to-Photoshop workflow. The final part of the lesson will focus on working in Photoshop to assemble the layers that you created in Maya to arrive at a finished illustration.

In this lesson you'll learn the following:

- How Maya's render layers differ from Photoshop layers;

- Effective scene set-up for layering;

- Output layered PSD files from Maya;

- How to compose the final image in Photoshop.

Open the scene file

Begin by opening either the final scene file that you saved in Project 3 Lesson 13, or open *L10_OaktreeRL_start.mb* from the Lesson Project directory. You'll break the scene into renderable layers that will be composited later in Photoshop. Render layers in Maya work differently than layers in Photoshop and take some getting used to, but once you have a feel for them they can save you time and be the backbone of an efficient pipeline.

> **Tip:** Think of render layers as recordings of scene states, rather than the layers you're used to working with in Photoshop. In Maya, you are not adding one layer on top of another, but rather making an editable recording of your scene as well as all modifications made to lighting, textures, objects, and even which rendering engine to use.

- If you are continuing from Lesson 13, arrange the main scene in the **Perspective** view by selecting **View → Bookmarks → cameraView1**.

1 Create a render layer

- Press **q** to get the Selection Tool.

- **LMB+drag** select the front tree so you have both the trunk and leaves selected.

- Switch the Attribute Editor window to the **Channel Box → Layer Editor**.

- In the Layers section, click on the **Render** button.

- With the tree selected, click the farthest right icon → **Create new layer and assign selected objects**.

- Click on the newly created **layer1**. Notice that only the tree you selected is now in the scene.

Create new layer and assign selected objects button

- Double-click **layer1** and rename the layer *moneyTree*.

- Save.

- Press **7** to preview your scene with lights.

  The objects in your scene show up as black because no lights have been assigned to the render layer. This is intentional as Maya allows you to specify custom lighting as part of each render layer's attributes.

- From the menu, select **Window** → **Outliner** to open it and click on the **defaultLight** to select it.

- **RMB** on the *moneyTree* layer and **Add Selected Objects.**

  The light is now added to your scene. You can create additional lights for this render layer by placing them in the scene now. They will only affect this render layer and the masterLayer unless you intentionally add them to other render layers as well.

Tip: *From the beginning, get in the habit of paying attention to which render layer you're working in. Adding lights, creating new objects and modifying settings will only affect the layer you're currently in, unless it's the masterLayer. This can get confusing later on if you switch to another layer and wonder where the object you just created disappeared to. A good method for avoiding this is to make major additions on the masterLayer render layer, then selecting and adding to the preferred render layer as a second step.*

Note: *Pay close attention when hiding objects by turning off display layers, as those objects will be hidden from all render layers as well. In other words, when you're in a render layer and want to hide an object, turning off a display layer that it may be assigned to will hide it from all other render layers, which may not be the result you're after. Making objects visible or invisible in a particular render layer is done by adding them or deleting them from the render layer set.*

RMB on the render layer
to add or remove selected
objects to that layer

moneyTree render layer with light

2 Set-up compositing layers

- Go back to the master layer and select the two trees in the background. Place them on a new render layer as you did in the step before.

- Create a new render layer.

- Rename the render layer to *bkgdTreeLeavesRL*.

  This layer will be used for applying effects to the leaves later in Photoshop. To accomplish this, the leaves will need to be isolated and the trunk and branches knocked out to black. You will also apply a special shader to the trunk.

3 Load the TotalBlack.mb shader

- In the **Hypershade** window, select **File** → **Import** and navigate to **shaders** → **TotalBlack.mb** and **Import**.

- In the *bkgdTreeLeavesRL* layer, select both tree's trunks.

- In the **Hypershade**, **RMB** over the TotalBlack shader and **Assign Material To Selection.**

4 Do a test render

Notice that the trunks and branches are now knocked out to black. Click the Display Alpha Channel and notice that the trunk and branches are not included in the mask.

Render View Display Alpha Channel button

Normal rendering   *With TotalBlack shader applied to trunk and branches*   *Mask (Alpha) channel*

4 Set-up additional render layers

- Click the **masterLayer**.

> **Note:** The shader change you made previously has been only applied to the render layer that it was assigned to.

- Choose the two tree trunks (on either side of the large tree). Trunks only this time, no leaves.

- Create a new render layer with the selected objects and call it *bkgdTreeTrunksRL* . Press **Save**.

- Select the tree that is farthest back (both trunk and leaves) and create a new render layer for it.

- Rename the new render layer to *bkgdTreeFarRL*.

5   **Create a special effects render layer**

Rather than use traditional lighting and cast shadows, in this instance you'll create a special type of render layer called an *Occlusion Pass*. This creates a type of diffused shadow that will impart a nice look to the illustration when composited.

- Click on the *moneyTreeRL* and select the money tree, leaves and trunk.

- Create a new render layer with selected objects.

- Rename the render layer *moneyTreeOccRL* and **Save**.

- RMB and select **Presets → Occlusion.**

- Do a test render.

Ambient occlusion rendering

6 Set-up for rendering

Maya allows you to take all of your render layers and combine them into one layered Photoshop file.

- An *R* in the first box of each render layer indicates that it is flagged to be rendered.

- Click on the masterLayer.

- Open the **Render Settings** window.

- Select the **Common tab.**

- Change **Image Format** to **PSD Layered [psd].**

This is the setting that will save a multiple layer Photoshop file for you. The PSD [psd] saves a single layer (flattened) Photoshop file in native format.

Render layers selected for rendering

Setting Image Format to layered Photoshop

- In **Image Size**, set the resolution at which you want to output your rendering.

  You set the units and dpi for rendering output here. At the top of the screen you can see what size and resolution that translates into.

- Close the Render Settings window.

7 Save the scene file

- Save as *L10_Oaktree.mb*.

8 Render the image

You can only generate a layered PSD file by batch rendering.

- Select the **Rendering** module, then from the menu select **Render** → **Batch Render.**

  Maya will render each of the render layers one at a time, and then post-process to assemble them into a single Photoshop file.

Edit   Presets   Help

Render Using | Maya Software

Common | Maya Software | Maya Hardware | Maya Vector | ▼

Path: /Volumes/Onager II/_MAYA_docs/Maya_SupportFiles/Project_03/L▸

File Name: L14_Oaktree.psd

Image Size: 2400 x 1796 (8 x 6 inches 300 pixels/inch)

▼ **Image Size**

Presets | Custom

☑ Maintain Width/Height Ratio

Maintain Ratio ● Pixel Aspect   ○ Device Aspect

Width | 8.000

Height | 5.987

Size Units | inches

Resolution | 300.000

Resolution Units | pixels|inch

Device Aspect Ratio | 1.336

Pixel Aspect Ratio | 1.000

▼ **Render Options**

☑ Enable Default Light

Pre Render MEL |

Post Render MEL |

Close

Size and resolution settings

Note: *New folders will be created for each render layer inside the images folder with the names you gave to the render layers. These folders are part of the behind-the-scenes processing and are no longer needed once the rendering is completed.*

Lesson 10: Render Layers & Strategy

9 Open in Photoshop

You now have an image called *L10_Oaktree.psd* in the images folder.

- Open the image in Photoshop.

  Each render layer that you set-up in Maya has been assigned its own layer in the Photoshop file with the name you gave it in Maya.

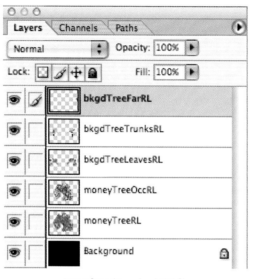

Layers from the rendered PSD file

- Rearrange the layers so they stack in the correct sequence.
- Change the **Blending mode** for the *moneyTreeOccRL* layer to **Multiply** and set the **Opacity** to **50%.**
- Create a color gradation for the background.

10 Add fog

11 Add shadows

> **Note:** Now start playing! By having the various elements broken onto layers you'll find that you have tremendous flexibility in arranging the pieces until you arrive at a finished composition. I've included the layered Photoshop file I worked on so that you can see how I approached it, but where you take this is up to you. Have fun!
>
> -Rob Magiera

Conclusion

In this lesson, you expanded your knowledge of render layers and learned the Maya-to-Photoshop workflow. By building on the Paint Effects model you created in the previous lesson, you were able to achieve a complete illustration. Congratulations!

Project 3
Special Effects

The primary idea behind this book is to introduce you to an entirely new spectrum of visual solutions that 3D has to offer. By expanding your CG toolbox to include three dimensions, many of the limitations that are encountered in 2D applications are easily overcome, and an entirely new universe of visual effects is yours for the creating.

You'll start by using Paint Effects, one of the most unique toolsets of Maya, to create two very different illustrations: an oak tree, complete with dense scenery, and a futuristic-looking cellphone. By utilizing the programmable nature of the Paint Effects brushes, very complex tasks can literally be accomplished with a few quick brush strokes.

In the second part of Project 3, you'll learn how to use image warping in Maya to create beautifully distorted graphic patterns that can be used for anything from surface textures to backgrounds and environments. These types of patterns would be tricky, if not impossible, to generate in any other manner.

Lesson 11
Paint Effects Illustration

Paint Effects technology in Maya provides an easy way to quickly integrate various 3D effects into your 2D illustrations. For example, you could use any number of nature type brushes (eg. grass, vine, flower or tree brushes) to enhance a landscape that you are creating in Illustrator. Vector rendering, one of the four rendering engines in Maya, allows for rendering 3D geometry to the Illustrator format, thereby giving you the ability to enhance your 2D illustrations with 3D graphics.

In this lesson you will learn the following:

- How to import Adobe Illustrator curves into Maya;

- How to create an Adobe Illustrator object within Maya;

- How to use Paint Effects brushes in conjunction with Illustrator objects;

- How to bring Maya rendered files back into Illustrator.

Bringing Adobe Illustrator text outlines into Maya

The following steps detail how to bring Adobe Illustrator text outlines into Maya and then convert them into 3D geometry. We will then apply Maya Paint Effects strokes to the text outlines and convert them to polygons. The resulting 3D objects will be rendered with Maya Vector and imported back into Adobe Illustrator.

1 Create a new Adobe Illustrator file

- Start Adobe Illustrator on your desktop and from the File menu create a new letter size file.

2 Create a text logo in Illustrator

- Select the **Type Tool** and change the character to Garamond and the font size to **72** points.

- Type **Spring Vibes** in your new document and then convert the text to outlines. Using the **Warp Tool**, deform your text outlines until they look similar to the following image.

> **Note:** You can use the file called Spring.ai from the supporting files CD-Rom.

Illustrator text logo that will be used in Maya

3 Save the Illustrator file for importing it into Maya

- In Illustrator, go to **File** → **Save As.** Name the file Spring and save it as an Adobe Illustrator file (.ai). In the Illustrator options window, choose Illustrator 8 as the version for the file (or turn off compression if you save it under the Adobe Illustrator CS format).

4 Create an Illustrator object in Maya

We will bring the Illustrator logo into Maya and create 3D geometry from it. For this task, we will use the new **Create Adobe Illustrator Object** functionality.

- In the Maya UI, go to **Create** → **Adobe® Illustrator® Object** and open the options box. Use the settings from the image below.

Choosing proper settings for the Adobe Illustrator object

- Click **create**, then locate the *Spring.ai* file and open it.

- The text outlines from Illustrator will be converted into 3D geometry and they will look like the following image.

Resulting 3D version of the text logo from Illustrator

5 **Import the Illustrator curves into Maya**

Now, we will import the same Illustrator logo into the Maya file containing the 3D logo. The outlines will be placed at the exact same location as the 3D logo. We will use these curves to attach Paint Effects strokes to them.

- In Maya, go to **File → Import**.

- Locate the Spring.ai file and click **Import**.

- In the Perspective view menu bar, select **Show** → **None** and after that select NURBS curves.

- Drag a selection around the text outlines, and then select **Edit** → **Group**.

- In the Perspective view menu bar, select **Show** → **All** to display all objects in the scene.

6 **Attach a Paint Effects brush to the imported curves**

We will now choose a brush that will be attached to all the imported curves. The effect will be that of flowers wrapping around the 3D text.

- In the Perspective view menu bar, select **Show** → **Polygons** to hide the polygonal text object from the view.

- Select one of the curves and press the up arrow to pick the *group* node.

- Click on the Paint Effects shelf tab in the Maya UI and choose the brush called *Daisy Large*. It is the brush *circled* in the following image:

Choosing the right PFX brush from the Paint Effects shelf

- In the Rendering module, go to **Paint Effects** → **Curve Utilities** → **Attach Brush to Curves**.

- You will now see the flowers wrapping around the text curves.

- In the Perspective view menu bar, select **Show** → **Polygons** to display the 3D text object.

- Your view should look like the following image:

3D logo adorned with Paint Effects strokes

Project 3: Special Effects

7 Modify the behavior attributes on the Paint Effects strokes

By adjusting some of the stroke attributes, the flowers will follow the text geometry even better. We will increase the curves' Path Follow and Path Attract attributes.

- Open the Outliner window, select **Window → Outliner**, and select all the stroke nodes.

- With the strokes selected, in the Channel Box scroll down to the Inputs section and select **daisyLarge**.

- Set **Global Scale** = 3.

- Scroll further down until you see the **Path Follow** and **Path Attract** attributes.

- Enter a value of **0.4** for both of them.

8 Create a material for the 3D text object

We will now create a new material for the 3D text object and give it a color that works better chromatically with the flowers.

- Open the Hypershade window, select **Window → Rendering Editors → Hypershade**.

- On the left side of the Hypershade window in the Create Maya Nodes section, click on blinn.

- Open the Attribute Editor window, and at the top rename the material to *SpringVibes*.

- Click on the color swatch and choose a light green color, H=82; S=0.64; V=0.96.

- In the Specular shading section, change the specular color to the same light green values.

- Select the 3D text object and assign the new SpringVibes material to it.

- Your view should now look like the following image:

Adding a material to the 3D text logo

9 Converting the Paint Effects brush strokes to polygons

In order to be able to render the Paint Effects strokes in Illustrator format, they will have to be converted to polygons and rendered with the Maya Vector rendering engine.

- Open the Outliner window, select **Window → Outliner**, and select all the stroke nodes.

- Go to **Modify → Convert → Paint Effects to Polygons → ❐**.

- In the **Poly Limit field** enter **1000000**. This will ensure that you have a high enough limit of polygons while you are converting the Paint Effect strokes.

- Click on **Convert**.

10 Choosing the proper render settings options for Vector Rendering

In order to be able to render to the Adobe Illustrator format, you will have to use the Maya Vector rendering engine. We will now choose the appropriate settings in the Render Settings window.

- Open the Render Settings window, select **Window → Rendering Editors → Render Settings…**

- At the top in the Render Using scroll down menu, choose Vector Rendering.

- In the Common Tab, set your image format to Adobe® Illustrator®.ai.

- Set your image size to **640** by **480** (8.9 x 6.7 inches at 72 pixels/inch). Since we will render to a vector format, the relatively low resolution will not be an issue.

- In the Vector Rendering tab, choose the following settings:

- Appearance Options:

    Curve Tolerance = 7.5;

    Detail Level Preset = Automatic;

    Detail Level = 0.

- Fill Options:

    Fill Objects should be **on**;

    Set **Fill Style** to **Two Color**;

    Show Back Faces to **on**;

    Shadows to **off**;

    Reflections to **off**.

- Edge Options:

    Include Edges should be **off**.

- Render Optimizations:

    Render Optimization should be set to **Aggressive**.

11 Bookmark the camera position for rendering

It is always a good idea to create a bookmark for the camera used for rendering your final image. This allows you to return easily to the desired camera position before rendering your file.

- Position your Perspective camera until you find the right position for viewing the 3D logo.

- In the Perspective View menu bar, select **View** → **Bookmarks** → **Edit Bookmarks ...**

- In the name field, enter a name (Render) for the bookmark, and then press Enter on your keyboard.

- Now, anytime you want to return to the bookmarked position just select **View** → **Bookmarks** → **Render.**

Creating a bookmark for the camera

12 Render the Maya scene to an Illustrator image format

Now that the Render Settings window is set for rendering to the Adobe Illustrator image format, you are ready to render. You will have to batch render your image since the Render view window will not allow you to save in the .ai format.

- Position your Perspective camera in the bookmarked position.

- In the Rendering module select **Render** → **Batch Render.**

- In the feedback line, you will see the percentage of the rendering's progress..

- The rendered image will be saved in the images folder inside your current Maya project. If you didn't create a new project, it will be found in your Default Project inside your Maya directory.

13 Open the rendered image in Adobe Illustrator

After the image is rendered you will want to bring it back into Adobe Illustrator where you can integrate it with other elements and add some color accents to it.

- Open Adobe Illustrator.

- Select **File** → **Open** and retrieve the .ai file from the images folder inside your current Maya project.

- The Adobe Illustrator file should look like the following image:

Vector rendered logo imported back into Adobe Illustrator

14 Bring some color accents to the text

We will now create some color accents for the text by filling certain portions of the letters with a lighter green tone.

- In Illustrator, with the Direct Selection Tool active, click on the front side of the letter S, and from the color swatches palette, fill the top area of the letter with *Fresh Grass Green* color. The results should look like the following image:

Adding color accents for the logo illustration

- After completing accents for all the other letters, the text should look like the following image:

The final version of the logo

Creating a background landscape for the illustration

We will now create a background landscape for our illustration using some of the other available Paint Effects brushes. The landscape will include houses in the background and a few trees closer to the viewer. The Spring Vibes logo will be used as the top layer in our illustration.

1   **Create a ground surface**

We will create a polygonal surface and use the Sculpt Geometry Tool to quickly create relief for the terrain.

- In the Modeling module select **Create → Polygon Primitives → Plane**.

- In the Channel Box, in the INPUTS section, select polyPlane1.

- Set the Subdivisions Width and Height to **50**.

- Change the Scale on X and Z to **80**.

2   **Sculpt the ground plane using the Sculpt Geometry Tool**

- Select the polygonal plane in Object mode.

- In the Modeling module, select **Edit Polygons → Sculpt Geometry Tool → ❑**.

- Set the **Radius(U) = 3**.

- Change the **Opacity** to **.5**.

- Under Sculpt Parameters, change the **Operation** to **Pull**.

- Start sculpting the surface until the results look similar to the following image:

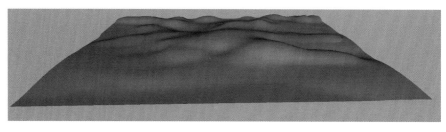

Sculpted ground plane surface

3   Make the ground surface paintable

In order to be able to paint on any surface, you have to first make it paintable.

- In the scroll down menu from the upper left side of the interface, scroll to the Rendering module.

- Select the ground plane surface.

- Select **Paint Effects** → **Make Paintable.**

4   Create geometry using Paint Effects brushes from the Visor

The Visor contains a series of pre-made brushes. We will be using some of these brushes to complete our landscape.

- Select **Window** → **General Editors** → **Visor ...**

- In the Visor window, click on the Paint Effects tab.

- Open the cityMesh folder.

- Select the brush named town.mel from the existing brushes.

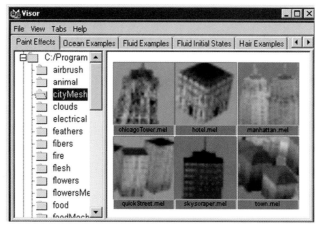

Visor Editor window

Project 3: Special Effects

- Start painting with the town brush at the back of the plane until you are satisfied with the results. The idea is to give the suggestion of a development or small town.

- Your Perspective view should now look similar to the following image:

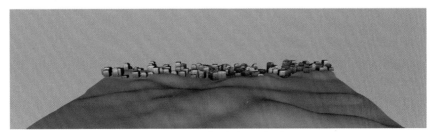

Houses painted with the PFX brush

Note: *You could adjust the Global Scale attribute if the houses are too big or too small.*

5 **Convert the Paint Effects brush strokes to poly geometry**

In order to be able to render the houses with Maya Vector, we have to convert the strokes to polygons.

- Open the Outliner window (**Window** → **Outliner**) and select all the strokeTown nodes.

- Go to **Modify** → **Convert** → **Paint Effects to Polygons** → ❑.

- In order to ensure that the conversion will not fail due to a low number of polygons set in the Poly Limit field, we can set this value to 1000000 and then click Convert.

6 **Add some flowers to the landscape**

Now that we have created the buildings in the background, we will create some trees and flowers using other existing brushes from the Visor.

- Select the ground plane surface.

- Select **Paint Effects** → **Make Paintable.**

- Select **Window** → **General Editors** → **Visor ...**

- In the Visor window, click on the **Paint Effects tab.**

- Open the flowersMesh folder.

- Select the brush named rosesClimbing from the existing brushes.

- Start painting on the ground plane surface.

7 **Convert the new Paint Effects brush strokes to poly geometry**

- Open the Outliner window, select **Window** → **Outliner**, and select all the strokeRoseClimbing nodes.

- Go to **Modify** → **Convert** → **Paint Effects to Polygons**.

8 **Add trees to the landscape**

Using the same technique as before, you will add some trees to your landscape.

- Select the ground plane surface.

- Select **Paint Effects** → **Make Paintable**.

- Select a tree brush from the TreesMesh folder (in the Visor window).

- Start painting on the ground plane surface.

- Open the Outliner window, select **Window** → **Outliner**, and select all the strokes for the trees.

- Go to **Modify** → **Convert** → **Paint Effects to Polygons**.

- After adding the flowers and trees, your file should look similar to the following image:

Trees and flowers added to the landscape

9 **Choosing the proper Render Settings options for Vector Rendering**

We will now choose the appropriate settings in the Render Settings window for rendering with the Vector rendering engine in Maya. The settings will be the same as when we rendered the 3D logo.

- Open the Render Settings window (**Window** → **Rendering Editors** → **Render Settings...**).

- At the top of the Render Using, scroll down the menu and choose Vector Rendering.

- In the Common Tab, set your image format to Adobe® Illustrator®.ai.

- Image size to **640** x **480** (8.9 x 6.7 inches at 72 pixels/inch). Again, since we will render to a vector format, the relatively low resolution will not be an issue.

- In the Vector Rendering tab, choose the following settings:

- Appearance Options:

    Curve Tolerance = 7.5;

    Detail Level Preset = **Automatic**;

    Detail Level = 0.

- Fill Options:

    Fill Objects should be **on**;

    Set Fill Style to **Two Color**;

    Show Back Faces to **on**;

    Shadows to **off**;

    Reflections to **off.**

- Edge Options:

    Include Edges should be **off.**

- Render Optimizations:

    Render Optimization should be set to **Aggressive.**

10 **Display the resolution gate for the Perspective camera**

In order to know which region from your Perspective view window will get rendered, you will have to display the resolution gate and increase the Overscan value.

- In the Perspective view menu, select **View** → **Select Camera.**

- With the Perspective Camera selected, go to **Window** → **Attribute Editor.**

- Scroll down to the Display section and turn on Display Resolution.

- At the bottom of the Display section, set the Overscan to **2**. This will allow you to see boundaries of the area that will get rendered.

11 Render the Maya scene to an Illustrator image format

Just like in step #12 in the first part of this lesson, now that the Render Settings window is set for rendering to the Adobe Illustrator image format, you are ready to render. Again, you will have to batch render your image since the Render view window will not allow you to save a file in the .ai format.

- In the Rendering module, select **Render** → **Batch Render.**

- Check the feedback line to see the rendering progress.

- The rendered image will be saved in the images folder inside your current Maya project. Again, if you didn't create a new project, it will be found in your Default Project inside your Maya directory.

12 Open the rendered file in Adobe Illustrator

We will now open the .ai file in Adobe Illustrator and see where minor changes need to be made.

- Open Adobe Illustrator.

- Select **File** → **Open** and retrieve the .ai file from the images folder inside your current Maya project.

- The Adobe Illustrator file should look similar to the following image.

The resulting Illustrator line-art after Vector rendering in Maya

13 Integrating the landscape with the logo

Now it is time to bring the previously created logo into the Illustrator file containing the landscape.

- In the Illustrator file containing the landscape, create a new layer.

- Open the Illustrator file containing the logo rendered previously.

- Select the logo and paste it into the file containing the landscape onto the new layer.

- Add some color accents to the houses and the rest of the landscape.

14 Save Your Work

Conclusion

In this lesson you learned how to use the Paint Effects brushes in Maya to integrate 3D elements into Adobe Illustrator files. You also learned about the possibilities with Vector rendering, namely how it gives you the ability to enhance your 2D illustrations with 3D graphics.

Lesson 12
Warped Patterns

By using some of the inherent capabilities of the 3D workspace in clever ways, you can generate an entire spectrum of image effects that are difficult or cumbersome to do otherwise. I like to think of Maya as an image synthesizer - an additional toolbox that allows me to generate anything from photoreal images and effects to components and parts that will be assembled later into a finished illustration. Because Maya is designed to mimic the real world, many of the working methods that you employ can logically follow how you would envision solving a particular problem in real life.

In this lesson you'll learn the following:

- How to create geometric patterns;

- How to warp them in a highly controllable manner;

- How to set-up rendered layers as masking channels;

- How to use masking channels to create a composition in Photoshop;

- How to layer in Photoshop for maximum adjustability.

1 Create a new scene file

- Open Maya. It will automatically create a new scene document.

- Using the View Selector, change the workspace to **Hypershade** → **Render** → **Persp Vertical**.

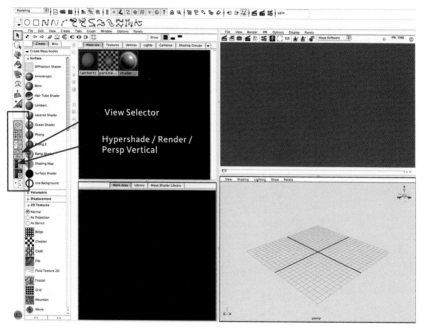

Workspace layout

2 Create a Ramp shader

You'll start by setting up a master shader that can be duplicated to give you variations. This will save you from having to build a shader from scratch each time.

- In the Hypershade, check under **Create** → **Create Options** and make sure **Include Placement with Textures** is checked; if not, select it now.

- In the **Create Maya Nodes** bar under 2D Textures, click the **Ramp** icon.

The Ramp node should be visible in the Attribute Editor on the right-hand side of your screen. You'll modify this ramp to create a repeating dot pattern.

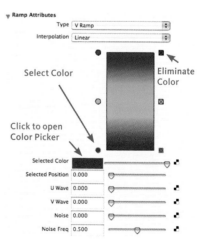

Ramp texture node in the Attribute Editor

Project 3: Special Effects

- Click the box to eliminate the blue color.

- Select the green color and change it to white.

- Select the red color and change it to black.

- Change **Selected Position** of the black color to **0.485**.

- Change Type to **Circular Ramp**.

- Click on the **place2dTexture** node to select it.

- In the Attribute Editor, change **Repeat UV to 10** and **10**.

- In the Hypershade, **RMB** on the **Ramp** node and **Assign Material To Selection**.

  This creates a lambert node with the Ramp assigned to the color input.

- Rename the texture *DotGraphicTex1*.

- Select the DotGraphicTex1 node and in the Attribute Editor set the **Diffuse, Translucence Depth** and **Translucence Focus** values to **0.0**.

- **MMB+drag** the Ramp node onto the DotGraphicTex1 node and select **incandescence** to make a new connection.

  The Ramp node is now connected to both the Color and Incandescence inputs for the shader. You can eliminate the color connection as it won't be needed.

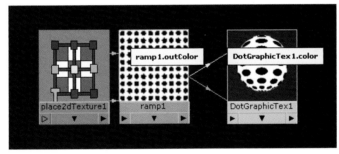

Mouse over the lines to see the input connections

- Select the Ramp **outColor to color** connection and press the **Delete** key.

3 **Create a surface to assign the shader to**

- Change the workspace to 4-view.

- Click in the side view window to select it.

- From the menu, select **Create** → **NURBS Primitives** → **Circle** → ❑.

- Select **Edit** → **Reset**.

- Change **Normal Axis** to **X Up**.

- Change **Sweep Angle** to -180.

- Change **Radius** to 6.

- Change **Number of Sections** to 4.

- **Create**.

4 **Modify the curve shape**

- Show the Channel Box and change **Scale Z** to 3.

Curve to be used for extrusion

5 **Extrude a surface**

- Select the curve in the Perspective window.

- From the menu, select **Surfaces** → **Extrude** → ☐.

- Select **Edit** → **Reset**.

- Set **Style** to **Distance**.

- Change **Extrude Length** to 20.

- **Extrude**.

6 **Center the surface**

- With the surface still selected, from the menu select **Modify** → **Center Pivot**.

- In the Channel Box, change **Translate X** to 10.

- From the menu bar select **Modify** → **Freeze Transformations**.

7 **Assign the shader**

- Change your workspace back to **Hypershade** → **Render** → **Persp View**.

- With the surface selected, in the Hypershade **RMB** on DotGraphicTex1 and **Assign Material To Selection**.

- Click the Persp view window to select it and press **6** for Textured preview.

8 **Center the camera view**

The following steps will show you how to center the camera view with the surface.

- In the Perspective view, select **View** →
  Select Camera.

- Change the settings in the Channel Box
  as in the image to the right.

Channels	Object	
persp		
	Translate X	0
	Translate Y	0
	Translate Z	25
	Rotate X	0
	Rotate Y	0
	Rotate Z	0
	Scale X	1
	Scale Y	1
	Scale Z	1
	Visibility	off
SHAPES		
perspShape		
	Horizontal Film Aperture	1.417
	Vertical Film Aperture	0.945
	Focal Length	35
	Lens Squeeze Ratio	1
	F Stop	5.6
	Focus Distance	5
	Shutter Angle	144
	Center Of Interest	44.822

Channel Box settings

9 **Do a test rendering**

- While in the Render view window, select **IPR** → **IPR Render** → **Current (Persp).**

- Drag a selection box to select a region to begin tuning.

  *You now have a basic repeating pattern of dots that take on the visual distortion that's
  imparted from the surface. This is a very interactive way to work and allows for a great deal
  of freedom and real-time feedback. Next, you'll take this basic setup and tweak some of the
  variables within it to get more dramatic results, as well as generate variations on a theme that
  will later become the structural building blocks for your illustration.*

10 **Modify settings**

- In the Hypershade, click on the place2dTexture node to view it in the Attribute Editor.

- Change the **Repeat UV** settings to **25** and **10.**

- In the Perspective view, select **View** → **Select Camera.**

- Change **Focal length** to **15.**

- Zoom the view to come in closer on the surface. Note the amplified distortion.

Project 3: Special Effects

Tip: *Holding down the Shift key while you zoom will constrain the camera movement and keep it centered.*

Note: *There are an infinite number of ways to achieve these distortions and experimentation is definitely the name of the game.*

- With the surface selected, press the **r** key for the Scale Tool.
- Grab the red handle (X-axis) and stretch the surface widthwise to fill the screen.

Note: *The IPR does not reflect changes to geometry. You must generate a new IPR in order for it to update.*

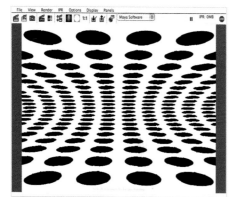

IPR in the render view window

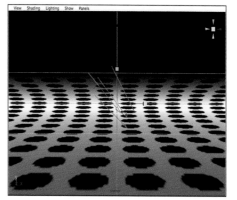

Perspective view window

Tip: *For a better onscreen texture display, open the shader in the **Attribute Editor**, scroll down to the **Hardware Texturing** section and set **Texture resolution** to **Highest (256x256)**.*

11 **Do a high quality rendering**

- Open the Render Settings window.

- Render using **Maya Software.**

- In the Common tab, change **Image Size Presets** to **1K Square (1024x1024).**

- Under Image File Output, change **Image Format** to **PSD layered [psd].**

- Click the Maya Software tab and change **Quality** to **Production Quality.**

- Uncheck **Use Multi-pixel Filter.**

- Close the Render Settings window.

12 **Render and save**

- In the Render view, click the Render icon.

- Click **File** → **Save Image.**

- Name it *DotPattern1.*

- Change the **Format** to **Photoshop (*.psd)** and **Save.**

DotPattern1 rendering

13 Assign the surface to a render layer

- Select the surface.

- Show the **Channel Box** → **Layer Editor**.

- Select the Render button to access the Render Layer Editor.

- Create a new layer and assign selected objects.

  A new layer is created and named layer1; it has the selected surface assigned to it.

- Change the render layer name to *DotGraphicTex1_RL* and **Save**.

14 Create a second render layer

- With the surface still selected, repeat the above steps.

- Name the layer *DotGraphicTex2_RL*.

15 Duplicate the DotGraphic shader

- In the Hypershade, click on the DotGraphicTex1 shader node to select it.

- Select **Edit** → **Duplicate** → **Shading Network**.

- Rename the shader *DotGraphicTex2*.

- In the Hypershade, double-click the shader node to open it in the Attribute Editor.

- Under **Hardware Texturing**, change the **Textured Channel** to **Incandescence**.

- **MMB+drag** the shader node to the surface to apply it.

16 Test render

- In the Render view, select **Options** → **Test Resolution** and set to **50% settings (512x512)**.

- Do an IPR render and drag-select an area for refresh.

17 Preview updates to the shader in the IPR

- **MMB** on the DotGraphicTex2 shader node and select **Graph Network**.

- Double-click on the Ramp shader for DotGraphicTex2 to open it in the Attribute Editor.

- Change the **Interpolation** to **Smooth**.

- Select the white color and change the **Selected Position** to 0.550.

- Select the black color and change the **Selected Position** to 0.170.

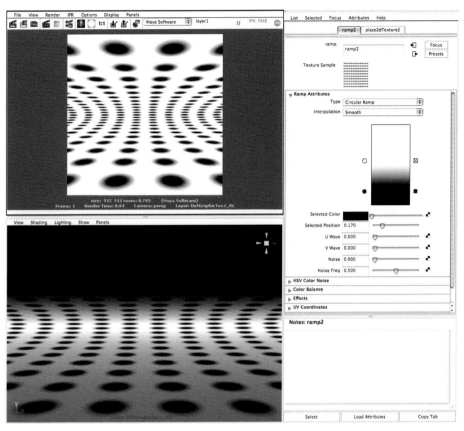

Variation of the original texture

> **Note:** You now have a scene file with two distinct textures. Each texture has been set-up to render as a separate layer in a single Photoshop (.psd) file. You can set-up as many layers as you like this way. Use this to set-up multiple variations of a texture that you can later render in one simple operation.

18 Create a new texture warp, this time modified by geometry

Another way to create variations in the pattern distortion is by assigning it to different types of geometry. This time you'll attach the same texture you just created (DotGraphicTex2) to an entirely new surface, which you'll generate from the curve you drew earlier in the lesson.

- Change to the 4-view workspace layout.

- In the **Layer Editor** → **Render Layers**, click on **masterLayer** to make it active.

> **Tip:** *Pay special attention anytime you are using render layers. It is a good practice to make any major edits your scene to the masterLayer.*

- In the Perspective view, select **View** → **Bookmarks** → **Edit Bookmarks**.
- Click **New Bookmark** and **Close**.
- Zoom out in the view to see your work better.

19 Make a new surface

- In the side view, click on the line to select it. Verify that only the curve is selected, not the surface, with a quick check in the Perspective view.
- Press **w** to get the Move Tool.

  The pivot point is centered within the curve space and needs to be relocated to an end point.

- Press and hold the **d** key.

  The Move Tool icon changes to reflect a new state that shows the pivot point is ready to be relocated.

- Continue to hold down the **d** key and move the pivot point anywhere over the curve.

- While continuing to hold down the **d** key, press the **c** key as well. This will constrain the pivot point to move along the curve. Drag it to either end of the curve.

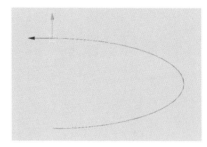

Relocated pivot point

20 Revolve a new surface

- With the curve still active, from the menu select **Surfaces** → **Revolve** → **❒**.
- Select **Edit** → **Reset**, then **Apply**.

21 Assign a texture to the revolved shape

- From the Hypershade, **MMB+drag** a shader node to the revolved surface to assign it.

22 Assign the revolved surface to a render layer

- Make sure the revolved surface is active, then in the Render Layer Editor select **Create new render layer with selection**.

- Rename the render layer *RevolvedGraphic_RL*.

23 Restore the camera view

- In the Perspective view, select **View** → **Bookmarks** → **cameraView1**.

24 Check surface tessellation

Tessellation is the process the rendering engine uses to convert NURBS surfaces to triangles. Tessellation determines how smoothly the surface is approximated so that it can be rendered with minimal faceting.

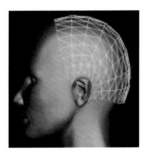 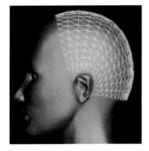

Surface tessellation

- Click on the revolved surface, and in the Attribute Editor expand Tessellation.

- Check on **Display Render Tessellation**.

- Check on **Enable Advanced Tessellation**.

- Expand the Advanced Tessellation section and check that **Mode** is set to **Per Span #** **of Isoparms**.

- Set **Number U** to **10** and **Number V** to **16**.

  This will increase render quality and keep the dots from having noticeable flat spots.

- Uncheck Display Render Tessellation.

- Test render.

Distorted pattern from the revolved surface

25 Do a layered rendering

- Show the **Channel Box** → **Layer Editor**.

- Make sure there is an **R** in the first box of each render layer, except for the masterLayer.

  R indicates which render layers are flagged for rendering.

- Change the menu to Rendering, and select **Render** → **Batch Render**.

  At the beginning of the lesson you set-up the renderer to produce layered Photoshop renderings.

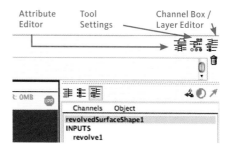

The Attribute Editor, Tool Settings, and Channel Box/Layer Editor buttons

26 Open the rendering in Photoshop

The next steps are all done in Photoshop.

- Navigate to the images folder in your project directory and open *L12_Warp_Start.psd*.

  The rendered file is automatically given the name of your scene file.

- Open in Photoshop. Note that there is a layer named for each of your render layers.

- From the images directory open *Satin_Pattern.psd*.

- Select **Layer** → **Duplicate Layer** and set the **Destination Document** as *L12_Warp_Start.psd*.

- Close the *Satin_Pattern.psd* file.

- With the imported layer selected, from the menu select **Layer** → **New** → **Background From Layer**.

  This places the Satin_Pattern layer at the bottom of the layer stack.

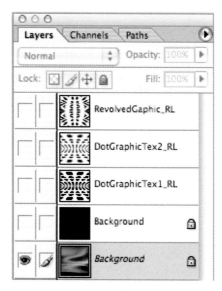

Layer stack in Photoshop

> **Note**: *Satin_Pattern.psd is an image from a bonus scene file called PatternBuilder.mb. When you're finished with this lesson, open the scene file to get additional ideas about how you can use this technique for creating patterns.*

27 Save the file

- Name the file *PatternArt.psd* and save it.

28 Add color to the base layer

- With all layers turned off, select the Background Layer you just made and choose **Layer** → **New Adjustment Layer** → **Hue/Saturation**.

- Check on **Colorize** and **Preview**.

- Dial in a color you like and then click **OK**.

29 Convert the pattern layers to Alpha channels

This is a multi-step process that you'll repeat for each of the three patterned layers.

> **Tip**: *Setting up layers in this manner gives tremendous flexibility when it comes to fine-tuning the color balance of the final composition.*

- Select the DotGraphicTex1_RL layer and press **Cmd a** (for Select All).

- Press **Cmd x** to cut the image.

- Switch to the Channels tab and click **Create new channel**.

  A new masking channel named Alpha1 is created.

- Press **Cmd v** to paste the cut image into the Alpha1 channel.

- With the pasted image still selected, press **Cmd i** to invert it.

- Press **Cmd d** to de-select.

Colorized background   *Alpha Channel*

30 Make a new layer from the Alpha channel

- Hold down the **Cmd** key and **LMB+click** on **Alpha Channel1** to load it.

  You'll know it's loaded by the "marching ants" marquee selection.

> **Note:** *Think of a mask as a constantly variable switch, where black is off, white is on, and the percentage of gray determines how much the area in-between is on or off.*

- Click the Layers tab.

- Click on DotGraphicTex1_RL to select it.

  You'll see the loaded Alpha channel selection.

- If the layer is not visible, click the eye icon to turn it on.

- From the menu, select **Edit → Fill**. For **Contents** use **50% grey**. Blending Mode should be Normal and Opacity 100%. Then click **OK**.

- Press **Cmd d** to de-select.

31 Repeat the steps for the remaining two pattern layers

32 Add color to the layers

- Select one of the pattern layers and create a new adjustment layer,
  Select **Hue/Saturation**.

- Before you make any adjustments, click **OK** to close the window.

- Group the adjustment layer to the pattern layer by pressing **Cmd g**.

- Double-click the adjustment layer to reopen it.

- Check on **Colorize** and adjust the color settings. Click **OK**.

33 Repeat for the remaining pattern layers

34 Save

Composited layers and adjustment layers in Photoshop

Conclusion

In this lesson you learned how to put some of the 3D capabilities of Maya to use to create patterns and geometric distortions that can then be used as the foundation for layered compositions in Photoshop. From here you should experiment with different blend modes, layer opacity, and color settings. Or, apply a filter and stretch and distort the layer with the Transformation Tool. It's completely up to you where you go with this!

I've included the layered Photoshop file I worked on with the DVD so that you can see where I ended with it. This is a method that I use quite frequently for creating environments, backgrounds, and textures. There is also a bonus scene file called *PatternBuilder.mb* that you can open to get some further ideas on how to use this technique to accomplish some rather surprising results.

To take this lesson a step further, make a shader from the texture you just created and map it back onto an object in Maya. You'll quickly discover how limitless this technique can be.

Lesson 13
Oak Tree Illustration

One of the truly unique features in Maya is the Paint Effects toolset. With each release, Paint Effects has grown more powerful and sophisticated, while at the same time becoming easier to use. It can make fast work of otherwise labor intensive tasks, so it is well worth learning. Paint Effects allows you to generate dense scenery with a few brush strokes, and then interactively edit the results to give you the desired effect.

In this lesson you'll learn the following:

- How to use Paint Effects to quickly create complex geometry;

- How to convert brush strokes to polygons;

- How to edit brush settings to revise your model.

Setting up your workspace

You'll begin by rearranging your workspace for an efficient workflow. As you'll soon see, the Paint Effects toolset approaches modeling differently than the typical workflow.

1 Set the project

The first thing to do when beginning a new project is to point Maya to the Project Directory you intend to work from, or set-up a new project directory if you are starting fresh. In this case, you'll show Maya where the files you copied from the DVD are on your hard drive.

- Select **File → Project → Set**.

- In the navigation window that pops up, locate **Project_03 Lesson_013_PFXOakTree** and click on the directory folder to select it.

- Click **Choose**.

1 Start a new scene

- Select **File → New Scene**.

2 Rearrange your workspace

- In the Persp window, choose **Panels → Saved Layouts → Hypershade → Render → Persp Vertical**.

- In the Hypershade window, select **Panels → Panel → Visor**.

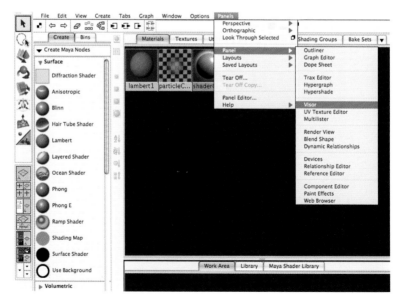

Changing to the Visor panel

3 **Start Paint Effects**

- In the Perspective view, select **Panels** → **Paint Effects**, or simply press the **8** key to enter Paint Effects mode.

  Paint Effects operates in two modes: **Canvas** *and* **Scene**. *In this case, you are painting three-dimensionally in the scene, so check that you are set accordingly by checking* **Paint** → **Scene** *in the Paint Effects window.*

  Note: *Pressing the* **8** *key will toggle you in and out of Paint Effects.*

- In the Visor, make sure the **Paint tab** is selected and open the **treesMesh** folder.
- Select the **birchSpringHeavy.mel** brush preset, and in the Perspective window drag a short stroke to create the tree. Maya will complete building the tree as soon as you release the brush.
- Press the **Spacebar** to zoom the Perspective view.
- Press the **8** key to exit Paint Effects.
- Press **f** to center the tree in your camera view.
- Press **5** for shaded view.
- Press **q** to switch to the Select Tool – so you don't accidentally paint more trees!

4 **Experiment with settings**

While it's fine to paint with the brush presets, more often than not you'll want to fine-tune the stroke to fit your specific needs. Here, you'll play around with the settings to get a feel for how they affect the geometry you just placed, and find out where the key controls are to quickly adjust your model.

- In the view, click on the tree to select it.
- Ensure the Attribute Editor is visible.

Attribute Editor button, far right of screen

Edit   Help

Vertex Color Mode	● None ○ Color ○ Illuminated
Quad Output	☑
Hide Strokes	☑
Poly Limit	0

Convert	Apply	Close

Convert to polygons, options box

5 Convert Paint Effects geometry to polygons

- Select **Modify** → **Convert** → **Paint Effects to Polygons** → ❑.

Note: *When history is on, all of the controls that determine how your brush stroke looks are still connected to the polygon mesh and allow you to update the mesh by changing the brush settings.*

Tip: *Setting the Poly Limit to zero removes any limitation on how many polygons can be created during the conversion.*

- In the Perspective window, enable **Shading** → **Wireframe on Shaded.**

- In the Attribute Editor, select **the birchSpringHeavy1 tab** and expand the **Mesh** section.

- With the tree branches and trunk selected, move the tube and sub-sections' sliders to see how they effect the polygon settings. Note that these settings also effect the polygon count of the leaves.

- Adjust the sliders until you have a nice balance to the polygon mesh.

Project 3: Special Effects

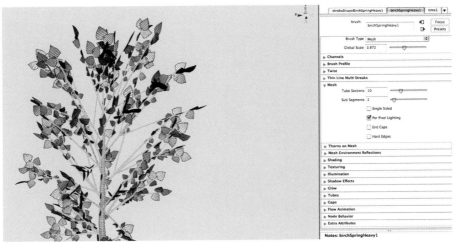

Poly mesh settings

5 Adjust the leaves

- Expand the **Tubes** section to reveal the **Growth** → **Leaves** section.

- In the Leaves section, experiment with different slider settings to see how they affect the size and quantity of the leaves.

- In the **Leaf Width Scale** section, note how the shape of the leaf is determined in the Curve Editor box. Modify the curve and watch how it updates in the Perspective window.

- In the **Leaf Curl** section, change the **Selected Value** of the Curve Editor to **.620** and notice how the leaf shape changes.

- Change the **Leaf Segments** to **4**. This is where you can control the polygon density of the leaves in the mesh.

- Save your work.

Leaf Width Curve Editor

Leaf Curl Curve Editor and settings

Shaded preview of test tree

> **Tip:** You have quick access to many of the key components that determine overall polygon mesh quality settings for the model from one central location. Make sure you're in the Rendering module, then from the menu select **Paint Effects** → **Paint Effects Mesh Quality**. Notice that most of the settings you were adjusting have been collected for you and are available here.

Set-up a new scene

Now that you have a general feel for the brush controls and how they affect your geometry settings, you're ready to set-up an illustration.

- Create a new scene.

- Set-up your workspace as you did at the beginning of the lesson.

- In the Perspective window, select **View** → **Camera Settings** → **Resolution Gate** to see your renderable view.

Project 3: Special Effects

- Press **8** to enter Paint Effects mode.

- In the Visor, have the **meshTree** folder open and select the **oakWhiteMedium.mel** brush.

- Paint a stroke near the center of the grid (X,Y 0,0) to place a tree in the scene.

- Press **8** to exit Paint Effects.

- Press the **Spacebar** to zoom the window.

1 **Scale the tree**

- With the tree still selected, go to the Attribute Editor and select the **oakWhiteMedium1** tab.

- At the top change the **Global Scale** to 10.

- Press **w** for the Move Tool.

- Open the Outliner by selecting **Window** → **Outliner.**

  The entire Paint Effects mesh actually springs from the curve you drew on the grid, so you'll need to select that in order to move the tree without it wandering off the pivot point. This curve is hidden by default, so select it in the Outliner (curveOakWhiteMedium, colored blue to signify the hidden state), and then move it in the Perspective view and the tree will follow. If need be, you can speed up your screen redraw by temporarily turning off the polygon display of the tree. To do so, from the menu select Display and uncheck Paint Effects Mesh Display. You can turn it back on once you have arranged the scene as you like.

2 **Compose your scene**

- Position the tree towards the back of the scene.

- Rotate, pan and zoom the camera view to get a nice angle.

3 **Convert the trees to polygons**

- Frame the closest tree by selecting it and pressing the **f** key.

- Convert the Paint Effects tree to polygons.

- Adjust the polygon density as you did earlier in the lesson.

- Open the **Window** → **Outliner**, select **oakWhiteMedium2MeshGroup** and **Edit** → **Duplicate** it.

- Move the copied tree to a new position.

- Repeat the same steps for another tree.

Modified small oak tree and settings

4 **Add a detailed tree to the scene**

This tree will be the focal point of the illustration, so you want an interesting, highly detailed tree to be your star.

- In the Visor, select **oakHeavy.mel** and place it in your scene.

- In the Attribute Editor, select the **oakHeavy1 tab** and increase the **Global Scale** to **14.**

- Position the tree and camera view to get a pleasing composition.

- Select **View** → **Bookmarks** → **Edit Bookmarks** → **New Bookmark** and close the window.

> **Tip:** *Anytime you have a composition that you like, bookmark it so that you can easily return to it down the road.*

5 **Convert the tree to polygons**

As soon as you select the tree, it will be obvious that you're dealing with an extremely dense polygon mesh this time. Before converting to polys, optimizing the brush settings will lower the density and make the model easier to handle.

Project 3: Special Effects

Overly dense polygon mesh

- With the tree selected, in the Attribute Editor click on the **oakHeavy1** tab.

- Zoom the Perspective view.

- Expand the mesh section and change **Tube Sections** to **12** and **Sub Sections** to **2**.

- Expand **Tubes** → **Growth** → **Leaves** and change **Leaf Segments** to **4**.

Revised mesh settings

- Convert the Paint Effects tree to polygons.

Paint Effects tree converted to polygons

Converted tree group

6 **Make a money tree**

If only it was this simple in real life - you'll replace the leaves on the big tree with dollar bills. The first task is to create a two-sided texture that you'll use as the leaf replacement.

- Change the workspace to **Hypershade** → **Render** → **Persp Vertical**.

- Select the **oakHeavy1LeafShader** material.

- In the Hypershade, select **Edit** → **Duplicate** → **Shading Network**.

- Rename the texture to *dollarBill*.

- Graph the network.

7 **Make a two-sided shader**

Since the dollar bill uses a different texture file for either side, you'll create a shader that correctly shows the front and back of the bill.

- In the General Utilities section of the Hypershade, click on both the **Condition utility** and the **Sampler Info utility**. This places two new nodes that you'll connect to your network.

- In the 2D Textures section, click once on the **File** texture node to add that to the work area.

  You now have a view of the shader network plus three new nodes that you'll connect together to create a new shader. If the File node has a place2dTexture4 node connected to it, simply select that node and delete it.

- Select **Graph** → **Rearrange Graph**.

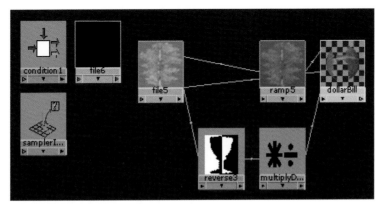

Graph view in the work area with unconnected nodes

- Select the new **File** node and in the **Attribute Editor** → **Image Name**, navigate to sourceimages/USD20_back.tif and **Open**.

- Click on the **File** node that is already connected to the shader network, and in the Attribute Editor navigate to **sourceimages/USD20_front.tif** and **Open**.

8 Make node connections

- **MMB** the connected **Ramp** node on top of the **Condition utility** node. In the pop-up box select **colorIfTrue.**

Since the color of the dollar bill texture is being modified by the Ramp node, that's where you want to make your connection into the Condition node.

Note: *The Condition utility node determines which texture map is used for color depending on which side of the leaf is facing the camera. Since it is the last piece in the chain the last piece in the chain determines what color is used, it is the one that will connect to the color input on the material node.*

- **MMB** the unconnected **File** node and drag-on top of the **Condition utility** node, in the pop-up box select **colorIfFalse.**

- **MMB** the **Sampler Info utility** node on top of the **Condition utility**, and in the pop-up box select **Other.**

- In the **Connection Editor,** click on **Flipped Normal** and then click on **Second Term** to make the connection between nodes.

- Close the Connection Editor.

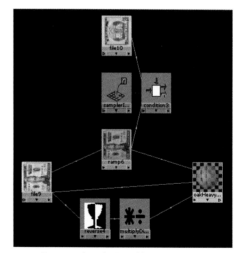

Rearranged graph view with new connections

9 Revise the existing connections

There are some qualities of the leaf that you'll want to keep, such as the green tint and specular light quality. Doing so is relatively easy by simply changing how the nodes are connected to one another.

- Delete two of the incoming connections to the material node (Color and Transparency).

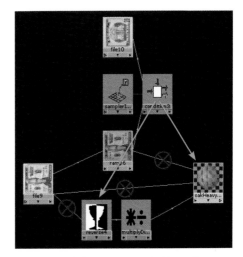

Break these connections by deleting them, then reconnect where the blue arrows point

- Delete the connection coming into the **Reverse** node.

- **MMB** the **Condition node**, drag it on top of the **Material node** and select **Color.**

- **MMB** the **Condition node**, drag it on top of the **Reverse node** and select **Input.**

There is no longer a need for transparency in this new shader.

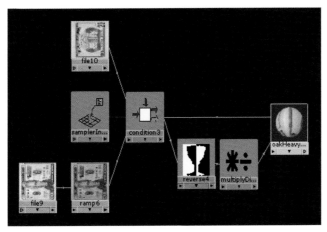

Shader with revised connections

10 Replace the leaf shader with the dollar bill shader

- In the Materials window, **RMB** on the **oakHeavy1LeafShader** and **Select Objects With Material.**

- In the Materials window, **RMB** on the **dollarBill shader** and **Assign Material To Selection.**

11 Modify the leaf shape

- Click on the leaves to select them, and in the Attribute Editor make sure the **oakHeavy1 tab** is selected. Now find **Leaf Segments** and change to **1.**

- Do a preview render.

Dollar bill leaves with incorrect texture orientation

For some reason the front texture is reversed. A quick and simple fix is in order.

12 Reverse front side texture

- In the graph view, click the front bill texture node to select it.

- In the Attribute Editor, under **Image Name,** click the **Edit button** to open the image in Photoshop.

- Flip the image vertically and save it.

- In the Attribute Editor, press the **Reload button.**

- Redo the test render.

> **Note:** *Photoshop has built-in currency detection that may block you from opening the image, per the request of the U.S. Treasury Department. In that case, use any other image processing program (such as Graphic Converter) to flop the image.*

- In the Perspective view, select **View** → **Bookmarks** → **cameraView1** to return to the camera view you set earlier.

- Save your work.

Conclusion

In this lesson, you learned about the effects that become possible with use of the Paint Effects toolset. The more you use the toolset and become.

Lesson 14
Image Warp

Let's say that you need to create a flat graphic that will precisely fit and reflect the distorted topology of a 3D surface. If you're very familiar with Photoshop you have undoubtedly come across the need to warp an image in a precise manner in order to fit a given shape, but the available tools don't offer a particularly effective way to accomplish this. The technique explored in this lesson was born from necessity. It was developed for a client that had a unique requirement; they needed graphics for a manufacturing / printing process called IMG — In-Mold Graphics. In this case, the graphics are printed flat and must be distorted to accurately fit the molded parts. This workflow makes quick work of a tricky image deformation. The final image will be a futuristic-looking cellphone.

In this lesson you'll learn the following:

- How to precisely fit a flat image to an existing shape;

- How to develop an intuitive workflow.

1 **Open the scene file**

- Open *L14_MobilePhone_start.mb.*

2 **Arrange your scene**

- Change your view to 4-view if you are not already there.

- Zoom the top view so that the phone wireframe comfortably fills the pane.

3 **Isolate the parts that you'll be working on**

For this project you want to fit a texture you'll create in Photoshop to the silver part of the front of the phone model. Cleaning up the scene by assigning pieces to a display layer and hiding the parts you don't need will make it easier to see what you're doing.

- To open the Hypershade window, select **Window** → **Rendering Editors** → **Hypershade**.

- **RMB** on the **brushedmetal** texture and **Select Objects with Material.**

- Group the selected objects by pressing **Cmd+g (Ctrl+g).**

- Unparent the new group by pressing **Shift+p.**

- Show the Channel Box / Layer Editor.

- Create a new display layer.

- **RMB** on the layer and **Add Selected Objects.**

- Double-click the layer and rename it *faceplateLayer.*

- Hide phoneLayer by clicking in the first box to **toggle v** off.

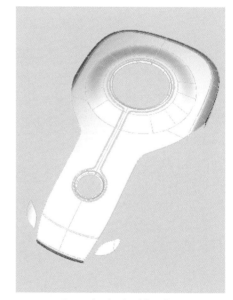

Grouped and isolated face plate

4 **Take a snapshot**

- Select **Window** → **Rendering Editors** → **Render View** to open the Render view window.

- Set **Options** → **Test Resolution** to **Render Settings (1800x1200).**

- Select **Render** → **Snapshot** → **Top.**

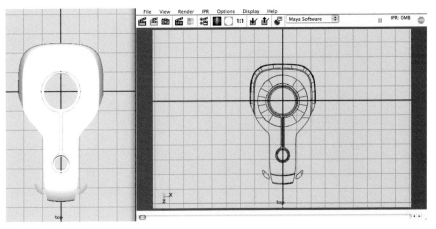

Take a snapshot of the top view of the model

You'll use this snapshot in Photoshop as a template for the texture you'll be making.

- **RMB** in the Render view window and select **File** → **Save Image.**

- Change the format to **Photoshop (.psd).**

- Name the texture *Template.psd* and Save.

5 **Open Photoshop**

You'll now be working in Photoshop for the next several steps.

- Open Photoshop, navigate to the snapshot and open it.

- Drag guidelines to mark the boundary of the faceplate.

  Drag to the outermost edge of the wireframe, not the middle, as this is where Maya fits the graphic to.

- From the Photoshop folder in the lesson directory, open *Graphic.tif.*

- Hold down the **Cmd (Ctrl)** key for the Move Tool and drag the *Graphic.tif* image into the *Template.psd* window.

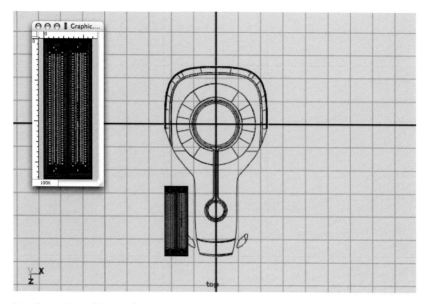

Drag the graphic you'll be using for the new texture to the template window to copy it and create a new layer

- Press **Cmd+t (Ctrl+t)** to get the Transform Tool and resize the placed file to fit the guidelines.

6 **Make the snapshot more usable as a template layer**

Although you don't need to do this for the graphic that's being used right now, setting up your working file in this way makes it more flexible for later applications.

- Double-click the background layer to convert it to a layer.

- Name the layer *Template.*

- Drag it up in the layer stack.

- Select the Magic Wand Tool and click the grey background to select it.

- From the menu, select **Select → Similar.**

- Delete the selection.

- Press **Cmd+d (Ctrl+d)** to de-select.

- Presss **Cmd+I (Ctrl+I)** to invert.

- Change the Blend Mode to **Screen.**

  If you are working over a light image set the Blend Mode to Multiply.

- Lock the layer.

Project 3: Special Effects

7 Crop the window

- Select the Crop Tool and snap it to the guidelines. Crop.

- Turn off the visibility of the Template layer.

- Save the file into the sourceimages folder as *Graphics.psd*.

  Saving in the native Photoshop format will let you easily update the texture file later on by simply turning layers on or off.

Note: *When using a layered Adobe Photoshop .psd file as your source texture file, keep in mind that Maya only sees the flattened result. If you are using a layered PSD file multiple times within the same scene file, be aware that any changes you make to it will affect all the previous placements of that file.*

8 Create a warp plane in Maya

- Click in the second box of the facePlateLayer to template it.

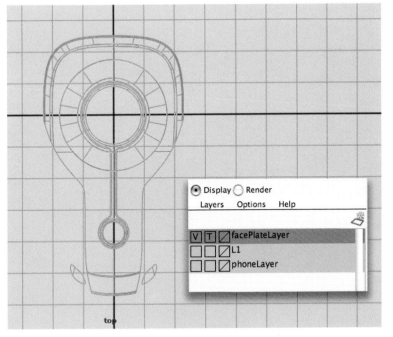

Template the facePlateLayer

Lesson 14: Image Warp

- From the menu, select
  Create → NURBS Primitives →
  NURBS Plane → ❑.

- Select Edit → Reset.

- Set U V Patches to 3 and 3 and Create.

9 Fit to shape

- Reposition and resize the NURBS plane
  to match the outer diameter of the
  templated face plate.

- With the NURBS plane still selected,
  from the menu select Display →
  NURBS Components → Custom → ❑
  and check on Hulls and CVs, then Apply
  and Close.

10 Create a shader

Begin by making a duplicate shader of the
brushedmetal shader network.

- Click on brushedmetal to select it.

- In the Hypershade window, select Edit → Duplicate → Shading Network.

- RMB over the newly created texture node and Graph Network.

- Rename the shader *graphicsTex1*.

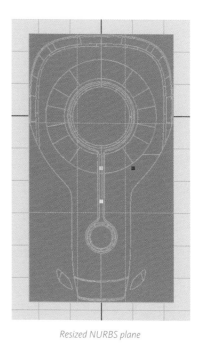

Resized NURBS plane

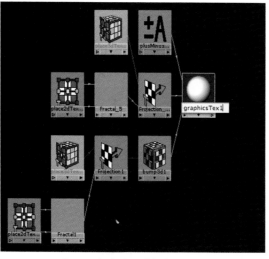

Rename the duplicated shader network

Project 3: Special Effects

- Select **Create** → **Create Options** → **Include Placement with Textures.**

- Click the **File texture node** in 2D Textures to create one.

- Double-click the file texture node to make it active in the Attribute Editor.

- In the Attribute Editor, under **File Attributes** → **Image Name,** navigate to the lesson's sourceimages directory and select *Graphics.psd* as the image file.

- **RMB** on the lower right corner of the file node, then select **Out Color** → **Out Color.**

- Attach the connection string by **RMB+clicking** over the lower left corner of the texture node and connecting to Color.

  This creates a new connection utilizing the Graphics.psd file as the color information for the shader.

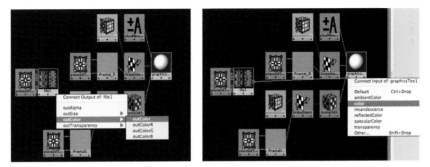

Make the new color connection by RMB+clicking on the lower corners of the nodes

11 **Assign the shader**

- Click on the NURBS plane you created earlier to select it.

- **RMB** on the *graphicsTex1* texture node and **Assign Material To Selection.**

- Go to the top view and press **6** for shaded preview.

12 **Warp the texture**

By modifying the shape of the surface the texture has been applied to, you can apply a smooth and precisely controlled distortion to the image.

Note: *NURBS surfaces assign texture coordinates by a method called* parameterization. *Parameters are the unique numeric values (like coordinates) of points on a curve or surface. Just as every point along the length of a curve has a U parameter, every point across a surface has U and V parameters. By changing the shape of the surface you simultaneously change the UV texture coordinates.*

- Change the selection mode to Select by Component Type and enable Hulls.

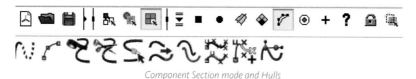

Component Section mode and Hulls

- Click on the topmost hull to select it.
- Press **r** to get the Scale Tool.
- Scale the Hull width-wise to fit the shape.
- Repeat by moving down the model from hull to hull and continuing to modify the shape to fit the template as close as you can.

13 Add isoparms for more detail

- **RMB** over the NURBS shape and select **Isoparms**.

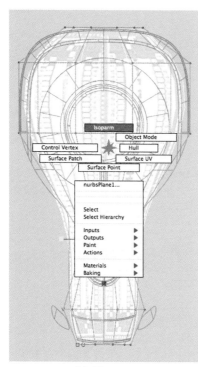

Select isoparms

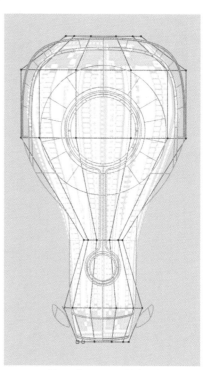

Additional isoparms added to the NURBS surface

Project 3: Special Effects

- Click on the top-most edge of the shape and drag a new isoparm to where you need more control.

- Hold the Shift key and continue to add isoparms in this same manner.

- From the Modeling menu, select **Edit NURBS** → **Insert Isoparms.**

Tip: *The trick to good NURBS modeling is to use as few curves (isoparms) as possible to achieve the shape you want. Fewer curves and control points will yield smoother surfaces, which are easier to control.*

- Add additional isoparms, if needed.

- Add **Points** to **Select by Component Type** to move the CVs (points on the hulls) to gain a better fit.

- Using the Scale and Move Tools, continue to adjust the hulls and CVs until you are satisfied with the fit.

Tip: *It's better to have the NURBS shape edge be ever so slightly outside of the templated shape rather than inside of it.*

14 **Test render**

You'll need to add a light, as the existing lights in the scene are assigned to one of the hidden layers and won't show.

- From the menu, select **Create** → **Lights** → **Directional Light.**

- Rotate the light on the X-axis to -90 so it shines straight down.

- With the light still selected, open the Attribute Editor.

- In the directional light's attributes, uncheck **Emit Specular.**

- Do a test render (test resolution 1800x1200).

- **RMB** on the rendering and **File** → **Save Image**. Select the sourceimages folder and name the image *WarpImage1*. Change Format to Tiff (*.tif) and Save.

15 Open WarpImage1.tif in Photoshop

- From the menu, go to **Select** → **Load Selection** and press **OK**.

  The Alpha channel (which was generated with the rendering) is loaded.

- With the marquee selection active, from the menu select **Image** → **Crop**.

- Press **Cmd+d (Ctrl+d)** to de-select.

- In the Channels window, select the Alpha channel and delete it.

- Save the file.

Note: At this stage, you have the primary workflow for fitting flat art into a specified shape. With a bit of ingenuity and a basic understanding of how image files are mapped to NURBS surfaces, it becomes possible to warp images to fit virtually any shape imaginable.

16 Apply to model

The last shader you worked on should still be graphed in the work area. Now you'll reconnect it and apply it to the model.

- **RMB** on file1 and select **outColor.**

- Connect to the Projection_13 node and select Image from the pop-up box**.**

- **RMB** over Projection_13 **outColor** and connect to graphicsTex1 **color.**

- **Double-click** the file1 image texture node to open it in the Attribute Editor and in Image Name load *WarpImage1.tif* .

- In the Layer Editor, uncheck **t** (untemplate) on the facePlateLayer.

- Turn on the remaining layers.

- In the Hypershade, **RMB** on the brushedmetal texture and **Select Objects With Material.**

- **RMB** on the graphicsTex1 and **Assign Material To Selection.**

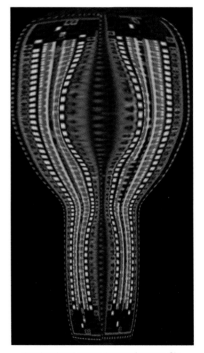

Rendered and cropped warped texture file

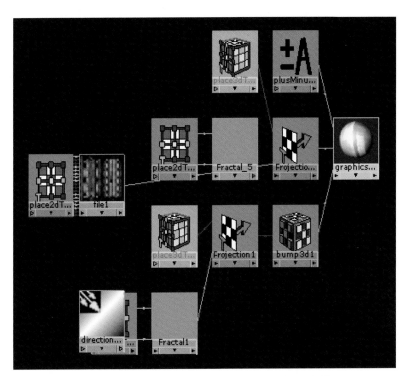

Hijacking the earlier texture placement node to make it do your bidding

17 Render and fine-tune

Do a test render to make sure that the new shader you've assigned is working as expected, and adjust as necessary.

- In the Render view, select **Options** → **Test Resolution** and set to 25% (450x300).

- Do an IPR render.

  The texture is not fitting correctly and will need to be adjusted.

- In the Hypershade, click on the Projection_13 node to select it.

- In the Attribute Editor in the Projection Attributes section, click on **Fit To Bbox.**

  The texture placement marker is now visible and you can see why the texture does not fit the surface properly.

- Adjust the texture placement to fit the surface.

  The IPR render will update as you make the adjustments.

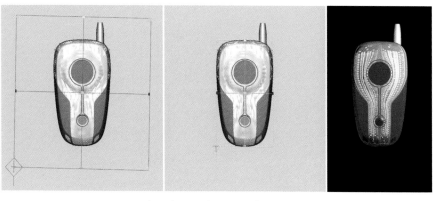

Adjusted texture placement and IPR view

18 Render

- Go to the Perspective view.

- In the Render view window, change your **Test Resolution** to **Render Settings** (1800x1200).

- Select **mental ray** as the rendering engine.

- Open the Render Settings and open the mental ray tab.

- Change the **Quality Presets** to **Production.**

- Render the image.

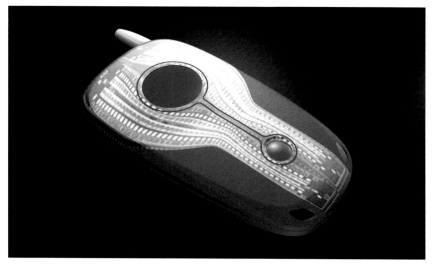

Final render

Conclusion

Utilizing the inherent image mapping of NURBS surfaces to freely distort and reshape an image adds a powerful tool to your image editing arsenal. While this lesson covers a highly specialized use of this technique, the fundamentals explained here can be utilized in an unlimited number of creative ways.

IMAGEGALLERY

Rob Magiera Noumena Digital

Rob Magiera Noumena Digital

Rob Magiera Noumena Digital

Rob Magiera Noumena Digital

Rob Magiera Noumena Digital

Rob Magiera Noumena Digital

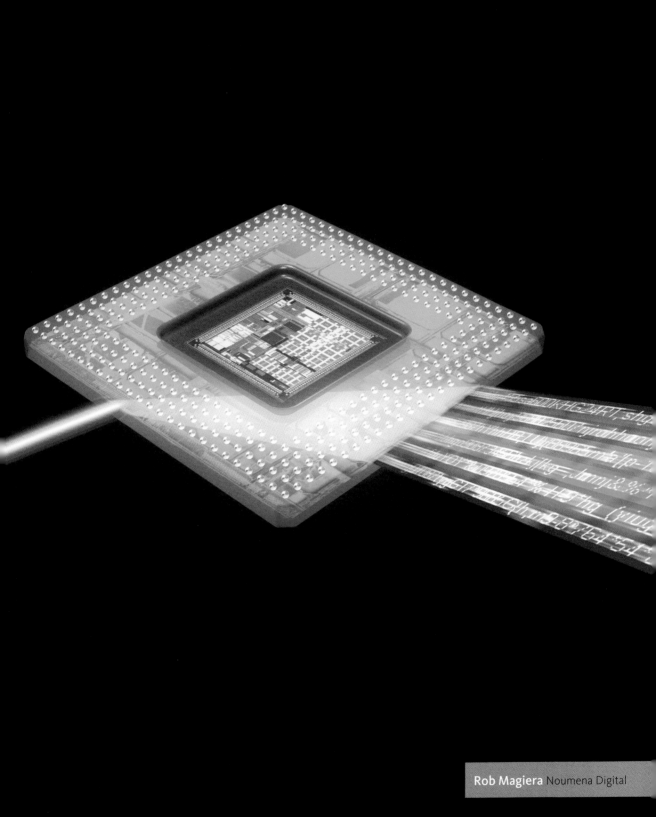

Rob Magiera Noumena Digital

Rob Magiera Noumena Digital

Rob Magiera Noumena Digital

Rob Magiera Noumena Digital

Rob Magiera Noumena Digital

Loïc Zimmermann E338

Loïc Zimmermann E338

Loïc Zimmermann E338

Loïc Zimmermann E338

Project 4
Yatoer, The Bus Stop Boxer

The content in Project 4 has been created by Loïc Zimmermann. In Proect 4 You'll be working on Yatoer, the bus stop boxer as a reference, but you will also use templates for explanations, crops of the final image and sometimes different basic pictures. This is to help you understand some effects and manipulations that could be more difficult to see on the final illustration otherwise. Once you've understood the concepts behind a tool, it'll be your job to find the other applications.

Consider, for example, that two passes of paint will always give a better result than one; well, in the same way, making things appear, little by little, is also a good way to work with digital images.

Lesson 15
Texturing Tricks

In this lesson, although it's not the focus of this book, we will have a look at textures. You can use Photoshop to sketch the picture you want, but you can also use it for creating textures and to finalize the image after the 3D is rendered. Basically, you could say that Photoshop is essential for every stage of the image and animation creation process.

In this lesson you will learn:

- How to create photo blendings;

- How to use UV snapshot;

- How to add detail, refine areas and play with color;

- How to merge photos together in Photoshop;

- How to post-process the final render.

Making a UV snapshot

Once your UVs are laid out, the first thing to do is make a high quality UV snapshot. This will be your guide for the entire texturing process. You'll make a global texture, without paying attention to details at this stage.

- Open *faceForTextures.ma*.

- Using the Selection Tool, select the polygon geometry.

- From the main menu, select **Windows** → **Texture Editor**.

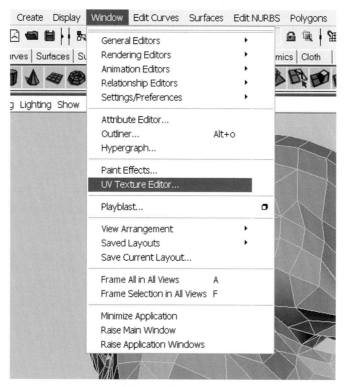

UV Texture Editor location

You should have a new window for the 2D layout of the geometry. On the top left, there is a polygon menu. At the bottom of this menu, there is the UV snapshot option. Select it.

- In the UV Texture Editor window, select **Polygons** → **UV Snapshot**.

Follow the images on the right for the settings.

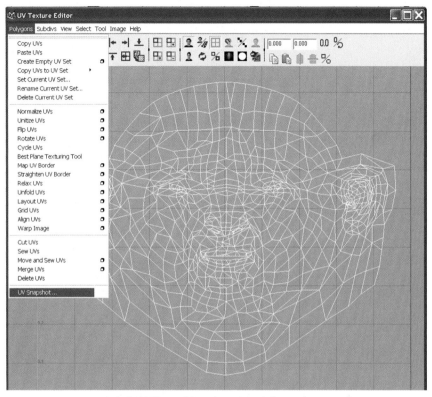

In the UV Texture Editor, the geometry is flattened out

UV snapshot options window

UV snapshot will create a picture from the information in the UV Texture Editor. Here, you can set the resolution, the file name and the file format. Make sure to set the file format to *tga*, unless you have the *.iff* plug-in for Photoshop. Choose **2048** x **2048** (2K) for the resolution in this example. Once this is done, go back to Photoshop and open the resulting image that should be in your Maya project images folder.

Let's say you need a profile and a face shot to start with. For the textures, I use references from 3d.sk, but you can also decide to make yourself a bank of photos (you will learn more about creating a bank of textures in Lesson 18 of this section). The good thing with 3d.sk is that it covers all kinds of morphologies, ages and races.

Note: *A free 3DSK samples folder is included with this book on the accompanying DVD.*

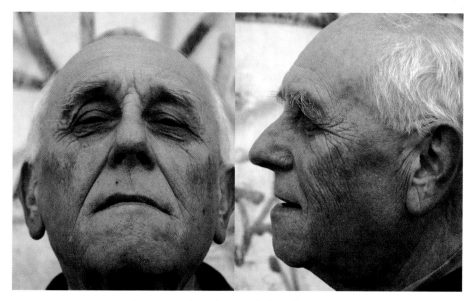

Two pictures to be used to create the base of your texture

- In Photoshop, open your UV layout.
- Duplicate the background and create a negative of the picture (Ctrl+i) .
- Set it to **multiply** in the blending mode of the layer tab.

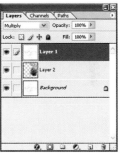

- Open the profile image.

- Copy and paste the profile texture between the background and layer01.

- In the layer tab, for each layer except the background, you have access to a blending mode option.

  Try to adjust the profile on the UVs very roughly by using the freeTransform Tool. You should get something like the following picture:

> **Note:** *To select your image layer, RMB+click holding Cmd (Ctrl) over the image layer you want to transform. Then click* **Cmd+t** *(***Ctrl+t***) or go to* **Edit** → **freeTransform***.*

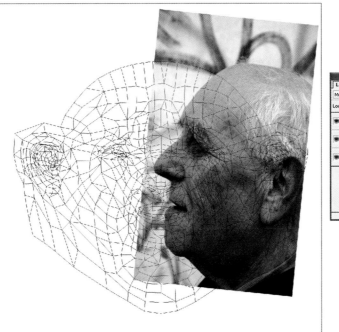

UV layout duplicated and set to Multiply. The profile picture has been pasted, scaled and rotated to globally match the UVs.

- Hide the layer01, and save the result as a template.tga file in your sourceimages folder. When Photoshop asks you which resolution you want to use (16, 24 or 32 bit), select 24 bit. You can use 32 bit when you want to keep the alpha channel, which is not the case here. It's not useful to use RLE compression here.

> **Note:** .iff is the native file format of Maya. There is a useful plug-in for opening and saving .iff in Photoshop. You can convert a picture to .iff for Maya with a basic command line. In Windows, go to **Start** → **Execute**, and type cmd. Now, browse to access the folder in which you have files to convert by using regular DOS commands. Once you're in, simply type imgcvt fileName.xxx fileName.iff.

Working with shaders

Back in Maya, create a lambert and plug your texture in the color slot. Assign this lambert shader to the geometry.

- Open the Hypershade window, select **Window** → **Rendering Editors** → **Hypershade.**

- In the menu on the left under **Create Maya Nodes**, select **lambert**.

- From the same menu under **2d textures**, make sure normal is checked and select **file**.

- Double-click on the file node and go to the **Attribute Editor**.

- In the Attribute Editor, click on the folder where it says **Image Name** and choose *Template.tga*.

- With the polygon geometry selected go back into the Hypershade, and **MMB** on the "**out connector**" arrow of *file1* and connect it to the lambert you created. Select **Color**.

- Press **6** in the Perspective view to display this texture in the viewport.

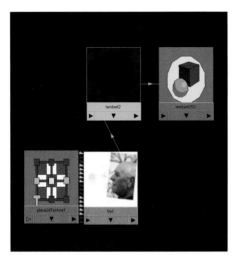

File imported back to Maya and connected to a regular lambert shader

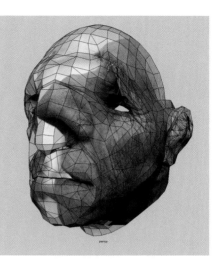

Displayed texture on the geometry. It looks strange at this stage of the process.

It's important to check that what you're doing in Photoshop is correctly positioned on the character. Using the front view picture, copy and paste the elements again to fill the UV layout. Try to focus on the big areas first, paying no real attention to details at this point. Save the result by replacing the first file you created.

To check your work in Maya, go in the Hypershade, **RMB+click** on the file node and select **Reload** to update the file.

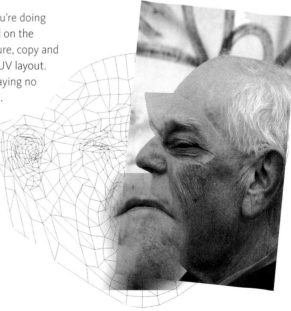

New layout with some more elements roughly pasted

Project 4: Yatoer, The Bus Stop Boxer

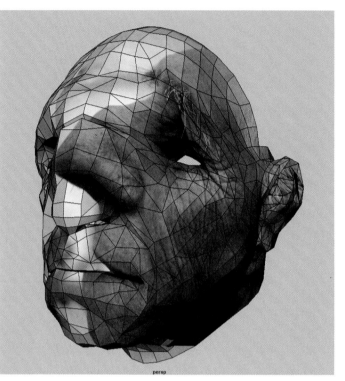

The result in Maya

Back in Photoshop, put the facial photo elements on your layout. Try to match the forehead, the front of the nose and the other facial features.

> **Tip:** *Don't spend time creating masks on your texture patches. Because the image is not properly aligned, you will only succeed in losing time.*

Using the Liquify Tool

As you will see in the following lesson, the Liquify Tool is useful for the illustration process. Right now, you will use it to adjust elements to your UVs. It is rare to have pictures that completely match your UVs, because matching is dependent on so many factors: morphology, the way your layout was done, the sources, etc.

In the following picture, you can see a patch for the area between the nose and the upper lip. The green area is there for clarification only; don't pay attention to it.

The red line represents the wrinkle on the character's face that you should match with this patch. Since using the freeTransform Tool is not enough here, the Liquify Tool will be useful.

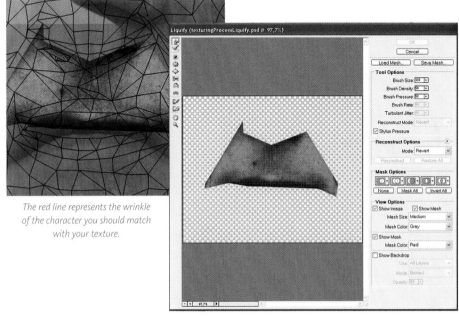

The red line represents the wrinkle of the character you should match with your texture.

Liquify creates its own window. The selected layer appears with a grid on top.

- Open the file called *TexturingProcessLiquify.psd*. Select the layer called **Patch to Liquify**.

- Create a selection with the Rectangle Selection Tool that contains the entire area you want to work on, even a bit wider. The Rectangle Selection Tool is the first tool in your tool window (top, left). Instead of working on the entire picture, it's good to create a selection of the area you want to focus on. By doing this, the preview is faster for the Liquify Tool, especially on large pictures. It works well with filters too, for getting the idea of an effect before applying it to the entire picture.

- Go to **Filter** → **Liquify**. You should get something like the picture at the top of the next page.

  *There is an option called **Show Backdrop** on the bottom right of the window. Activate it and choose to display the layer called Shape1.*

Project 4: Yatoer, The Bus Stop Boxer

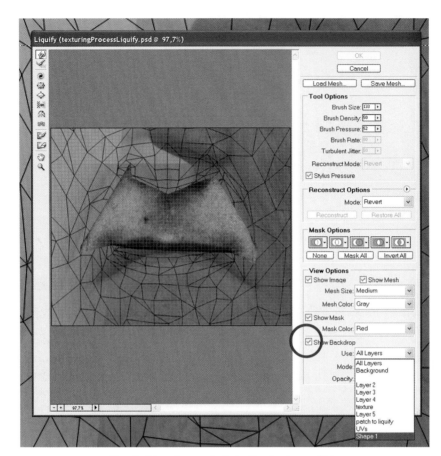

*Show Backdrop allows you to display the other layers, which
is helpful for matching elements together.*

At this stage, you don't need to go to the other options of the Liquify Tool. Simply push
things so they match your reference line. Don't hesitate to change the brush size for some
soft deformations. When it looks good, press OK on top. The modifications you made
are computed and applied to your picture. In fact, when you use the Liquify Tool, what is
onscreen is a preview of a lower resolution image. This is beneficial, because it would take
ages to see things on the high resolution image. In this case, it's only 2K, which is easy for
the Liquify Tool. In the future, you will probably push the resolution further.

You could do the texturing entirely with this method, going back and forth from Maya to
Photoshop. There is a complementary workflow that you will learn now.

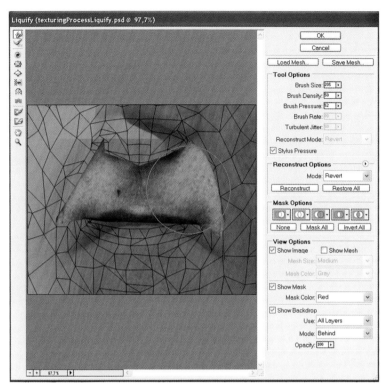

*With a brush, you push things so they match the
reference line (red one)*

Projection mapping

If you knew the angle to be used for the final picture, *projection mapping* would be the
only method you would need. Since that's not the case here, we will use projection
mapping in conjunction with other methods. We're going to use projection mapping to
fine-tune the placement of a specific area, and then, by using Bake to Texture, we will get
the result of this projection unwrapped to our UVs.

When you make a projection, you've got a virtual plane that projects the texture on the
object, without taking care of the UVs. It's useful for matte paintings, and to texture a
piece of geometry to look good in a camera angle.

> **Note:** This method is also called camera mapping, when the projection plane is the
> camera itself.

For this method, we use the projection to get an unstretched texture on the face, and, by baking it on the UVs, we can assemble it with the rest of the layout in Photoshop.

In Maya, go to the Hypershade and create a file node with *projection* checked on. Use *nose.tga* as a source.

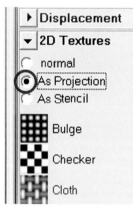

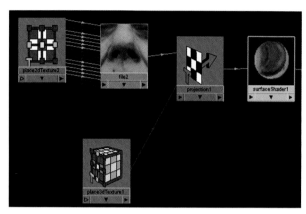

Click on "as projection" and create a file node

The resulting network - the texture goes into a projection node that is connected to a surface shader

- Browse the *sourceimages* to select the *nose.tga* file.

- Connect the projection node to a surface shader.

- In the *place2dTexture*, uncheck **wrapU** and **wrapV** as you don't need a tile here.

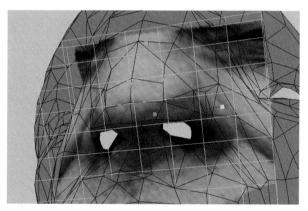

Projection is aligned to the nose. It is oriented and scaled so the tip of the nose matches the geometry.

By default, the projection is set on planar, which is exactly what you want.

- Select the *place3Dtexture1* node and align it to the nose.

- In the viewport, rotate and scale it. Do everything you need to have the node scaled properly and in the correct place. You can't get everything matching at once; the anatomy is too dissimilar, so focus on only one area. Try to match the bottom tip of the nose, for example. Nostrils are black in the photo, but you will make them neutral in the end.

Project 4: Yatoer, The Bus Stop Boxer

- When this is done, select the shader and **Shift**-select the geometry.

- In the Hypershade, go to **Edit** → **Convert To File Texture** (Maya), and click in the hotbox.

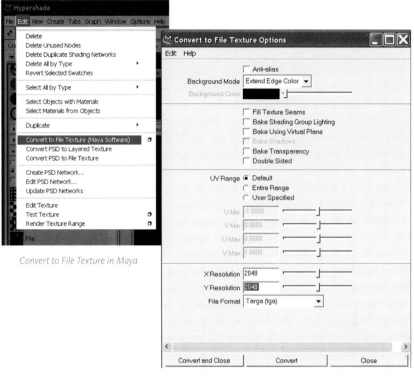

Convert to File Texture in Maya

Resolution set to the one you started with in Photoshop (2K in this case)

- Set the resolution to **2048** x **2048** and select **tga**, unless you have the *.iff* plug-in for Photoshop.

- Click on **Convert**.

  This will compute the result of the projection, baked onto your UVs.

  When this is done, a new shader with a file connected to it appears in the Hypershade. If you select this file and get its attributes, you will notice that it was saved in your sourceimages folder.

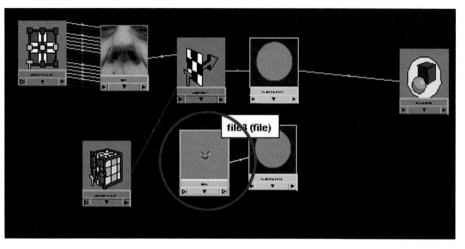

A new file is generated and plugged to a new surface shader

Go back to Photoshop and, in the Hypershade tab, open the file in which the **Bake to Texture** is done. Copy and paste it on your existing layout.

Your texture work opened in progress

Now, you can start creating some nice masks for all those elements. The Bake to Texture technique is a long process, but it can yield very good results. You should experiment with several pictures and various angles.

Project 4: Yatoer, The Bus Stop Boxer

Back in Photoshop, you have many tools to help you fill the empty areas. You will learn more about the Stamp Tool in the next lesson. It's a fast way to copy a pattern and repeat it where it's needed.

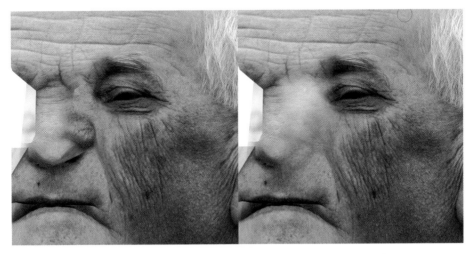

By uing the Stamp Tool, you can blend areas together and fill holes between patches.

You should now have a nice base to work with. If you multiply the sources and patches, you can end up with something very detailed and neat.

> **Tip:** In this example, you've been using a 2K map. If you plan to work on a high resolution illustration in the end, try to use higher resolution. It's better to work on a 4Kmap in Photoshop and reduce it later, rather than trying to increase the size of your texture in the end; you would miss sharpness that way.

Painting techniques will be covered in subsequent lessons. Have a look at them, and then go back to the texture to experiment. The example on the following page is one of the many texture levels of Yatoer. It's a mix of projections, regular work on UVs, and a lot of paintover, cloning and color adjustments.

Tip: Check your UVs before texturing. You can still tweak them a bit, but it would be better not to. Use a checker for that, and also some circles and/or a tile like the skin one. Fix as many issues as you can, keep in mind the major shot angle and don't pay much attention to the hidden areas.

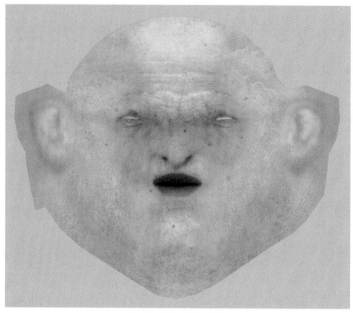

Final result for Yatoer's face

I've been using many reference pictures for Yatoer's face, and it would take pages and pages to redo it the exact same way. It's important for you to consider the different techniques when you start the texturing process. There's not one ultimate method, rather a combination of many, depending mostly on the morphology.

Note: Depending on the renderer you use, you should also convert your textures to the most appropriate file format to avoid memory crash. Maya and mental ray convert textures during render time. Use .iff or .bot files for Maya's native renderer. Use .map for mental ray.

Conclusion

Texturing a face and/or an entire character cannot be done in a few seconds. It's a long process. Always keep in mind the purpose of your character. I would say, if it's for illustration only, that you should focus on the main axis, almost as a rough projection, and that's all. When you texture a character, you should also take your time on the main color map, because most of the others are extrapolated from this one. If it looks good, it'll be easy to create the others. The opposite is also true: if you're not fully satisfied with it and you start creating the others, such as the bump map or the specular map, corrections and updates will become tedious because of the new details added.

For Yatoer, I even made my first shader tests with colorMap used for bump and the rest. It was just to get the idea, and when I was finally okay with the main aspect, I started to create the other textures.

In the next lesson, you will learn how to integrate render passes together.

Lesson 16
Integrating

In this lesson you will learn how to integrate render passes together. You will use the Liquify Tool to correct some artifacts and learn the basics of working with a CG render. The steps outlined in this lesson are designed to apply to any kind of render pass work. You will also see how to increase the quality of a fur pass, how to add density and how to smooth out areas. At the end of this lesson, you will create a rough background from an existing photo and learn how to tweak perspective.

A note about the render: Classical lighting was used, with a couple of extra light sources to enhance brightness in some areas. I had to render everything separately because of the size of the initial maps, which represented almost 2GB in the end. This is pretty huge for a single character, but some textures were made in 6K, and once converted to *.map*, file size became gigantic. These textures were done for close-up purposes; in the final animation, there would be various resolutions available, depending on the shot itself. Anyway, this means the computer was unable to render the scene, as there wasn't enough memory in the system. The fur required a different anti-aliasing and was also rendered separately. So as you can see, you can render elements separately for many reasons, such as optimization of the memory, anti-aliasing parameters, renderer used (mental ray, Maya, other), etc...

In this lesson, you will learn:

- How to load a selection;
- How to save a selection;
- How to transfer a selection from one document to another;
- How to use the Liquify Tool;
- How to use the freeTransform Tool;
- How to use the Stamp Tool;
- How to use the Healing Brush Tool.

Getting started

When you start to work on a picture in Photoshop, it is smart to create a set of selections early in the process so you can then focus on other tasks.

> **Note:** A benefit of using CG is that you automatically get nice alpha channels (selections).

Once you select some areas, be sure to save those selections each time.

In your Lesson 16 folder, you should find four .psd files (they could have been in *tga* or *tif*), that correspond to the renders done within Maya.

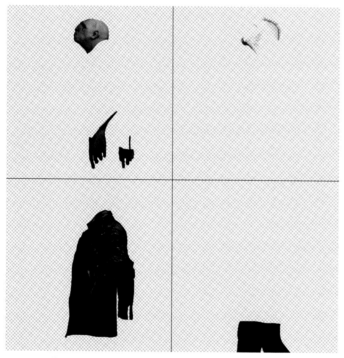

All rendered passes assembled together (for presentation purposes)

- Open the file *flesh.psd* as a starting point.
- **RMB+click** with the Lasso Tool, load the selection and select **Alpha1**.

The Lasso Tool is the best tool by default (you find it just beside the Rectangle Selection Tool), when you work on layers. With your RMB, you have access to cool features such as Load Selection, Save Selection, Color range, and freeTransform once the selection is made. With the spacebar pressed, you can pan on the picture, and with Ctrl pressed, you can move elements instead of selecting the Move Tool.

- Now, create a new layer from this selection with the **Ctrl+j** shortcut.

- Rename the layer by double-clicking on it in the **layer tab**. You should use descriptive names for your files. In this case, *flesh* will be fine.

Reviewing render passes

Open the three other render passes: **Jacket.psd**, **Fur.psd** and **Pants.psd**.

There are three ways to copy those pictures to the main composition. The first one is to simply load the selection and drag and drop the picture to your Flesh.psd document, but this is a bit messy because you could have difficulties aligning it properly with the other passes.

The second way is to select it all (**Ctrl+a**), copy it (**Ctrl+c**) and paste it in the final destination (**Ctrl+v**). Then, you would also have to get the mask back. For this, go back to the source (**Jacket. psd**), load the selection and then save it by specifying that you want to save it to a different document. Select *Flesh.psd* in the list, and you're done.

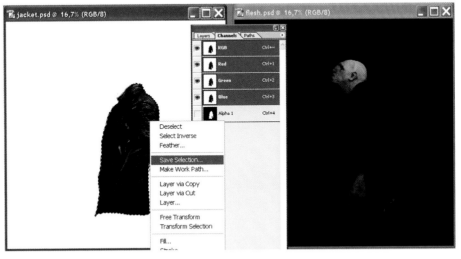

Save selection option

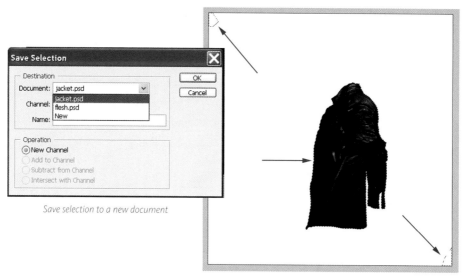

Save selection to a new document

Selections at the top left and bottom right of the picture, in addition to the main jacket selection

For the third method, once you've got the alpha loaded, **Shift-select** both the top left corner and bottom right corner of the picture.

Copy this, **Cmd+c** (**Ctrl+c**), and then paste it, **Cmd+v** (**Ctrl+v**), to your main document. Then, quickly remove the areas you don't want. This way, you will be able to make all your layers match together.

Tip: *Rename your layers. This is important because good descriptive names can help you in the end when you're working with numerous layers.*

At this stage, you should have a single document open with four layers respectively called *Flesh*, *Jacket*, *Pants* and *Fur*.

When you create a character for illustration, it is not ideal to spend too much time on the skinning in Maya; it's a long process, and, for this lesson, it's not necessary to reach perfection.

Instead, you'll use the Liquify Tool in Photoshop to correct artifacts and add details.

You can find the Liquify Tool in the filterTab of Photoshop. This tool is very useful at several stages, including texturing. By using a virtual grid, it deforms the picture as you would, for example, with Artisan within Maya.

For this picture, you don't need to work on proportions and skinning because they were already adjusted in Maya. You will work on both later in this lesson to further tweak a few things.

Note: *You can save a deformation (called a* filet*) for future use.*

Using the Liquify Tool

For now, the idea is to make corrections to all the skinning artifacts, volume loss, etc.

You can also use the Liquify Tool to reshape the character and change its proportions.

- Select an area to work on.

- Go to **Filter** → **Liquify**; the Liquify Tool opens in a new window with new buttons. This is because when you use the liquify, it creates a low resolution version of your picture, to work faster than it would with the high resolution one.

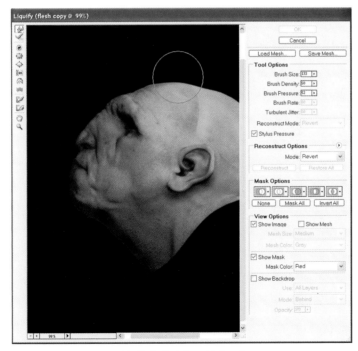

Liquify Tool window with its options

On the left side, you have access to the main tool. For this lesson, you will focus on the first two options. The first one allows you to push the filet to distort your image. The second one allows you to reconstruct the filet.

> **Note:** At this stage, you can decide to merge all the layers together, giving you one render pass, or you can keep them separated. What I usually do, once the liquify process is complete, is to load selections for each element (clothes, face, etc.), save them (**RMB+click** and **Save Selection**) and merge the layers (not the background). You can also decide to make a group of those layers, duplicate this group and then merge it down. This way you can keep track of the elements you had, and you'll be able to load a specific element in the future if it's required.

It is important to keep a record of the various steps in this document. You can, of course, use incremental saving, but having various stages of your character hidden in your document is a great idea, as you can then reference them even if it's only for a minor detail.

Consider an example: You've been working on some texturing and what you did for the hand is a not quite right (I'm speaking from experience). Follow these steps:

- Display an earlier release of the character and select the hand.

- Duplicate it and hide the source again.

- Move this new copy on top of the recent version you have and mix it with the textured area that needs some work.

This is a fast and easy way to go back in time to fix present mistakes.

This liquify stage can also be done later, but you must pay attention to one essential detail: if you add, for example, a paper texture and merge this texture after some time while using liquify to correct the shape, the texture will be deformed as well, giving you some unnatural effects. This might be your intention, but it is important to be aware of this result.

> **Tip:** At this stage, you may also want to consider having a look at some rendering artifacts before the texturing is created.

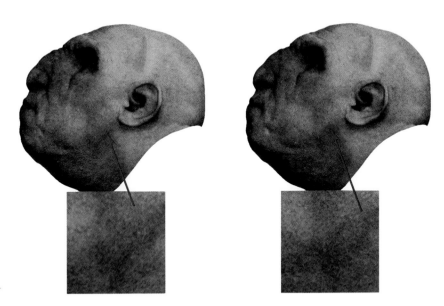

On the left, liquify made on the picture with textures applied.
On the right, textures applied after the liquify is done.

On the left, you can see the result of the Liquify Tool after some texturing work. Notice there are stretches in the grain, which is not ideal. On the left, you can see the results of the liquify done before the texture work.

Keep this in mind before you run from grainy and noisy effects on your render. Try to fix as much as you can when you still have the original layers available.

The Stamp Tool and the Healing Brush Tool

As you can see, the texture on the head is not seamless. You will use the Stamp Tool and Healing Brush Tool to meld things together.

Basically, the Stamp Tool gives you the ability to clone an area and paste anything in this area that you want. You will use it later for fur, but here it will be used to create a basic blending area.

My advice when working with the Stamp Tool is to duplicate the layer you want to work on. This will save you from losing anything from the original. Then, when you're happy with the work that is done, you can merge them together.

- Select your flesh layer and duplicate it (**Ctrl+j**).

- Select the **Stamp Tool** in your **tool tab**.

- With Alt pressed, **click** on the area you want to clone.

- With Alt released, **paint** using this cloned element where you need to blend.

  It is important to clone as many areas as you can to avoid creating a tile aspect. Alternate between choosing areas from the left and then the right and repeat until you have the look you want.

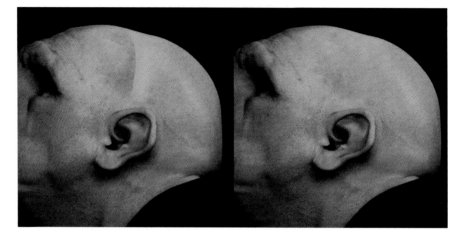

On the left, no corrections made; on the right, stamp reduced the seams in the texture

This is a good start, but you're not done yet! With a lot of patience, you could use the Stamp Tool to create something clean and impressive. But, nowadays, things have to move quickly, right? There is a new tool in Photoshop that does the job even faster. It's called the Healing Brush Tool, and it allows you to clone the texture of one area to replicate it elsewhere. By texture, I mean the grain, the pattern, etc., not the area itself. Its basic use is to clone a clean skin area to paste onto a spot or wrinkle.

The Healing Brush Tool works in a similar way to the Stamp Tool. With Alt pressed, copy the reference area and then paint over what you want, creating the blending between your background and this new information.

My advice, once again, would be to duplicate your layer (the one with stamped areas) to avoid losing what you did previously; history has its limits.

Go ahead and experiment. Don't hesitate to clone several areas to achieve a richer, seamless space.

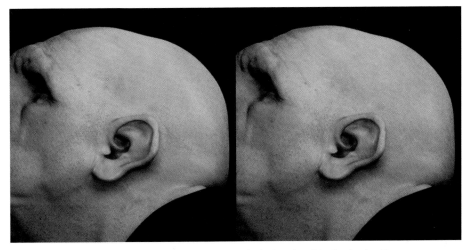

On the left, stamp corrections made; on the right, final result with healing brush add-ons.

> **Note:** In this specific case, the Healing Brush Tool could work on its own, but it's not true for all cases. The combination of Stamp Tool and Healing Brush Tool is often the best and fastest way to get the exact blending you want.

The background

You may not want to keep the black background to work with, but it's not a good idea to change it. First, the contour of the character may change drastically if you use a different environment. Also, for the *chromis* (in post-processing, the work done on the colors and hues of the stills and animation), it's good to make the blending progressive.

Load the file *CH_03_background.jpg*, and copy and paste it in your document.

The point here is to have an idea of what the backlights are and to keep working on the character. This is the interior of a wagon, and you will turn it into an outdoor view.

In order to do so, you need to play with the freeTransform Tool to correct the perspective of this picture and make it match with our character.

- Press **Ctrl+t** to activate the **freeTransform Tool**.

- Scale the picture as you want, and RMB to access more options.

- In the Free Transform tool (RMB), use the Perspective and Distort functions to achieve a cool mood. Once again, it's only to get the idea; you will work specifically on the background at the end of this lesson.

On the left, the original photo as a guideline for the background. On the right, the same picture after transformations, to match the character's perspective.

In **Layer → Create New Adjustment Layer**, or at the bottom of the layer tab, create one colorBalance and one BrightnessContrast adjustment Layers. **ColorBalance** is used to warm up the left part of the picture. **BrightnessContrast** is used to darken the picture behind the character.

On the left, no color corrections. On the right, levels and colors have been adjusted a bit.

How to use and enhance a fur pass

Some elements require more attention than others. This is usually the case for hair and fur. In most cases, it's better to have only a couple of layers for them.

Duplicating your hair layer and slightly blurring it is a good start. You can put this new layer behind the sharp one, and play with opacities and small translations to get some depth.

In this case, although it looked good during the tests, the final render of hair is lacking some density. Since the fur was rendered all at once, it would be a good idea now to separate it by elements: beard on one layer, punk hairdo on a second layer. To do so, select your fur layer, select (roughly) the beard area, and by pressing **Shift+Ctrl+j**, you'll make a new layer.

There are two pictures that show the work done for this: *Po4_L17_vFurwork.psd* and *Po4_L17_FurworkOK.psd*.

You will have a better understanding of these steps by checking **Offets** and **Patches**.

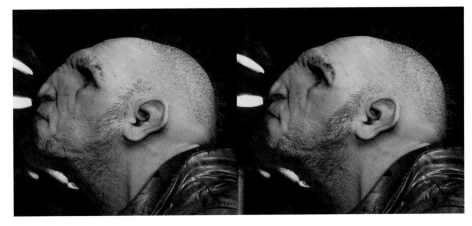

On the left, fur before corrections. On the right, fur after corrections.

Since there is some density missing from the fur, copy the entire layer and offset it down so it fills the empty spaces as much as possible. Focus on one area, such as the connection between the beard and ears. If you pay attention to the beard itself it will look odd, one inch from the chin, on its own.

When you think the density has been restored, create a mask and remove all the unwanted areas.

On the left: basic passes. Middle: a new copy of the fur layer with no mask. On the right: result with a mask applied.

 Tip: *By fading transitions with the airbrush on the mask and removing some fur here and there, it will look like a brand new render pass.*

You can also use the Stamp Tool on a new layer to duplicate some of the beard, hair, etc., to use as a patch later.

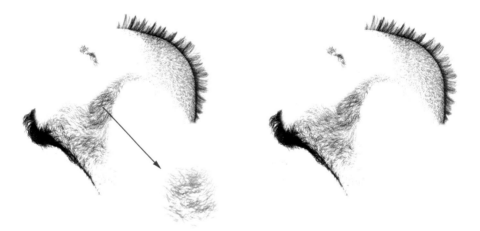

On the left, fur pass without patch and detail of the clones' elements. On the right, cloned elements integrated into the fur pass.

When you use the Stamp Tool, create a new layer to clone elements on. Don't work directly on the main fur layer, because it would become messy. You can also check **Use all Layers** to clone all displayed layers at once.

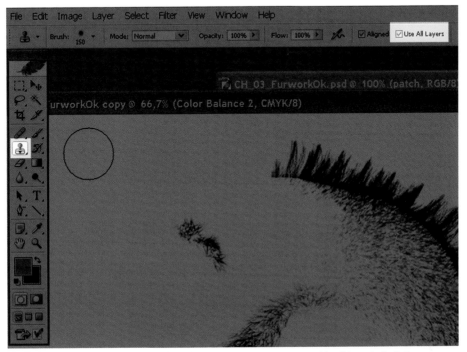

Stamp Tool on the left, and its options on top. As you can see, Use all layers is checked.

- Press **Alt+LMB** to specify the area you want to clone, then paint a patch beside the picture. You will place this patch in the correct area later.

- Return to your hair selection and shrink it from 1 pixel by selecting **Selection → Modify → Contract**. Make a copy with merge (**Ctrl+shift+j**), and colorize this new layer by playing with color balance or hues (**Ctrl+b** for color balance). Make it warm. Tune down the opacity to something around 20%. This adds to the complexity in the fur and begins to create a reaction with the background.

*A copy of the fur pass is added, slightly
shrunken and colorized*

Note: *Copy with merge means that you're not only copying elements from one layer,
but rather elements from several layers at once.*

Finally, you will end this fur session with the eyebrows. They definitely lack density, and you now know how to add some. However, for this step you will use an external picture of an eyebrow. By combining the freeTransform Tool and the Liquify Tool, you will make it fit as shown at the top of the next page.

Open *Eyebrow.psd* in the source folder.

Use **Ctrl+a** to select the entire picture, then **Ctrl+c** to copy it, and go to your main document and paste it **(Ctrl+v)**.

In the blending mode of the layer tab, set the layer to **Multiply**.

With the freeTransform Tool, scale down the eyebrow patch, then, with **RMB** (still using freeTransform), select **Distort** to get an idea of the perspective. When you're satisfied with the result, apply those transform modifications.

Now, make a rectangular selection that contains the eyebrow area (always select a bit more than what you need). When it's okay, go to **Filter → Liquify**.

With the Liquify Tool, reshape the eyebrow so it looks more natural. Try to make it fit inside the area of the existing eyebrow made with fur. It's only here to add density.

- Save your work.

On the left, eyebrow as it was rendered. On the right, eyebrow
with an external picture added to it.

Conclusion

In this lesson, you learned some of the basics required to deal with CG renders. You are now able to copy and paste elements. As well, you know more about selections: the way you can retrieve them, create them and transfer them from one document to another. You also worked with the Liquify Tool, the Stamp Tool and the Healing Brush Tool. Keep in mind that Photoshop is great at playing with selections, and we will use them more and more in the following lessons. Don't hesitate to create new layers each time you work on a specific area; you don't want to end up with patches for fur and patches for the jacket on the same layer!

In the next lesson you will learn how to use adjustment layers to increase detail and contrast.

Lesson 17
Creating Primary Highlights

By using adjustment layers, you're going to increase contrast and detail on the character, without losing any information from the render itself. Adjustment layers are based upon masks, and there is a wide variety of blending possibilities with them.

In this lesson you will learn:

- How to work with a color balance adjustment layer;

- How to use the Gradient Tool;

- How to manually paint contrast;

- How to create a patch and apply a mask to it.

Getting started

It is a good idea at the beginning of the project to know how the character and background will react together. For this, you will create a color balance adjustment layer.

- Go to **Layer** → **New Adjustment Layer**, or click on the icon at the bottom of the layer tab.

Icon to create a new adjustment layer

- Set it to a warm global red. Then, choose a good starting point and fill its mask with black.

    As you can see, a color adjustment layer opens the same window that a regular color balance function would. The main difference is that this color correction is made through a layer and not directly on the picture. This allows you many blending and history possibilities.

Tip: *When you render something for an illustration, be careful not to go too far into the highlighted and dark areas. Rather, try to keep details everywhere you can. If an area is burned out of render, which means that the highlights are completely white with no remaining information in them, it will be harder to correct than it would have been to sharpen a soft render and increase the highlights.*

On the left, picture with no effect. In the middle, adjustment layer set with no mask. On the right, picture with the adjustment layer with its mask.

With a white airbrush and some gradients, reveal the effect of the layer on the left side of the picture and on the face, so it looks like it's affected by the warm light. Keep it basic at this stage; you'll refine it later.

The Gradient Tool

The Gradient Tool allows you to fill a picture, selection or mask with a progressive transition from one color to another. Although it is not necessary for this lesson, you can make more complex transitions if you decide to create your own gradient presets. For our purposes, there are already enough existing presets. Once you've selected the Gradient Tool, you simply **LMB+click** (On Mac, **click+drag**) where you want it to start, and without releasing the mouse button, go where you want it to end. When you do this, a line is drawn that represents a vector, giving you the direction and length of this gradient. When you think it's okay, release the **LMB** and the gradient is done.

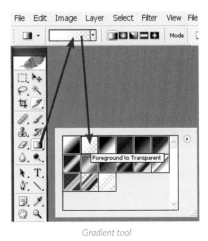

Gradient tool

When you select the Gradient Tool, notice its options in the upper tab of Photoshop. You have the choice between predefined gradients (foreground to background, foreground to transparent, etc.) and the type of gradient (linear, radial, etc.).

Try to use the foreground to transparent option for your masks. The following picture on the next page roughly represents the mask that was made for the background's color balance.

Once the background and character are working better together, you're ready for the next step.

Create a second color balance adjustment layer that you will place under the fur group and on top of the skin (in the layer tab).

This color balance adjustment layer will help integrate the fur with the skin. In a regular illustration, one would probably paint some green/blue areas to symbolize the beard; it's the same case here. This slight color change helps the blending.

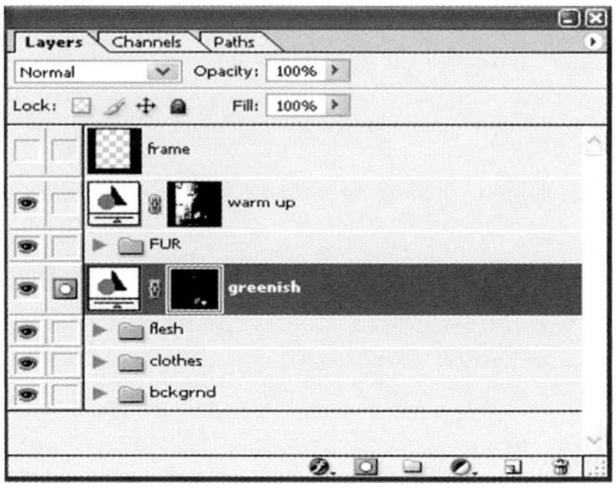

Position the greenish layer between the flesh and the fur

The values on the picture below are just for reference; feel free to set them as you want. By playing with the midtones, you can get pretty good results as they usually cover a wide range of values. But, you can also tune dark and bright values with some different tones in order to obtain richer colors. In this case, the midtones are set to some green/blue values, but you can set the dark values to something a little bit warmer, and the bright values to cyan.

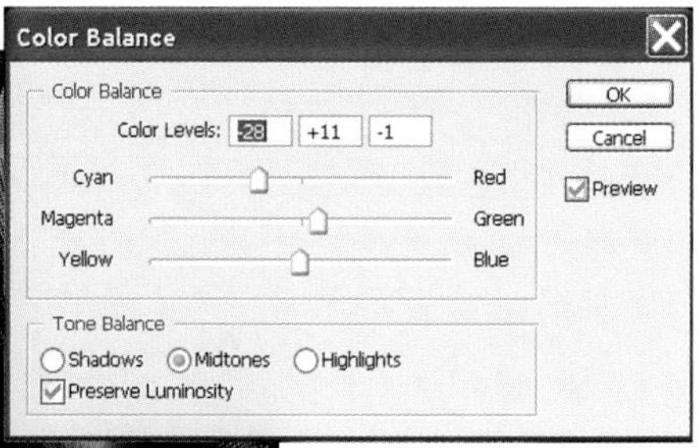

Values used for the greenish adjustment layer.

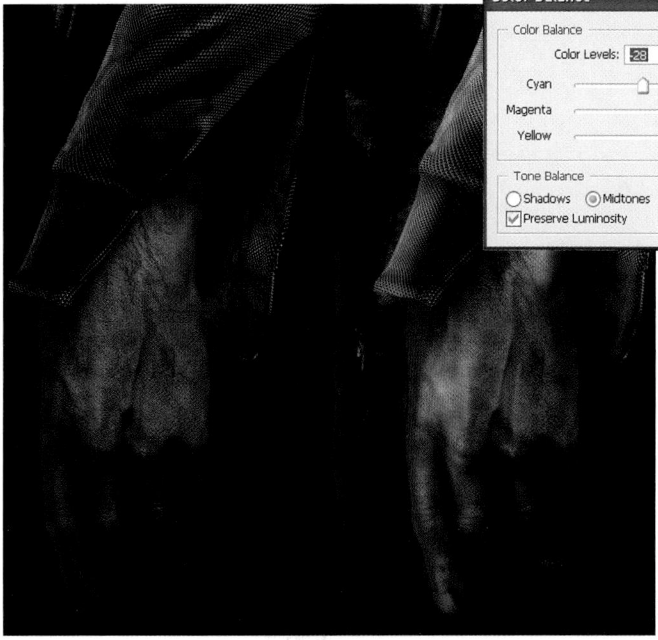

On the left, out of render image. On the right, result with a couple of adjustment layers for levels.

Adjustment layers for highlights and contrast

When you paint areas on adjustment layers, make them soft. Brush one area slightly, go on to another and so on. Return to the first to increase the effect and continue this permanent loop. Use all the values between black and white to get what you want. If you prefer, you can also press the pen of your tablet. The key idea to understand is that *black means no opacity and white means full opacity*. In other words, 50% grey means 50% opacity. By using a tablet, you can simply use pure black and pure white and deal with the opacity by pressing on the pen more or less. If you're using a mouse, you need to adjust those colors manually and you might have to pick up variations of grey to get what you want.

> **Tip:** Use **x** to switch background and foreground colors. This is useful for painting masks with back and white, adding and removing elements and adjusting.

Now, create a levels adjustment layer and make it dark. Rename it with a descriptive name so it will be easy to identify later on.

Create a levels adjustment layer set to darken the picture

Create a second levels adjustment layer and make it bright. You're going to use both layers to darken and lighten parts of the picture.

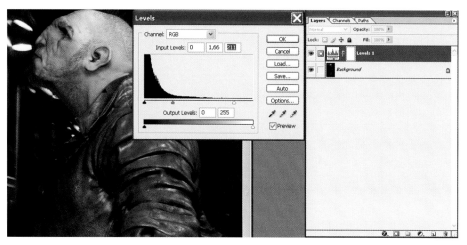

A levels adjustment layer set to lighten the picture

The technique is the same as it was for colors: tune the layer by focusing on a couple of points on the picture, like the face and the sleeve. Fill with black (**Ctrl+i**) to apply and mask it. For Mac OS, press **command+i**. Then, paint where you want to with the brush. For these sorts of adjustments, the brush itself is not a critical factor because you are not painting details, but rather enhancing them. The regular soft airbrush works fine for this.

A benefit of adjustment layers is that you can change their settings by double-clicking on them in the layer tab. This way, if the effect you've done is not right, you can tune the layer up or down while keeping the work (masking) you've achieved by painting. You can also quickly tune down the effect by changing the overall opacity of the layers in the layer tab, as shown below.

Overall opacity changed on an adjustment layer

The idea here is to increase the contrast on the character. The leather jacket can be pushed a bit, and the skin could match the clothes and environment better with some brighter and darker areas.

> **Note:** *Effects, adjustments and filters should always be done on only part of the picture, not globally. Global adjustments come later on, when everything already fits together.*

You might think that for adding contrast to the picture, brightness and contrast would be enough. It's not entirely wrong, but as you are seeking an illustrative look, it's better to manually paint this contrast. This way, you have more control over the areas you want to tune, and by using levels instead of contrast, you also have greater control on highlights and shadows, dramatically reducing the loss of detail.

If you feel more comfortable with brightness and contrast (also available as an adjustment layer), you can achieve almost the same results as you would with levels, as long as you use the same method: one to lighten the picture, the second to darken it. The main difference is that with levels, you have much more control on dark, medium and bright areas. This is true if you work with the entire channel or channel by channel (red, green, blue). You can also manage output levels to clamp your values.

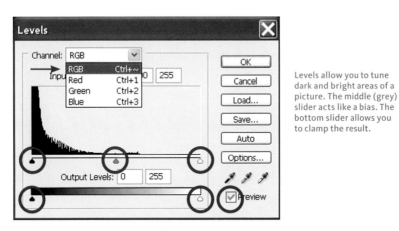

Levels allow you to tune dark and bright areas of a picture. The middle (grey) slider acts like a bias. The bottom slider allows you to clamp the result.

Levels window

Another option is to practice this two-step method (bright, dark) with the curves function. It's up to you to choose the one you're more comfortable with.

On the left, picture before the levels were tuned. On the right, levels applied.
Notice how highlighted and dark areas are increased.

Some people like to paint directly on top of the picture. Although this is something we will do later on, you may want to keep as much of the 3D render as you can. By using adjustment layers, you only add work on what already exists, i.e. if there is a pixel here, you'll keep the pixel, if there is some texture there, you'll keep the texture.

You need to do one more thing before you start texturing this picture. As you can see, the collar is still messy. UVs were done in a hurry, and the procedural pattern used for the fabric is irregular. You need to replace it with a clean patch that you will create from the sleeve, for example. Using the exact same method as the one for the beard patch, create a new layer on which you will clone a neutral piece of the sleeve.

Take your time and try to get something that's large enough to cover the collar (fig. A on following page).

When you're done, align it on top of the collar (fig. B). Hide the layer, and with the Lasso Tool, make the selection of the collar (fig. C). Create a mask on your patch so it remains visible only inside the collar area (fig. D).

It's impossible to achieve fantastic results with just one pass of work, but you will see that, little by little, textures will blend together, creating something new and organic.

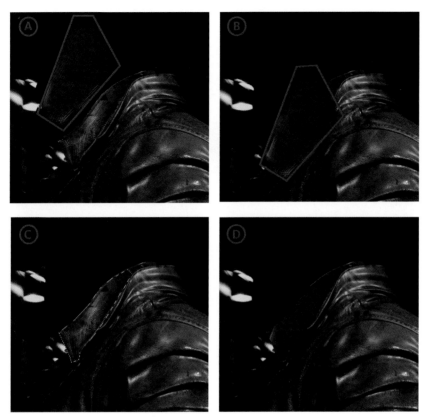

Fig A, patch being made. Fig B, patch positioned. Fig C, patch hidden and selection of the needed area. Fig D, mask applied to the patch.

It is time to update your adjustment layers. The new patch is too flat, and you need to paint some bright and dark areas. As well, you need to add red here and there so it matches with the rest of the background.

Of course, it's possible to make this patch later on, but it would be more difficult. It's better to get rid of all the improper elements first so you can focus on the creative work.

• Save your work.

Conclusion

Adjustment layers are excellent tools for increasing contrast and detail. Now that you know about the color balance adjustment layer, the Gradient Tool and how to manually paint contrast, you are ready to expand on this knowledge in Lesson 18.

In the next lesson you will work in greater detail with brushes and texturing.

Lesson 18
Brushes and Textures

Photoshop contains several presets for brushes and it takes time to gain understanding of each one. Knowledge is all about experimenting and testing, at the end of which you'll probably focus on a small number that really fit your needs.

To begin, you can start from an existing brush and tune it to make it your own, then save it for future use. The purpose of this lesson is not to review every brush preset, but rather to teach you where to find them, how to choose and tweak them and, finally, how to save them.

In this lesson you will learn:

- How to use the Brush Tool;

- How to update a list of brushes for your own use;

- How to use flow and opacity jitter;

- How to use textures to paint an organic surface;

- How to work with comparison modes.

Getting started

When you select the **Brush Tool** (shortcut: b), options appear in the top tab of Photoshop.

The Brush Tool allows you to draw on your picture with various options ranging from a soft airbrush feel to a big noisy brush, and from a thin pen to a rattle with paint.

Note: A brush is similar to the good old "sprites" in the early videogames. They both create a pattern, repeated many times in space, that end up creating a line or a shape.

If you click on **Brush**, a list with icons is displayed. In this tab, you can simply pick up a brush and paint with it.

But, if you click on the small arrow on the right of this tab, you will also have access to a new menu with plenty of options and brush types. There are many ways to display those brushes, including text and thumbnail. You will also find a **Load Brush** and a **Save Brush** option. To the right is a list of predefined brushes classified by category. Have a look at them to see if they will be beneficial to your work or not. Then you'll be able to save and update a list of personal brushes.

The brush menu rollover, set to organic brushes

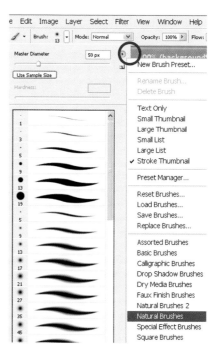

Access to presets, classified by categories

Project 4: Yatoer, The Bus Stop Boxer

Most of the brushes I work with are found in the **Natural Brushes** category. If you load them now, you can see how to change their attributes.

A message appears onscreen asking: *Replace current brushes with the brushes from natural brushes.abr*? Click **OK**. You will be able to load the default brushes back anytime you want by clicking on **Reset Brushes**.

As you can see, a new set of brushes appears. Select one set and create a new 1k square (1024 x 1024px) document to test it. Paint a couple of strokes.

Now, on the upper tab of Photoshop, click on the Brush option to toggle to the Brushes palette.

This icon gives access to all the options of a brush

In this new window, you'll be able to set everything you want to tweak on a predefined brush or create your own brush. Some of the most important options are outlined to the right.

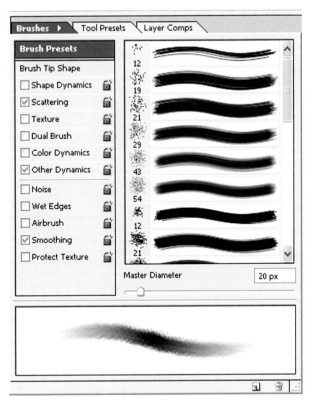

All the options are classified in this window

293

Controlling opacity

First, absolutely necessary, is the ability to control opacity with the pressure of the pen.

> **Note:** If you really want to have fun with Photoshop, digital illustration in general, and many functions and tools of Maya, you definitely need to get a tablet. If you don't have a tablet for the exercises in this lesson, click the brushes tab to see the list of settings. In most cases, you will choose the fade setting. Once you've chosen your setting, enter a value and test it to see how it affects your stroke.

To open this option, select **Other Dynamics** on the left. You have access to two options.

The first option, *opacity jitter*, produces a random opacity effect with the brush. You can set it by using the slider, or, go to the control tab and pick a specific parameter of the pen to control it. If you select *Pen Pressure*, opacity will be proportional to the pressure you put in the pen. If you set the slider to the right, it will also create a nice random effect.

Other Dynamics allows you to set opacity control to your brush

The second option is *flow jitter*. At first, it might appear to produce the same effect as opacity jitter, but the difference is subtle.

Let's say that a stroke you make is a succession of shapes that are very close to each other and in the end create a continuous line. Flow jitter affects the regularity of this flow, creating "holes" in areas. They appear as holes, but in reality, the space is simply a lack of density.

These two options combined together are the basis of a good brush.

The tab called **Shape Dynamics** is also an important one. With the same slider/control system, you'll set-up both random and pen control to the size of your brush. This can be combined with the shape opacity, but that's not generally the best thing to do. You may want to keep the opacity of a line, while changing its size through the pressure on the pen, or, conversely, you may want to change the opacity of a line without changing its size.

After you use Shape Dynamics to achieve the proper brush size, you can also use it to control the orientation (angle) and roundness of the brush. It is best to create two brushes for that, but it's up to you to experiment and choose your preferred method.

Shape Dynamics gives you options for dealing with the size of the brush

The first tab allows you to select a brush from the preloaded ones; in this case, the natural brushes. You have access to the main diameter of the brush, although it can be changed anytime after its creation. You also have access to the brush orientation, roundness and jitter. Perform tests with these tools to fully understand what you can achieve with the various parameters.

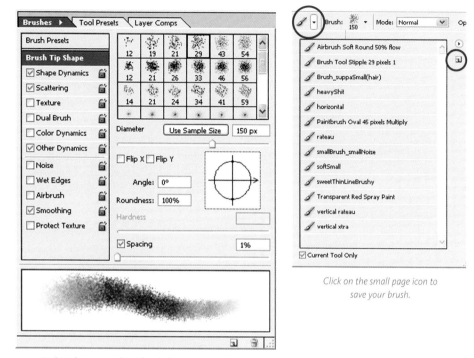

Click on the small page icon to save your brush.

In this tab you can select a brush shape to start with, and then change its global parameters.

Tip: If you are happy with a particular brush, save its settings so you don't have to redo the changes every time you want to use it. On the top left tab in Photoshop, there is a brush icon and a small black triangle. Click on the triangle and you will see a rollover displayed with some predefined brushes. On the right side, there is an icon that looks like a page. Click on it, set a name and you're done. Your brush now belongs to this list!

This section is just a primer for learning about brushes in Photoshop. There is much more to know, so feel free to explore and experiment. You have the framework of understanding now to comprehend how the other settings and options work together.

Using real textures to create an organic surface

Even if everything could be done within Photoshop, you may want to consider using external textures and photos to increase the detail in your picture. CG artists often create a bank of textures made from different media in addition to a variety of photos. Photo subjects can range from an interesting wall on a building, to a metallic item, or some broken glass and torn paper, etc. Some online Web sites offer free textures, but you will find that it's useful to keep a database of your own as well.

Photoshop does an excellent job of melding images together, so think of your collected images as potential resources of detail, rather than whole pictures. For example, a shot from a piece of fabric on its own would most likely not be an interesting picture, but the texture combined with something else could reveal a noteworthy image.

My bank of favorite textures scanned over the years include a basic noise/gritty effect, skin, fabric, splashes on a piece of paper and close-ups of an abstract painting. The textures have provided a multitude of applications. The more extensive the bank, the richer the picture.

Color range

Now, to demonstrate what you've learned about textures, you're going to isolate them.

- Select → Color Range.

  You have access to color range by **RMB+clicking** *on your document with the lasso as current tool, or in the Select menu.*

The color range selection allows you to pick a color in your picture and increase the range of this selection with a slider. You can also add more colors with **Add to Sample**, or remove some with **Subtract from Sample**.

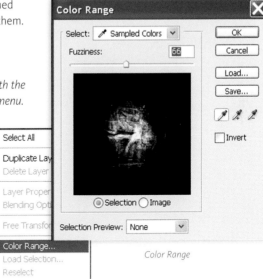

Color Range

Color range gives you a preview of the future selection, using black and white.

When you're happy with the selection you've made, press **OK**.

In most cases, I prefer using the color range function to the magic wand, but it's up to you to choose. Color range offers more possibilities at once, but magic wand has its advantages in specific cases.

- Open the file *CH_04_scratches.psd*, and select the **Color Range Tool**. Select the black areas of the picture and play with the range to achieve the image you want. When it's done, press **OK**.

- **Select** → **Color Range**.

- See image below for settings:

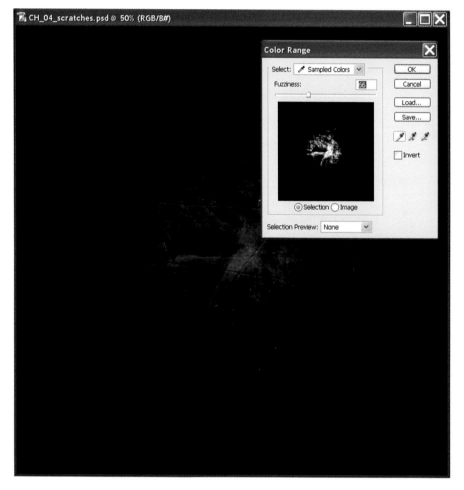

Color range preview and the source picture in the background...

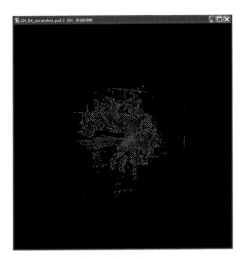

Now you have many possibilities. One would be to simply copy the texture inside the selection and then paste it on your picture.

Another one would be to use this selection in combination with an adjustment layer to create something new. The following steps will achieve this.

...and the resulting selection.

- Open the file *Yatoer_Wip_tmpPict01.jpg*. Once your selection is done on the texture file (*P04_L19_scratches.psd*), with the **Lasso Tool** activated, click on your selection without releasing the mouse button and drag it onto your picture. Position it where you want.

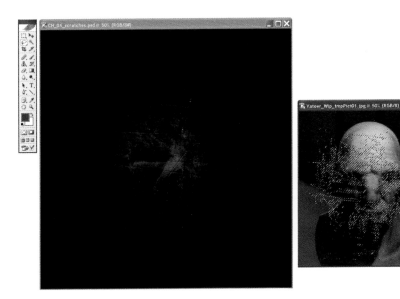

Drag and drop the selection from the left picture to the destination on the right with the Lasso Tool.

Because this texture is bigger than what we need, we're going to use the freeTransform Tool once it's on our final picture. You could scale down the texture before making the selection, but the freeTransform is really user-friendly and more convenient to use in this particular case.

With your **RMB**, you can now use the freeTransform selection to scale it to the size you want, or to alter the texture in other ways. One possibility is to use Perspective mode to match an element of your picture.

Because this texture is huge, the handle of the freeTransform is out of frame. It's not a problem, you simply need to scale down the picture to make it visible. Use the shortcut (**Ctrl** + "-") to do so. You can then use the opposite shortcut (**Ctrl**+ "+") to scale up the picture.

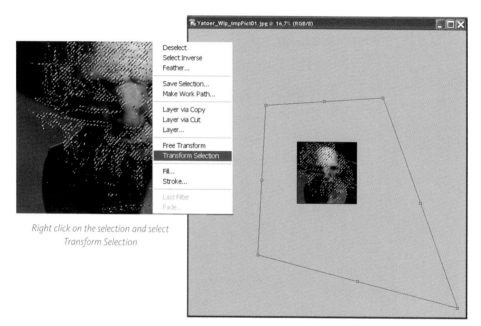

Right click on the selection and select Transform Selection

FreeTransform your selection to get the aspect you want

When you're happy with your selection, create an adjustment layer (levels, for example). Tune it to achieve a nice effect on your image.

Once it's done, you can simply remove unnecessary areas with the Lasso Tool or with a black brush on the mask.

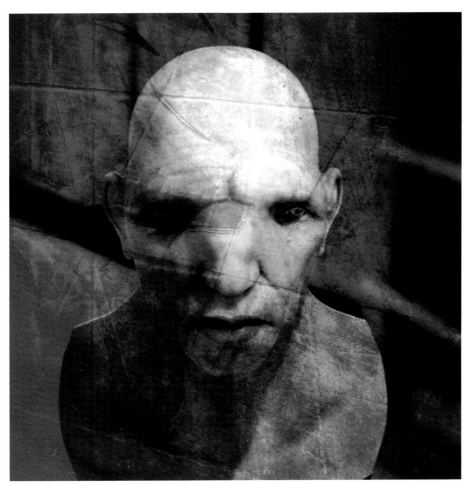

Resulting picture, with levels applied to the selection.

Note: Instead of copying an entire texture on top of something, with this method you can choose an aspect of the texture that you like and use it in many ways.

Tip: You can save your chosen color and the way it was tuned for future use. This can be helpful, especially when you want to use it in a script job. In this case, by saving a specific color range on your base picture and loading it back when you create the script, you'll be sure Photoshop picks the right color on the other pictures you want to process.

Comparison modes

Comparison modes are the ideal companion for textures.

Instead of using a texture, say, an inkbrushed piece of paper with only a control on the opacity, you can use comparison modes to achieve more layered effects.

Basically, modes are different ways to add your picture to a background. Some will lighten your background using light areas of the picture. Some will darken it and some will do both. Each one takes into consideration the colors you've got.

The different modes depend upon what your background and texture look like. A benefit of working with modes is that once you've selected one, you can simply jump to another by pressing the vertical arrows on your keyboard. This way you can test every mode, one after the other.

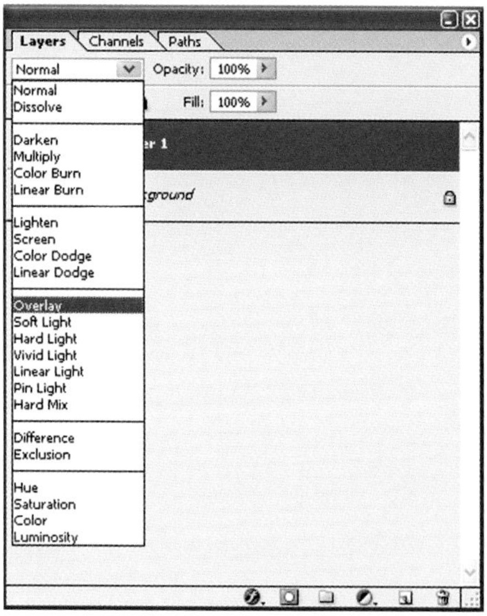

In the layer tab, click on Normal to access the available modes.

- Paste a texture on your document.

- Test all modes and then pick one.

- Use a mask and only keep the effect where you want it to be (just like we did with adjustment layers), by painting this mask, and/or by using another texture as a selection.

Try this workflow with the following picture: *CH_04_comparisonModeSample.psd*.

As you can see, everything can be combined. Combinations like this are the best way to get an organic result on a picture.

Even filters can be incorporated in an interesting way with this workflow. For example, by making a copyMerge of your picture and pasting it on top, you can filter this layer, add noise, brightness, outline, solarize, etc.

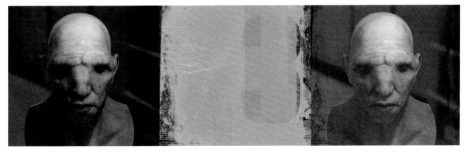

On the left, the "original" picture, in the middle, a texture sample pasted on top. On the right,
the result with a soft light comparison mode.

> **Tip:** A copyMerge is a copy that takes all visible layers into account. To create one, go to
> **Edit → Copy with Merge** or **Ctrl+Shift+c** (Mac OS **Command+Shift+c**).

> **Note:** Do not post-process an entire image with a filter. The result is too flat and obviously
> visible, i.e. people could recognize the effect, diminishing the efforts you've done to
> make it look natural. Always use a combination of filters applied by area and tuned
> individually to give life to your picture.

Conclusion

Now that you understand the options inherent in the predefined brush sets in Photoshop, the
possibilities are endless for the images you can create. In addition to learning about Photoshop
brushes and how to control opacity, you also experimented with using real textures to create
an organic surface to paint on. This skill will serve you well in much of your future CG work.

In the next lesson you will continue working with adjustment layers as you learn advanced
blending options.

Lesson 19
Advanced Blending Options

Thus far, we have learned some of the concepts for working with layers as a way to create an organic feel in a picture. You have combined render passes together, seen how to increase detail on some elements and played with adjustment layers to enhance contrast. Then, you used color balance to do some color bleeding between the background and the character. Focusing on blending options, you've learned how to create illustrative effects and how to blend textures.

There is one more essential area to learn, which is the focus of this lesson. It's time to go back to adjustment layers and work with levels, color corrections and color bleeding, while taking into consideration all the new details visible in your picture.

Each lesson in this project builds on the one before it, so rest assured that when you combine functions, everything will look natural.

In this lesson you will learn:

- How to tune transparency with sliders;
- Blending options for adjustment layers;
- How to soften a mask interactively;
- How to work with filters on masks.

Getting started

Open your latest version of the picture, which should be the result of Lesson 18.

Right-click on a layer in the layer tab to see your blending options. When you click on it, a window should pop up.

On the left, there are categories listed of different effects, including drop shadow, glow and bevels. These are mostly used by Web designers to create buttons. For the purposes of this lesson, you will focus on the right side, where the two sliders are.

On the left, dark slider moved toward the right. On the right, light slider moved toward the left.

- The top slider relates to the layer itself, while the bottom slider affects the background, i.e. everything that is under your actual layer. By experimenting with your sliders, you can learn how to fade areas of your picture to enhance depth.

- Open the file called: *CH_04_comparisonModeSample.psd*.

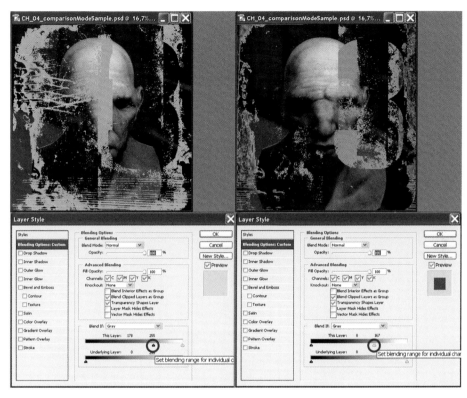

Access blending options by double-clicking on a layer in the layer tab or with RMB blending options

If you use the top slider, you will actually fade areas of your layer and make the background appear. If you move the left (black) slider toward the right, dark areas of your picture will disappear. If you move the right slider toward the left, bright areas will fade.

Tip: *Click on one of the sliders with Alt pressed (option on Mac) to create an additional slider that will work as a transition range. This way, you can tune the transparency you want with the main slider, and then with Alt pressed you can tune the soft transition.*

Note: *Once the secondary slider has appeared, you can release Alt.*

Project 4: Yatoer, The Bus Stop Boxer

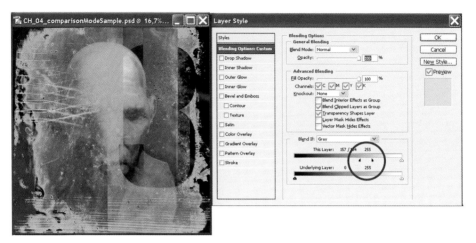

A secondary control created to smooth transitions

The bottom slider, meanwhile, works on how the background will go through the foreground. The two sliders work in tandem, and if you want to soften the blending they create, just use Alt. Depending on what you want to achieve, you will fade the background, the foreground or both.

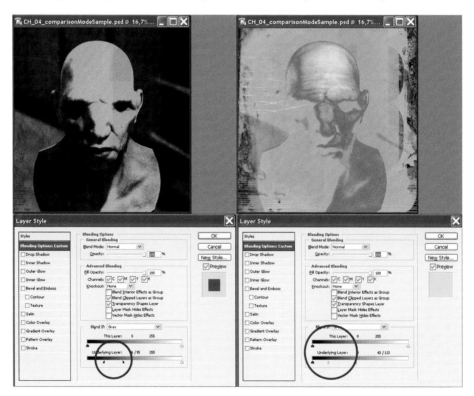

By playing with the bottom sliders, your background goes through the foreground

This is a perfect technique for painting on top of a picture while maintaining details through the paint. This way, you can use a few layers of the same color to achieve a nice, believable painterly feeling.

As you can see, a comparison is being made on a greyscale range, but you can manually tune it differently on the three (RGB, or four for CMYK) channels of your picture if you need to.

A CMYK picture with advanced blending options

Blending options for adjustment layers

Blending options work the same way on adjustment layers. What you've learned about color corrections, lighting, etc. can work in combination with these new options.

If you want to use a level adjustment layer in order to highlight some areas, you may want to keep the darker areas as black as they were, and only clamp the highlights.

By dragging the bottom left slider toward the right, underlying dark elements will appear through the new adjustment layer.

• Open the files *blendingOptAdjLayer.psd* and *blendingOptAdjLayer_DONE.psd*.

Project 4: Yatoer, The Bus Stop Boxer

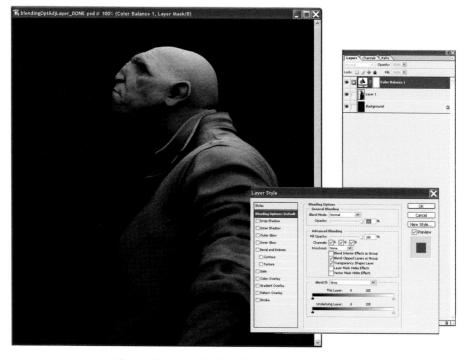

*Adjustment layer is set globally on the picture without any mask
or advanced blending options*

- Using the Alpha of the character, remove the background from the effect of the adjustment layer. To do that, load Layer1's selection, invert it and fill the result with black.

Tip: *To invert Layer1's selection, **RMB** with the Lasso Tool selected and press Invert, or go to the selection menu and select Invert.*

- **RMB+click** on the adjustment layer's name and select **Blending Option**. Tune it so the dark areas are no longer affected by the color balance. It should look greenish instead of red.

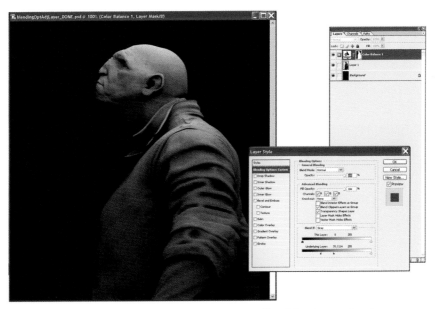

By setting the underlying layer options, the effect of the adjustment layer is
removed from the dark areas of the picture.

Filters on masks

When you create a selection with the Lasso Tool or any kind of selecting action, you can soften
it by right-clicking on the selection and using the **Feather** option. This allows you to smooth the
selection on a specific amount of pixels. However, this can be a time-consuming method unless
you know exactly what you want, because often you have to enter a value, test it, undo, enter
another value and so on.

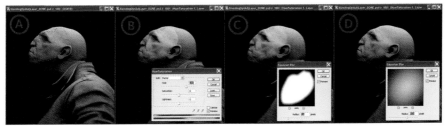

The workflow

To try this workflow, make a selection and keep it sharp (**A**), without using the feather option.
Then, create your adjustment layer (**B**), and use a gaussian blur to soften the mask interactively.
The preview on the blur acts on the mask, and you can see interactively how it looks (**C** & **D**).

- Open *blurringMasks.psd*. The selection and adjustment layer have already been done.
  Simply go to **Filter → Blur → Gaussian Blur**, and see how it affects the mask.

> **Note:** Since a mask is basically a black and white picture, it can be worked on almost the same way as everything else. Keeping this is mind, note that you can use filters on masks to add radial blur, noise, distortions, etc.

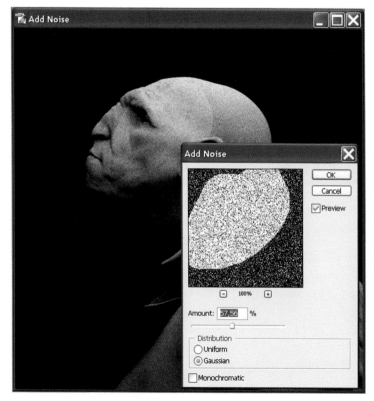

A noise effect achieved using a filter on a mask

Illustration details

Now let's have a look at some details of the illustration. To combine what you've learned about the brushes with what you've learned about the advanced blending options, you will work on the sleeve of the character. The blood on the fabric was achieved using 2-3 layers and a red brush.

- **Create** a new layer and paint some red strokes on it for a global effect.

- Go to the blending options of your layer, and by using the bottom slider, push the dark values up so the black areas of the shirt (mostly the pattern of the fabric), go through the paint.

- **Reduce** the overall opacity of the layer to something around 50%.

- **Create** a second layer and paint some more red strokes on it. As mentioned earlier, you'll always get better results with two layers of paint instead of one.

- Go to the blending options and repeat the steps you followed for the first layer. One option is to paint only one stroke to set the blending options and then to paint with the final effect, seeing what remains throughout the blending.

- **Create** a third layer and paint the high density blood areas with no blending option activated. This way, you have achieved a progressive painterly effect that should look as if several layers of paint were used.

Final result obtained with 3 layers of red paint, using various advanced blending options.

Considering the background

Before you begin to work on the background, which is the focus of the following lesson, it would be good to uniformize things a bit. There are some details in the picture that you don't want to keep, and, instead of simply removing them, you will create some additional painterly areas. The method is similar to what you did for the sleeve, but the main difference is that you will use a texture that is pasted first.

- Open the files *paintTexture.psd* and *paper.psd*. Copy and paste them on top of your picture, align them to the left and scale them using freeTransform (**Ctrl+T**) to cover most of the area of the train. When this is done, play a bit with blending options to get a decent effect. The purpose is not to have a large texture effect, but more to match the complexity of the character and remove the photo aspect of the background.

- Using a new layer, paint over some remaining details to blend everything together.

Textures pasted on the background with paint added on top

- Play with blending options again and create as many layers as you need to. On the right side of the picture, as you can see, the character seems a bit lost in the background. Use a new layer, and paint some soft strokes of color to detach Yatoer's back and arm. Once again, don't be shy with layers. Create as many as you need to, combine blending options, opacities, etc.

- Open the file called *Kraft.jpg*. Copy and paste it on top of your picture. Play with blending modes to see how it affects the picture.

- Tune down the opacity to 10%. Then, keep on searching for a blending mode that you like. The idea is to put a soft texture to the entire picture and merge elements together before you continue with details and color bleeding.

- Save your work.

Conclusion

Compare the picture of Yatoer at the beginning and you will see marked improvement. The differences are based on what was learned in the last lessons about textures, brushes, comparison modes and advanced blending options. Technically speaking, there is nothing complicated about what was added.

Intuition is a primary force in successful CG work – by applying textures and colors, testing hues and hiding some details while increasing others, the picture will start to look the way you imagine it.

Nothing is planned at this stage, and you can't overestimate the importance of experimentation. Even on a high resolution picture, these operations are done in close to real time, i.e. you can see the changes happening right before your eyes. When you are truly comfortable with a tool and don't have to think about where a function is, you're ready to continue.

In the next lesson you will learn how to build a background from scratch.

Lesson 20
A Background From Scratch

At the end of the previous lesson, you were invited to use textures and layers with brush strokes, to globally enhance image quality and to meld things together. This lesson will show you how to create a background from scratch, but it is not a step-by-step instructional. The goal of this lesson is to use your understanding of the methods and tools described previously in this project to combine and blend things together.

In this lesson you will learn:

- How to achieve a nice backlight effect;

- How to match elements;

- How to finalize your picture with adjustment layers.

Getting started

At this stage, you have two options:

- You can make your own interpretation of the background using the file from previous lessons. You can choose the textures and color tones you want and place them to your liking.

- You can use the Lesson 20 version of the picture in the file called *newStartingPoint.psd*. This one is already textured and color tuned, but there is no history on it.

  If you would like to do option #1, choose textures in the texture folder and create your own version of the picture. Add some colors, increase details, modify shapes, switch the background, feel free to experiment. When you think it's close to what you want, continue reading for the next steps.

  Readers opting for option #2 should open newStartingPoint.psd in the Lesson 20 source folder.

Increasing the backlight effect

First, the idea is to get a nice backlight effect that slightly burns the character's contour. Because you are dealing with a leather jacket that has some very sharp speculars, it can be nice to integrate background tones onto it.

In order to do this, duplicate the background and go to **Filters → Blur → Radial Blur**. Select **Zoom**, tune it to a strong value and click on **Apply**.

The radial blur window

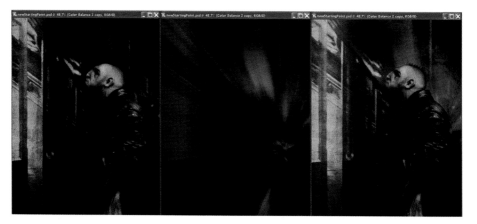

The blurred layer is set to screen in the blending modes and the character's alpha is used as an inverted mask

The radial blur is long to process, but provides amazing results. Change the blending mode of the blurred layer to **Screen** and create a mask, removing the entire character using its alpha. At this stage, you should be comfortable with selections and masks, which is why these steps aren't detailed. If you need to review the steps, go back to Lessons 16 and 17 in this project.

Once the blur effect is done, the idea is to use a combination of adjustment layers, regular layers with radial ramps and some brush strokes to enhance this backlight. Keeping in mind that the character has to be easy to read, you need to add light to some of the background areas around the important elements of Yatoer. His face, hands and the silhouette of his jacket have to be pushed forward by the effect of the background. Instead of detailing everything, here are a couple of stages to help you see the entire process.

From top left to bottom right, various stages of the process

As you can see, it's not a major revolution. By pushing some values higher and lowering others, things are somewhat clarified. Then, globally, you need to tweak levels to get the mood you want while maintaining a clear distinction between the character and the background.

Making the blending more painterly looking

One might consider these blur effects enough to create a nice picture. However, if you want to make them look more painterly, you can use them as guidelines for your painting. Because the blur created a coherent blending between the character and the background, you can now make a layer on top of everything, and, by choosing underlying colors, make some more defined strokes. Always keep in mind that the audience will focus on some specific element in your picture. Because of this, it's important to detach some things and, conversely, to hide others.

Tip: *Play with the zoom to reduce this picture to the size of a stamp. This way you can see what remains visible.*

On the left, Yatoer with radial blur only on the background. On the right, the result with some very soft gradients.

- Using brushes and/or the Gradient Tool, paint some light areas around the character on a couple of layers. This will increase the backlight effect and help read his face. This can be done just the way you did it with the blood on the sleeve, or with the greenish area on the background. I tend to use several layers with various blending options; you may prefer to use only one layer, with low opacity strokes. Create some radial gradients, using colors from the existing background (select some light values) with very low opacities.

- Use a hues and saturation adjustment layer to darken the background a bit. This will not remove what you've already done, it's just a way to globally affect the background so it doesn't distract the audience from the subject.

By creating a hues and saturation adjustment layer on the background, you keep the attention on Yatoer.

> **Note:** *Do not use a hues and saturation adjustment layer on the character; a mask is used for that.*

- Use a texture with a low opacity on the background to increase details in your backlight.

On the left, previous stage with no textures applied. On the right, backlight looks a bit richer.

Lesson 20: A Background From Scratch

321

- Press **Ctrl+a** to select everything, **Ctrl+Shift+c** to copy with merge and **Ctrl+v** to paste it on top, using a regular noise filter.

- Instead of keeping this noise on the entire picture, create a mask. The fastest way is to fill it completely with black. Then, create a gradient set to white to roughly get the area of the backlight being affected.

- Finally, load back the selection of the character (using his alpha in the channel tab), and fill it with black. Deselect all and slightly blur the entire mask with a gaussian blur to merge the contour of the character in the noise.

Your mask should look like this now:

Mask for the layer with noise

This is the result on the picture:

Layer with noise, with its mask applied

Now, if you are following the reference picture, the idea is to have urban lights everywhere, even some in the foreground, like a reflection on a glass or a lens.

> **Note:** *The reason I used these highlights is because the jacket was lacking sharpness in the environment. It's always good to have matching elements, like you should with a photo-realistic collage, for example. By identifying the significant elements of a picture or photo and replicating them in the element you want to combine, you will be able to merge things and make them look natural.*

If you want to merge CG into a photo, for example, it is understood that you have to match keylights and sharpness. However, if you focus on some specific details as well, you will be able to create a more complete illusion.

One of the 3 samples for the lights

Urban lights

Use some of the provided samples in the Lesson 20 source folder to create the highlights (night_lights01, 02, 03). As you can see, they are mostly photos from a town shot at night and not very attractive on their own. But, they do provide enough light information for what you need here.

- Open *urban night_light01.jpg* and copy and paste it on your picture.

- Set it to **Screen** to keep only the light effect visible.

- Place the highlights so they add complexity to the picture without taking focus away from the character. In order to do that, simply duplicate this layer as many times as you want. Play with the freeTransform to create some depth as well. You can also use hues and saturation adjustment layers to colorize some of them.

Copies of lights from the photos are made and positioned all around.

- Use masks to hide them behind the character.

Tip: *Don't make the transition too sharp. Color bleeding would be a good way of slightly covering the character's silhouette with light. It gives a nice glowing effect.*

A soft airbrush is used to make some of the lights appear on the borders of the character.

- To do this color bleeding, mask those patches of light with the alpha of the character through a mask. When the mask is done, use a soft airbrush and paint on the silhouette of the character with white so it creates a subtle transition.

Note: *This is a similar process to what you did for the backlight around the character.*

Then, you can add some scaled up light in front of the character, as if during the shot some lens effects and echoes appeared.

In order to do this, repeat the steps you followed for the previous lights. Copy and paste bright elements extracted from the night photos, and scale them up with the freeTransform Tool. Set those patches to screen in the blending modes, and, if required, blur them slightly with the gaussian blur filter. Once again, during this step, you have to focus on the composition; these foreground highlights shouldn't distract the audience from the character.

More lights are added in the foreground with no mask this time.

When you're done, you can enhance details or sharpness on your character with adjustment layers. It can be very cool to reveal elements at this stage using all the texturing you've done, while painting like you would with charcoal or paint on a canvas. If you experiment with some advanced blending options on your layer, you can achieve a similar feeling to one derived from traditional media.

Conclusion

In the lesson you created a background from scratch, building on the concepts explored in previous lessons regarding textures, layers and global enhancement of image quality. For the background you matched elements, created a backlight effect and finished your image with adjustment layers.

The next lesson is the final one of this project. You will use render layers to finalize your image of Yatoer.

Lesson 21
Freestyle (Render Layers in Maya)

One of the best additions in Maya 7 is definitely the render layers. In the past, you had access to render pass, which is basically a way to extract information of an image, such as speculars, shadows, diffuse, etc. If you have ever worked with compositing software then you must know how useful it is to have separate access to those channels in order to create the best integrations.

With render layers, Maya pushes the possibilities even further. Now you have the ability to change attributes of your shaders, lights and cameras on each layer of your object. When properly tuned, a layer is like a brand new scene. This means that instead of having to deal with many different files for creating your render passes, you can have them all at once in a single Maya scene.

In this lesson you will use render layers to generate four passes for a single illustration to be combined afterward in Photoshop.

As well, you will work on a new picture with our good old Yatoer, using a more sketchy/gritty approach. This is to demonstrate that you don't necessarily need high end shaders and lighting to work with CG for illustration.

The methods in Photoshop are similar to the ones you've already been introduced to in previous lessons, but this time the goal is to work as fast as possible (it took me 1h30 to make this rough and basic portrait).

In this lesson you will learn:

- How to use the occlusion pass;
- How to use the "Suppa Shadows" shader;
- How to use the Stamp Tool to create a clean patch;
- How to work with the proper blending mode.

Render layers

Take a look at the documentation in Maya to understand the basis of render layers. I'd like to focus on the workflow, i.e. the way you can split your scene into a few layers, switch to Photoshop and keep on working.

Since I already created the shaders for this scene, all you have to do is apply them to the proper object on the correct layer.

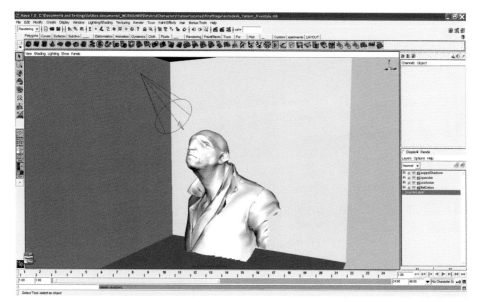

Final scene with its layers tuned

- Set your Maya project first. In your Lesson 21 sources, select the freestyle folder. *Open finishedScene.ma.*

- In the Channel Box, there is a tab, called **Display** and on its right, another one called **Render**. Go to **Render** → **Render Layers**.

As you can see, in the render layer tab there are four layers and the master layer. The master layer is automatically generated when you create a layer, and it corresponds to the scene without any necessary changes. The other layers are respectively called *Flat Colors*, *Occlusion Specular* and *Suppa Shadows*.

It's up to you to name the layers you create, using descriptive names.

For this example, you will use the basic shaders.

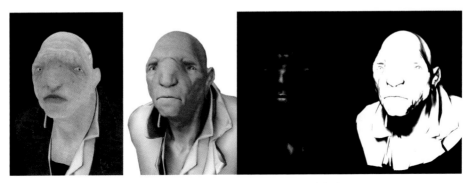

From left to right: surface shader, occlusion, specular and shadows

A *surface shader* is a very basic shader that doesn't react to lights, doesn't receive shadows and flattens things out. Usually, it is used for matte paintings and backgrounds. Here it will be perfect for receiving the color textures of the face, jacket and eyes.

Next is the *occlusion pass*. Occlusion is a mental ray node that you can connect to many different shaders. Usually, it is used to create a black and white render in which all contact between objects is darkened out. Occlusion is based upon a raytracing system, and you can find a multitude of uses for it. Here, you will generate a basic black and white pass of the character that will reveal every detail of the geometry.

The *specular pass* is also called "highlights", and you will use a blinn shader to get it. The easiest way to render a specular pass is to use a black shader with white speculars. Here, a specular map was connected to the shader. This is what you would do on a complex shader to control highlights on geometry. For example, on a character you know that the nose, forehead, chin and lips have more highlights than the rest of the face.

Suppa shadows is a homemade shader, created to generate a shadow pass. In our case, it will be closer to what we want than the regular shadow pass rendered through the Use Background shader.

In order to use all these shaders and generate the four pictures in a single Maya scene, the procedure is as follows:

- Open *StartUpScene.ma*. Select all your objects and create four layers with the second icon in the render layer tab.

> **Note:** *The first icon creates a layer and the second icon creates a layer that automatically applies selected objects in it.*

- Rename each layer by double-clicking on it.

- Select your flat colors layer and go to the Hypershade. Apply the color shaders to the respective objects.

- Apply *surfaceShader_face* to the face of the character, apply *surfaceShader_jacket* to the jacket and so on.

  For the occlusion layer, the procedure is simpler, as you only need one shader for all objects. Apply an *occlusion* shader to the entire scene.

- Select the light, and with your **RMB** on the occlusion layer, click on **Remove Selected Object**.

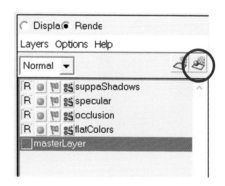

CreateLayerWithSelectedObjects allows you to create a layer and apply the selected objects to it

  For the specular layer, apply specularShader_XXX to each respective object.

- For *suppa shadows*, as you did for the occlusion, select all the objects and apply the suppa shadows shader (but keep the light in it).

  You could stop here, but because I want to introduce you to certain render layer specificities, you're going to make some more manipulations.

- Select the flat colors layer. Click on the **Render Settings** icon in it, or in the general **Render Globals** of Maya.

- In the mental ray tab, **RMB+click** on the word **Filter** and select **Create Layer Override**. By doing this, you can set an attribute for this specific layer. This is what you should do for any parameter; it works for everything on a shader, object and rendering attribute (also called a *rendering flag*).

- Set the **Filter** to **Mitchell**. Mitchell is very sharp anti-aliasing that will be perfect for the color pass.

Create an override for the filter; here, set to Mitchell.

- Select the occlusion layer, and in its **Render Globals**, RMB and set a new layer override for the maxSampleLevel. Set it to 1. This will render the pass faster than it would have set to 2. Of course, the pass will be a little bit less smoothed, but that is not a concern here.

Keep on experimenting with the override. Have a look around and you will notice that you can create overrides specific to each layer for almost every parameter of every object.

- Set your Render Globals and define a name and resolution. Set the file format as well – use *tga* if you don't have the *.iff* plug-in for Photoshop.

- Save, and batch render the scene (**Render** → **Batch Render**).

Note: *A batch render is a render that is not displayed in Maya's UI. This is faster, because as soon as you see the rendering started in the Status Line, you can exit Maya to save memory. The render is done through an executable called mayabatch that doesn't require Maya to function. To see if the render is finished, open a Task Manager in Windows (Ctrl+Alt+Suppr), and check the activity of your CPU.*

Mayabatch.exe in the Task Manager of Windows

Back to Photoshop

The batch is complete, and you should have four new folders in the Images folder of your Maya project. In each folder, there is a file in tga that you can rename properly using the name of the respective pass.

Open these files in Photoshop, and create a new document in which you will paste all the passes (just like you did for Lesson 16). You are now working with a combination of everything seen in the previous six lessons. Consider this lesson as a review, and if you feel confused, go back to the previous explanations and practice a bit more. The following first steps are new, but the subsequent ones are pure experimentation with adjustment layers, regular layers, advanced blending options and a few filters.

Appropriate blending modes

The base layer is the flat colors layer. If you set occlusion on **Multiply** and place it on top, you start to see that it is adding geometry details to the flat colors, creating something close to what you would have achieved with the colors on a regular shader and some light information. Because occlusion reveals every detail of a surface, it's the perfect companion for a surface shader, and an awesome way to give some weight to a render.

If you look at the last example, you will see that you still have to deal with the bad junction between the forehead and the skull. Use the **Stamp Tool** for that. Hide the occlusion layer, create a clean layer on top of your surface shader pass and make the patch.

You can also correct the messy blending on the jacket's collar and fix the nostrils.

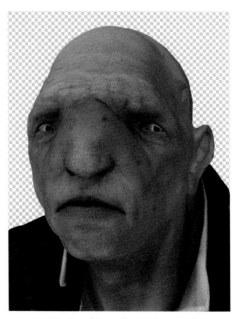

Combination of the surface shader pass with occlusion on top, set to Multiply

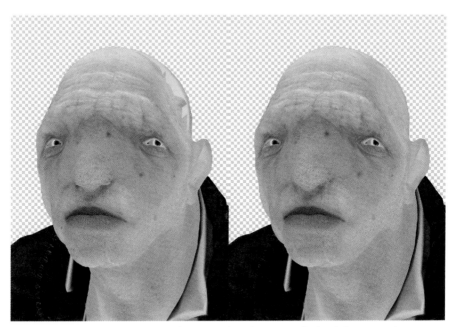

On the left, surface shader out of render. On the right, same pass fixed with the Stamp Tool.

- Display the occlusion layer again.

- Set the suppa shadows' blending mode to **Multiply** and tune down the opacity to 25%.

- Set the specular layer's blending mode to **Screen** and tune the opacity down to something around 50%.

- Get the fur pass and paste it on top (as you did in Lesson 16).

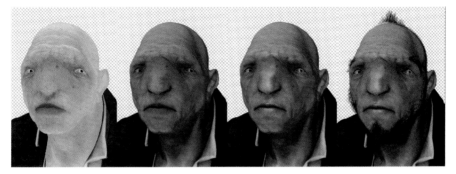

From left to right: surface shader, occlusion and shadows added, specular added and some fur

Note: I did not put the fur scene in the project or in the render layers, because it's a bit tricky to handle and I didn't want to confuse anyone. My apologies.

- Create a rough background using the samples you have in the source folders for all lessons. Use some adjustment layers for shadows and highlights. Use some color balance adjustment layers to enrich the face.

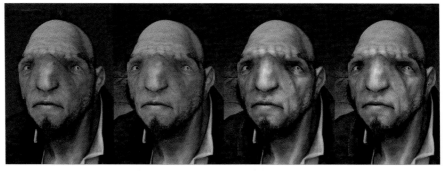

From left to right: background added, very low textures added globally, levels for highlights and dark areas, color balance.

- Create a layer or two, and use brush strokes to redefine the contour of the character.

- Play with adjustment layers to increase sharpness.

- Make a copy with blend (**Ctrl+Shift+c**) of the entire result, paste it on top, blur it with a gaussian blur, set it to soft light and tune it down.

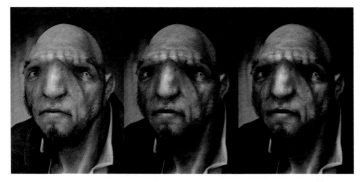

From left to right: paint added, levels and a copy of the entire result, set to soft light and blurred.

Continue enriching the picture using adjustment layers and copies with filters on (vertical blur copy set to **Color Dodge** here), as well as some paint. You can also use some of the basic passes, such as occlusion, to reinforce sharpness.

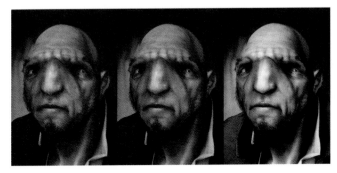

More paint added, vertical blur filter on a copy and another layer of occlusion on top to sharpen the image

Continue playing with the image: redefine some force lines, use a small brush to increase some of the contour highlights, add some more textures and put more density in the fur. Use adjustment layers to meld the background with the character.

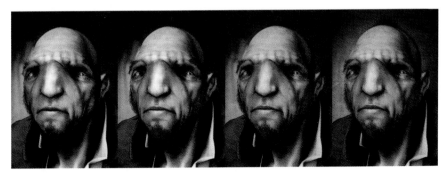

From left to right: light strokes added, textures, fur density and color balance.

Sharpness can still be added to some details. Now that the picture is really gritty and detailed, try to clear up certain areas. Use a small brush once again to draw the outline of the character. Use some paint on the background with a new tone and a big loud brush. Make this rough, so the character remains the only one with so many details.

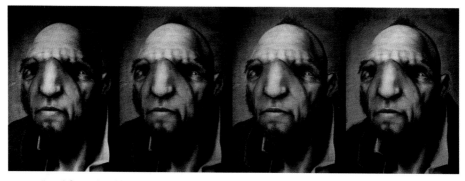

From left to right: global color with blending mode added, a new bright contour drawn and final picture

Here it is! As I said, it's a very rough picture, not designed for big prints, but it's pretty decent for a quick test. This is an example of the same method used to achieve a completely different result. Of course, results depend on the sources you use and on the way you use textures. Here, they were applied with stronger opacities than in the bus stop boxer image, which obviously provides a more gritty and noisy effect.

For an additional exercise, you could experiment colorizing a basic occlusion render, or any kind of basic render. It depends on what you want to do. Testing and retesting is the only way to feel confident with a method and its inherent tools.

Some final tips to end this project:

- Don't work too quickly when texturing. Try to match elements as much as you can initially, as they are easier to work with at the beginning.

- Save often, create copies of your document to test and compare different choices on a single effect. When you make a new incrementation of your document you can also flatten things out, allowing you to work faster with less memory.

- Use **Purge → History** in the Edit menu to avoid memory issues. Because Photoshop keeps a history of your work, usually 20 undos are available, requiring a lot of memory.

- Always get a good night of sleep before you show your picture to anyone!

- Have fun.

Thanks again for reading and good luck with all your future projects.

Final image

Glossary of Terms

3D
Three-dimensional. Descriptive of a region of space that has width, height and depth.

Algorithm
A procedure or formula for solving a mathematical problem. Algorithms are commonly used for such tasks as generating textures, rendering images and controlling mathematically based behaviour patterns.

Alpha Channel
The top byte of a 32-bit pixel that is used for data other than color. The alpha channel commonly holds mask data, enabling an image to be separated from its background for use in compositing.

Ambient Light
An artificial illumination level representing infinite diffuse reflections from all surfaces within a 3D scene, ensuring that even surfaces without direct illumination become visible to the user.

Animation
A medium that creates the illusion of movement through the projection of a series of still images or 'frames'. The term is also used to refer to the techniques used in the production of an animated film - in 3D animation, primarily those controlling the motion of the objects and cameras within a scene. These include keyframe animation, in which the artist sets the positions of objects manually at certain key points in the action, and the computer calculates their intervening positions through a process of interpolation or 'inbetweening', and procedural animation, in which the motion is controlled automatically via a series of mathematical formulae.

Animatic
A rough animation that is used by animators to give some idea about the timing of a sequence, used as a kind of animated storyboard.

Anti-aliasing
A method of reducing or preventing rendering artefacts by using color information to simulate a higher screen resolution. The term is often applied to the process of softening the unnaturally precise or stepped edges (sometimes known as 'the jaggies') created when a computergenerated object is placed against a contrasting background by using pixels of intermediate shades as a buffer between the two.

Aperture
In a real camera, the size of the opening that light passes through (usually given in terms of its f-stop) in order to reach the film. The larger the f-stop, the smaller the opening. 3D software packages sometimes mimic the effects of different aperture settings on a recorded image during the rendering process.

Aspect Ratio
The ratio of the width of an image to its height. Common aspect ratios for broadcast images include 4:3 and 16:9 (widescreen).

Axis
A hypothetical linear path around which an object can be rotated, or across which it can be mirrored. In the Cartesian co-ordinate system, the three world axes, X, Y and Z (width, height and depth) define directionality within the 3D universe. Hence, a co-ordinate of (0,0,0) defines the origin of the world.

Beauty Pass
When rendering multiple passes of a scene, the beauty pass is the one that features the most significant information about the objects within it. This usually includes the main, full-color rendering of those objects, including diffuse illumination and color. A beauty pass will not include reflections, highlights, and shadows, which are usually separate passes.

Bit Depth
The number of bits used to define the shade or color of each pixel in an image, a 'bit' being the smallest unit of memory or storage on a computer. (One 'byte' is eight 'bits'.) A 1-bit image is black and white. An 8-bit image provides a 256-color palette. A 24-bit image provides 16.7 million possible colors: a palette sometimes known as 'True Colour'. A 32-bit image provides the same palette, plus an 8-bit greyscale alpha channel.

Bitmap
Strictly speaking, a bitmap is a 1-bit black-and-white image. However, the term is often loosely applied to any two-dimensional image, regardless of bit depth. Still image manipulation packages such as Photoshop and Paint Shop Pro are sometimes referred to as 'bitmap editors'.

Blinn See: Shading.
Bluescreen Footage Live footage shot against a backdrop of a single uniform color (usually blue or green) with a view to compositing it into a computergenerated background. Every pixel with the same color value as the backdrop is replaced by the CG image.

Bone
A rigid object analogous to a real bone, placed inside the 'skeleton' of a character during the process of rigging it for animation. When a bone is moved, it acts upon the mesh of the character model, deforming it.

Boolean
An object created by combining two objects using mathematical operators. The two objects may be subtracted from one other, merged, or intersected to form the new object.

Bounding Box
The smallest regular-shaped box that encloses a 3D object, usually rectangular in shape.

Bump Map
A black-and-white image used by a 3D software package to simulate the three-dimensional detail on the surface of an object. When projected over the surface of the object, parts of the surface beneath white areas of the image are raised; those beneath black areas are depressed. Bump mapping is purely a rendering effect, however, and does not affect the underlying geometry of the model.

CAD
Computer Aided Design. The use of computer-based models of objects for visualization or testing as an aid in the design process. CAD software packages usually contain more precise real-world measuring tools than ordinary 3D packages, but fewer surfacing and animation features.

Camera
A virtual viewpoint in 3D space that possesses both position and direction. In a 3D scene, the camera represents the viewer's eye. When the scene is rendered at final quality, it is the camera view that is used, rather than the one seen in the software's workspace. This enables the artist to move around the workspace without disturbing the camera view.

Camera Mapping
A technique by which geometry matching the size and perspective of objects shown within a still image is constructed, and the original image mapped back onto those objects. This permits limited camera movement around the picture, giving the illusion of a 3D environment from a 2D image.

Camera Move
A movement of the virtual camera within a 3D software package analogous to one in real-world cinematography. Common camera moves include dollying, in which the camera angle remains fixed, but the camera moves towards or away from the subject; panning, in which the camera position remains fixed, but the camera tilts or swivels in any direction to follow the action; and tracking, in which the camera moves in a single plane at right angles to the area of interest.

Camera Path
The path in virtual space along which the camera moves during the course of an animation.

Camera Tracking
Also known as match moving, camera tracking is the process of 'extracting' the motion of the camera in space from a piece of live-action footage. This motion data can then be imported into a 3D software package and used to animate the virtual camera, in order to better match the rendered output to that of the source footage during the compositing process.

Caustics
Patches of intense illumination caused by the refraction of light through a transparent object or the reflection of light from a reflective surface. One common example would be the shifting patterns of light and shade cast on the floor of a swimming pool on a sunny day. Rendering software has only recently become sophisticated enough to mimic such complex real-world lighting effects as caustics.

CGI
Computer Generated Imagery. An image or images created or manipulated with the aid of a computer. The term is often used to refer specifically to 3D computer animation, although it is really more widely applicable.

Channel
For a two-dimensional image, a channel is a sub-image composed only of the values for a single component of a given pixel. A greyscale image has one color channel, an RGB image has three, and a CMYK image has four. When applied to materials, the term refers to one particular subset of the properties which determine the way in which a surface reacts to light, including color, reflectivity, transparency, diffusion, specularity and bump.

Character Animation
A sub-area of animation that deals with the simulation of the varied movements of living creatures. Usually, before a character model can be animated, it must be set-up with an underlying skeleton, constraints and controllers: this process is known as rigging. See: Hierarchy.

Color Bleeding
A physical phenomenon by which the color of one object is seemingly transferred to a neighbouring object by light bouncing from one surface to the other. Like caustics, color bleeding is a complex real-world lighting effect, and one that rendering software has only recently become able to simulate accurately.

Color Space
A mathematical method for defining the way in which color is represented within an image. Common color spaces include RGB (Red, Green, Blue), which has a bit depth of 24, and is commonly used in broadcast applications, and CMYK (Cyan, Magenta, Yellow, Black), which has a bit depth of 32, and is used for print illustration work.

Compositing
The process of combining multiple images into a single image. This is often performed in films to make a live actor appear on a computer generated background, or vice versa. It can also be used following multi-pass rendering to combine the various render passes in different ways to control the look of a scene.

Compression
A technique for reducing the quantity of data required to make up a digital image. Compression techniques can be non-destructive ('lossless') or destructive ('lossy'), in which part of the data set is discarded permanently. Converting still images into JPEG format is one example of lossy compression.

Constrain
To restrict the motion of an object to one or two planes, or to a certain range of values within a plane, in order to simplify the process of animation. Constraints are commonly imposed on joints within a skeleton during the process of rigging a character for animation, in order to prevent that character from performing actions that would be physically impossible.

Constructive Solid Geometry
A modeling technique that combines simple solid forms, or primitives, into more complex models, by means of Boolean operations. Common primitives include the plane, the cube, the sphere, the cone and the torus.

Co-ordinate System
A set of numerical values used to denote a location in 3D space. In the Cartesian co-ordinate system, three orthogonal 'world axes' (the X, Y and Z axes) are used to define the position of a point relative to the intersection of these axes, or origin. Other co-ordinate systems can be used for modeling and texture projection.

CV
Control Vertex. A control point used to manipulate the shape of a NURBS curve.

Deformer
Usually: a modeling tool that deforms the structure of an entire object. However, the exact meaning of the term varies from software package to software package.

Dirt map
See: Grime Map

Displacement Map
A recent advance on Bump Mapping. Like a bump map, a Displacement Map is a black-and-white image that a 3D software package projects over the surface of a model to generate surface detail. Unlike a bump map, however, a displacement map modifies the actual underlying geometry and is not merely a rendering effect.

Depth of Field (DOF)
The depth of field of a specific lens is the range of acceptable focus in front of and behind the primary focus setting. It is a function not only of the specific lens used but also of the distance from the lens to the primary focal plane, and of the chosen aperture. Larger apertures will narrow the depth of field; smaller apertures will increase it.

Environment Map
An image intended to entirely enclose a scene, either to provide a convincing background, or to project real-world lighting or reflection data onto the surface of an object.

Expression
A mathematical formula used to define the value of a given attribute of an object during animation. The use of expressions forms a procedural alternative to hand, or keyframe, animation.

Extrusion
A modeling technique in which a two-dimensional outline or profile is duplicated outwards along a linear path, and the set of duplicated profiles joined to create a continuous three-dimensional surface.

Face
The front or back of an extruded object. The shape from which a 3D object has been extruded.

Fall-off
The way in which the intensity of a light diminishes with the distance from its source. In the real world, the fall-off of light is governed by the inverse square law, which states that the intensity is inversely proportional to the square of the distance. However, in 3D software packages, it is possible to use a variety of different mathematical formulae to describe the relationship.

F-Curve
Function Curve. An F-Curve is displayed in the Graph Editor of a 3D software package, and is used during the animation process both to display and to control the way in which a particular attribute of an object varies with time.

File Format
The format in which the data making up a particular 3D object or scene is stored.

Flythrough
A type of animation in which the camera moves around a scene, rather than objects moving in front of a stationary camera.

Forward Kinematics
Often abbreviated to FK, Forward Kinematics is a character animation technique for controlling the motion of the bones in a chain – for example, a limb – in which rotations propagate from bone to bone towards the free end of the chain (in the case of a limb, towards the hand or foot).

Frame
A still two-dimensional image. In computer animation, the term 'frames per second' (fps) is a measurement of the number of still frames displayed in one second to give the impression of a moving image. For film work, this value is usually 24; for the European PAL broadcast format, 25; and for the US NTSC broadcast format, 30 fps.

F-Stop
See: Aperture

Global Illumination
A superset of the radiosity and raytracing rendering techniques. The goal of Global Illumination rendering is to compute all of the possible light interactions between surfaces in a given scene, and thus obtain a truly photorealistic image. All combinations of diffuse and specular reflections and transmissions must be accounted for. Effects such as color bleeding and caustics must also be included in a global illumination simulation.

Graph Editor
The part of the GUI of a 3D software package where a particular attribute of an object changes over time is displayed graphically, in the form of an F-Curve.

Grime Map
Also known as 'dirt maps', grime maps are two-dimensional images applied to a particular channel of a material. When the image is projected across the surface of an object, it breaks up that channel's flat, even value, creating realistic surface variations.

Group
A set of sub-objects within a model or scene that move and behave as a single entity, yet can still be split apart (ungrouped), if necessary. Most complicated models are constructed from several less complex parts that need to maintain the same spacing and orientation; grouping provides a way of locking the relative positions of the objects without joining them permanently.

GUI
Graphical User Interface. An icon based interface that controls a 3D software package. Although the GUI varies from program to program, there are certain basic conventions governing the layout of the main professional 3D applications.

Hard-Body Dynamics
Also known as rigid-body dynamics, hard-body dynamics simulate the physical behaviour of rigid objects that do not deform upon collision.

Hardware Rendering
Also known as display rendering, hardware rendering previews a 3D scene within the viewports on a 3D software package, providing real-time on-screen feedback about the effects of changes made to that scene, but omitting certain processor-intensive effects such as volumetrics, shadowing and realistic refraction.

HDRI
High Dynamic Range Image. A 2D image stored in a file format with a greater range of luminance values than a standard bitmap image. HDR images are often used as environment maps in image-based lighting techniques to create subtle, real-world lighting effects.

Hierarchy
The relationship of the sub-objects within a model or a scene to one another. Sub-objects may exist as parents, children or independents. A parent object controls the motion of all child objects linked to it, although the motion of a child object does not affect that of the parent.

History
A record of the previous values of the attributes of a 3D scene, enabling an artist to revert immediately to a particular earlier state. The history is especially valuable during the modeling process.

Hull
A series of straight lines connecting the CVs of a NURBS surface.

Image-Based Lighting
A technique in which a photographic reference image is used as an environment map to control the surface illumination of a 3D object, in order to create subtle real-world lighting effects. In-betweening: The generation of intermediate transition positions between two key frames. The term is drawn from traditional cel animation, where alead artist generates the beginning and end keyframes of a sequence (typically one second apart), a breakdown artist does the breakdowns (typically four frames apart), and an 'in-betweener' completes the rest.

Interpolation
The mathematical procedure by which a 3D software package calculates the in-between positions between two keyframes.

Inverse Kinematics
Often abbreviated to IK, Inverse Kinematics is a character animation technique in which the end bone of a chain - for example, a limb - is assigned a goal object. When the goal object moves, the bone moves with it, dragging the rest of the chain behind it. The movement propagates from the free end of the chain towards the fixed point: the reverse of Forward Kinematics.

Isoparm
Lines on a NURBS surface connecting points of constant U or V co-ordinate values, and representing crosssections of the NURBS surface in the U or V directions.

Joints
Points of articulation between the bones in a character rig.

Keyframe
An image, or set of attributes for a 3D scene, used as a reference point in animation. The artist usually sets up keyframes manually at significant points in the action, and the computer calculates the in-between values automatically.

Lathing
A modeling technique in which a two-dimensional profile is duplicated in rotation around a reference axis, and the duplicates joined up to create a continuous three-dimensional surface. Lathing is particularly useful for creating objects with rotational axes of symmetry, such as plates, glasses, vases or wheels.

Layer
A level of an image that can be edited independently of the rest of the image.

Lens
In a real camera, a lens is a curved piece of glass or other transparent material that focuses light onto the film. Modern 3D software is capable of simulating a variety of optical distortions created by imperfections in real-world lenses, adding realism to the rendered output.

Lens Flare
A bright pattern on an image caused by the reflection and refraction of light within a camera. Although lens flares are actually artifacts of the photographic process, many 3D software packages offer artists the opportunity to add them deliberately in order to increase the realism ofrendered output.

Light

A point or volume that emits light onto a 3D object. Types of light supported within 3D packages include Point lights, which emit light in all directions from a single point; Spot lights, which emit light in a cone; Distant or Directional lights, which emit light rays in parallel, illuminating all surfaces within a scene; and Area lights, which emit light from two-dimensional surfaces.

Lip Synching

The process of matching a character's facial movements to a spoken soundtrack during facial animation.

Lofting

A modeling technique in which a continuous three-dimensional surface is created by selecting and joining multiple two-dimensional cross sections or profiles.

Look Development

The process of developing the look of a 3D scene by compositing separate render passes together in different permutations.

Low-Poly Modelling

The process of creating simplified models with low polygon counts, usually for use in videogames, where scenes must be rendered in real time, by software with a limited ability to handle complex models.

Match-moving

See: Camera Tracking.

Material

A set of mathematical attributes that determine the ways in which the surface of a model to which they are applied reacts to light. These attributes are sub-divided into individual channels.

Mask

An area that can be protected and isolated from changes applied to the rest of the image.

Mesh

The surface geometry of a 3D model, made up of a series of linked geometry elements such as polygons, patches or NURBS surfaces.

Metaball modeling

A technique in which models are created using spheres (or, more rarely, other primitive objects) that attract and cling to each other according to their proximity to one another and their field of influence. Metaball modeling is particularly useful for creating organic objects.

Model

Used as a verb, to model means to build a 3D object. Used as a noun, it means the 3D object created as the end product of the modeling process. A variety of different methods are used in 3D.

modeling,

including polygonal, NURBS, Sub-D and metaball techniques. Modifier See: Deformer.

Morph

To transform from one state to another. Morphing is commonly used in lip-synching, in order to transform the head model of a character between a variety of preset states (or 'morph targets'), corresponding to common facial expressions, in order to create the illusion of speech.

Motion Blur

An artifacts of real-world cinematography in which the camera's target object is moving too quickly for the camera to record accurately, and therefore appears blurred. Many 3D software packages simulate motion blur as a rendering effect, in order to increase the realism of 3D images or animation.

Motion capture

Often abbreviated to mocap, motion capture is the process of recording the movements of a live actor, and converting them to a 3D data format which can then be applied to a virtual character.

Multi-pass rendering

To render out the lighting or surface attributes of a scene as separate images, with a view to compositing them together later. Multi-pass rendering can be used simply to speed up the rendering process, or in order to develop the look of a scene by compositing the different passes together in various permutations.

Negative Light

A light within a 3D scene that decreases the illumination on a surface instead of adding to it. Negative lights can be used to remove 'overspill' in brightly lit scenes.

Normal

An imaginary line drawn from the centre of a polygon (or other geometry object) at right angles to the surface.

Null

A point within a 3D scene that does not render out, but which is used as a reference for other objects.

NURBS

Non-Uniform Rational B-Splines. NURBS curves are two-dimensional curves whose shape is determined by a series of control points or CVs between which they pass. When a series of such curves are joined together, they form a three-dimensional NURBS surface. Such surfaces have a separate co-ordinate space (known as UV co-ordinate space) to that of the 3D scene in which they are situated. NURBS are commonly used to model organic curved-surface objects.

Object

A generic term describing any item that can be inserted into and manipulated within a 3D scene. Models, lights, particle emitters and cameras are all objects.

Object file

See: File format.

Origin

See: Co-ordinate System, Axis.

Parent

See: Hierarchy.

Patch

An area of a NURBS surface enclosed by a span square: the shape created by the intersection of four isoparms, two in the U direction, and two in the V direction.

Particle System

An animation system consisting of a large number of very small points whose behaviour is determined mathematically. A particle system typically consists of an emitter (which may be a point, surface or volume, and may emit particles directionally or in all directions) and a series of fields that determine the motion of those particles. Individual particles have a finite lifespan, and may possess attributes (such as color, radius, and opacity) that vary over the course of that lifespan. Particle effects are commonly used to simulate fire, smoke, steam and other fluids, or to control complex animations such as crowd scenes.

Phong
See: Shading.

Photogrammetry
Also known as image-based modeling, photogrammetry is the process of generating a fully textured 3D model from a series of photographs of a real object. Although it was once an expensive high-end technique, there is now a range of increasingly inexpensive photogrammetry software packages on the market.

Plane
A two-dimensional surface in Cartesian co-ordinate space. Essentially a flat sheet extending infinitely in all directions, a plane may be used to aid object manipulation, positioning and construction, and is not usually made visible in a final render.

Plug-in
A small piece of third-party software that is loaded into a 3D application in order to extend its functionality. Plug-ins commonly perform such specialized tasks as file conversion or data export, texture generation, and physics or fluid simulation. There are thousands of plug-ins currently available on the Internet, both commercially and as free downloads.

Point
A one-dimensional point in coordinate space. Points can be linked up to form polygons, used as control vertices for NURBS curves, or employed as nulls to control lights or cameras, amongst other functions.

Polygon
A geometry element formed by connecting three or more points. A triangle, or three-point polygon, is the simplest form of polygonal geometry. Polygonal modeling is a fast, intuitive method of creating 3D objects, but does not easily generate smooth curved surfaces.

Post Processing
The manipulation of a rendered image, either to improve the quality of that image, or to create effects that cannot easily be achieved directly within the 3D software itself. Some 3D software packages can be set to automatically apply post-processing effects, such as motion blur or depth of field, after a frame is rendered.

Preset
A pre-generated list of settings for a particular 3D software package. Presets are usually used to control and customzse properties such as rendering or lighting styles. Like plug-ins, they may either be commercial products, or freely downloadable from the Internet.

Preview
A time-saving method of checking the progress of a project by rendering it at a lower quality, resolution or frame rate than will be used for the final project.

Primitive
A simple three-dimensional form used as the basis for constructive solid geometry modeling techniques. Typical primitives include the plane, the cube, the sphere, the cone and the torus.

Procedural Texture
A texture map that is generated by a mathematical function, rather than a real-world bitmap image projected over the surface of an object.

Projection
The process by which a two dimensional texture map is applied over the surface of a three dimensional object, as if it were an image projected from a slide projector. There are several common projection types, including Planar, Cubic, Spherical and Cylindrical. Which one is most appropriate depends on the type of map being projected, and the shape of the object it is being projected upon.

Quad view
A method of displaying 3D scenes adopted by many high-end software applications, in which a scene is shown simultaneously in Top, Side, Front and Perspective views.

Radiosity
A technique for rendering 3D scenes. Radiosity simulates the way in which light bounces from surface to surface within a scene, and is more accurate, but also more processor-intensive, than raytracing.

Raytracing
A technique for rendering 3D scenes. Raytracing traces the path of every ray of light from its source until it either leaves the scene or becomes too weak to have an effect. The term is also sometimes applied to the reverse method: tracing the path of every ray of light from the camera backwards to the light source.

Reflection Map
An environment map used to simulate real-world reflection effects on the surface of a 3D object. Reflection maps render more quickly than methods that generate true surface reflections, such as raytracing.

Rendering
The process of converting the 3D data stored in a software package into the two-dimensional image 'seen' by the camera within the scene. Rendering brings together the scene geometry, Z-depth, surface properties, lighting set-up and rendering method to create a finished frame. Rendering comes in two forms: Display or Hardware rendering,

used to display the scene on-screen in the software package's viewports; and the more processor intensive final-quality or software rendering, which generates an image for output, and takes account of properties that display rendering overlooks, such as shadows, reflections and post-process effects.

Resolution
The size of the final image in pixels when rendering out a scene. Higher resolution renders contain more detail, but take longer to complete.

Rigging
The process of preparing a character model for animation, including setting up an underlying skeleton, complete with constraints, controllers and kinematic systems, and linking it to the mesh of the character model.

Scene
A set of 3D objects, including the models themselves and the lights and camera that will be used when rendering them out. Scene file See: File format.

Script
A small piece of code created in a 3D software package's own internal programming language, and used to automate common or complex tasks.

Shading
The mathematical process of calculating how a model's surfaces react to light. A variety of alternative algorithms can be used for the task, including Phong, Lambert, and Blinn shading models.

Shaders are often built up as node-based shading trees, with each node controlling a specific aspect of the process.

Skinning
The process of binding the surface of a model to the underlying skeleton during character rigging.

Skeleton
An underlying network of bones used to define and control the motion of a model during character animation. Moving a bone causes the mesh of the model to move and deform.

Snapping
The automatic alignment of one object to another or to a reference grid, intended to aid the precise placement of objects within a scene or modeling hierarchy.

Soft-Body Dynamics
The simulation of the behaviour of soft bodies that deform on collision with other objects, such as cloth or fluid flows.

Specularity
A surface property of an object that determines the way in which highlights appear on that surface.

Spline
See: NURBS.

Subdivision Surface
Also known as Sub-Ds, subdivision surfaces are surfaces created using a technique midway between polygon and NURBS modeling. They consist of an underlying polygonal base mesh, which is automatically subdivided by the software to create a smoothed final form.

Sub-Ds combine much of the power of NURBS surfaces with the intuitive characteristics and ease of use of polygonal modeling tools.

Sweep
A modeling technique similar to extrusion in which a two dimensional profile is replicated along a path, then joined to form a continuous three-dimensional surface. Unlike extrusion, however, this path need not be perpendicular to the profile. By sweeping a circular profile along a helical path, for example, it would be possible to model a coiled cable of the type commonly found on telephones.

Symmetry
A modeling option in which any changes made to the model are duplicated across an axis of reflectional symmetry. This makes it possible to create complex symmetrical objects, such as a human or animal head, without having to work directly on more than one half of the model.

Texture
A bitmap image that is applied to the surface of a 3D object to give it detail. Texture maps may be either photographic images or procedural textures, and may be applied in each of the material channels of an object using a variety of mapping or

projection methods.
Three-Point Lighting. A system of CG lighting derived from real-world cinematography, in which a scene is illuminated by three light sources: a Key light, which acts as the

primary source of illumination for the scene; a Fill light, which illuminates shadow areas; and a Rim light, which illuminates the edges of objects and helps them stand out from the background.

Tiling
The process of duplicating a texture across the surface of an object. Tiling textures must be created so that the edge of one aligns perfectly with that of its neighbor, otherwise the result is a series of ugly seams. High frequency textures are those in which patterns repeat at short intervals over an object's surface; low-frequency textures are those in which the intervals are larger.

Timeline
A fundamental element of the graphical user interface of most modern 3D software packages which shows the timing of the keyframes in a sequence of animation. Playback of the animation may be controlled either by a series of VCR-like controls, or by clicking and dragging with the mouse to 'scrub' a slider to and fro along the timeline.

Trimming
The process by which NURBS surfaces are edited. The trimming tools allow 3D artists to define areas on a NURBS surface that will be made invisible and not render out, even though their CVs still exist. Separate trimmed surfaces may be joined together by using a variety of techniques, including Attaching, Aligning, Filleting and Stitching.

UV Texture Co-ordinates

The co-ordinate system used for assigning textures to polygonal models. Since UV co-ordinate space is two-dimensional, one of several projection methods must be used to 'unwrap' the UVs from the model and lay them flat on a plane. Once unwrapped, the UV map may be screen-grabbed and exported to a paint package for texture painting.

Vertex
See: Point.

Viewport
The region of the interface of a 3D software package in which the scene is displayed to the artist.

Volumetrics
Volumetric lights are lights whose illumination can be observed throughout a volume of space, rather than simply where the light strikes a surface. In similar fashion, volumetric textures are textures applied throughout a volume of space, rather than to a surface.

Walk Cycle
A short sequence of animation containing the keyframes necessary to make a bipedal character take two consecutive steps. The sequence may then be repeated over and over again to animate the character walking forward. Walk cycles may be modified in many subtle ways to suggest information about a character's age, gender, emotional state or personality.

Weighting
The process of determining which bone in a skeleton affects which part of a model's surface mesh. In many cases, this is achieved by painting weight maps onto the surface of the model that delineate a particular bone's area of influence.

Wireframe
A shading method in which a simple grid of lines is used to represent the basic contours of the underlying model. For many 3D artists, this is a favored mode to work in, since it permits them to see faces and surfaces that would otherwise be hidden by overlying geometry.

World axes
See: Co-ordinate systems.

Z-depth
The distance a particular point or surface lies inside a scene. Z-depth information is used to calculate where a light casts shadows, and also to calculate which surfaces are visible to the camera during rendering, and which are obscured by nearer geometry.

Index

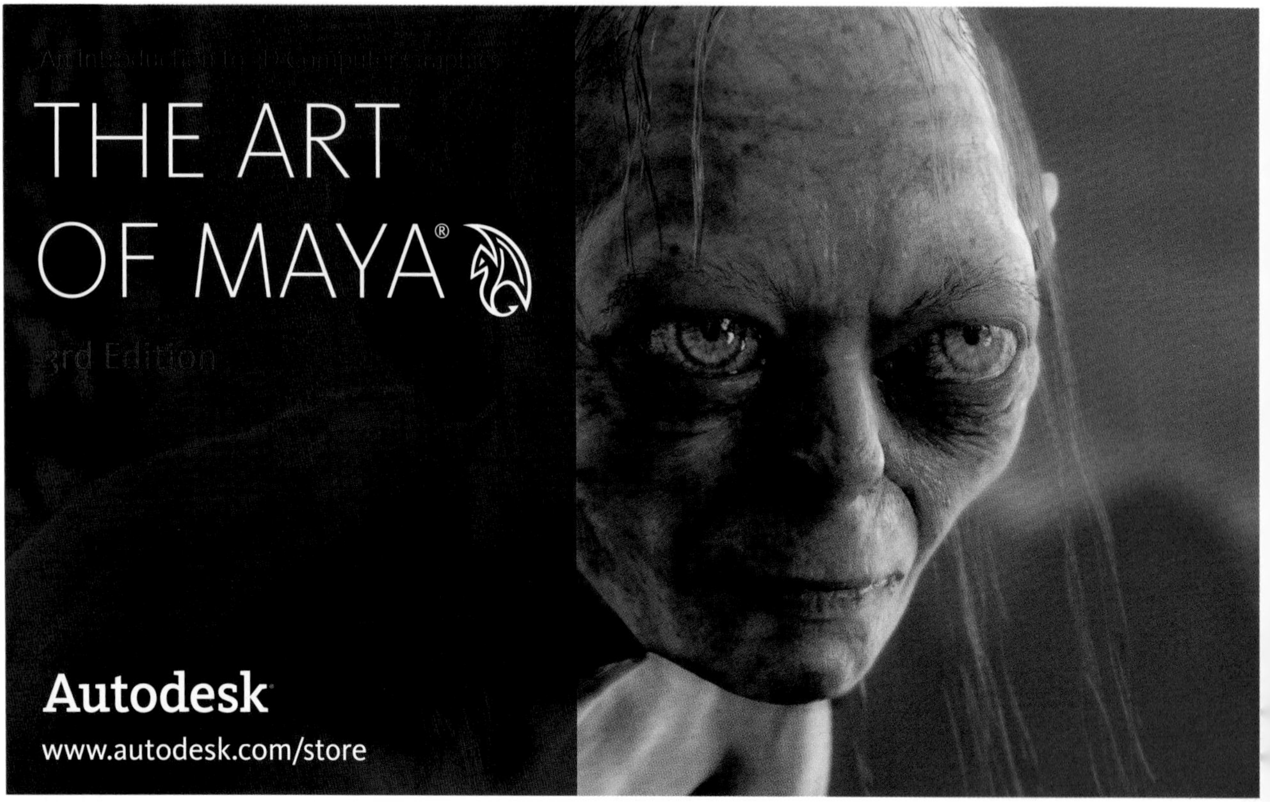
THE ART
OF MAYA®
3rd Edition
Autodesk
www.autodesk.com/store

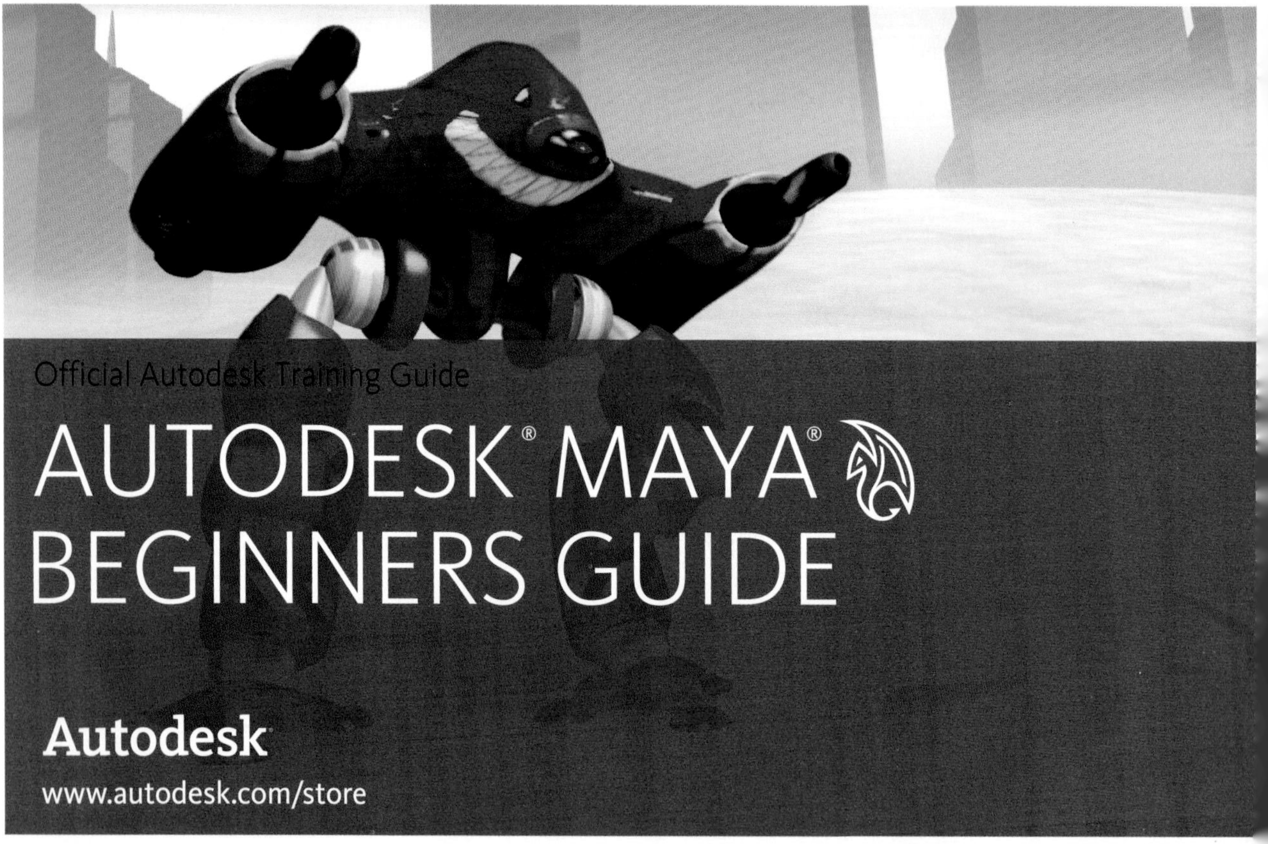
Official Autodesk Training Guide
AUTODESK® MAYA®
BEGINNERS GUIDE
Autodesk
www.autodesk.com/store

Official Autodesk Training Guide

LEARNING
AUTODESK® MAYA® 🐉
8.0

Foundation

www.autodesk.com/store

Autodesk

Autodesk Paint FX plug-in for Adobe® Photoshop®

Discover unlimited creative possibilities with the Autodesk® Paint FX plug-in for Adobe® Photoshop®. With over 190 brushes you can't find anywhere else, you'll be able to create trees, flowers, fire, clouds, smoke and other elements with a few simple brush strokes.

Save time, energy and frustration by achieving the results you want effectively and efficiently. The only limit is your imagination! Work with: jet trails, daisies, ferns, raw meat, oil brushes, watercolors, grasses, and many more...

Autodesk® Paint FX plug-in for Adobe® Photoshop®

Included on DVD
(SEE INSIDE FOR SYSTEM REQUIREMENTS)

PLUG-IN

Autodesk